The Final Words of Jesus
A Discipleship Manual

*"All authority has been given to Me in heaven and on earth.
Go therefore and make disciples of all the nations, baptizing
them in the Name of the Father and of the Son and of the
Holy Spirit, teaching them to observe all things that I have
commanded you; and lo, I am with you always, even to the
end of the age." Amen. (Matthew 28:18-20)*

JESUS THE CHRIST

Travis Hunt
Moses Paulose   David Witt

Published and Distributed by Martus Publishing
PO Box 101
Clarkdale, AZ 86324
Contact@SpiritofMartyrdom.com

Layout and Format completed by Jay Myers
The Yetsirah Company
www.yetsirah.com

ISBN 978-1-4507-2602-3
Printed in the United States of America

DEDICATION

To my wife and children, who are dearer to me than any on earth. You have sacrificed a great deal of "family time" that others might know our Jesus. Your rewards are eternal. I love you all dearly: Loriena, Amanda, Theran, Jared and Daniel

To M. Paulose who is like a father to me. For bringing to light the simple truth of God's Word and challenging me to let go of this world and cling to the Lord.

ACKNOWLEDGMENTS

I would like to thank Pastor M. Paulose for his obedience to the Lord in teaching biblical discipleship. His outstanding work and Bible study on this subject has been the backbone and impetus for writing this book. Most of the material in this book is based upon tattered handwritten notes, which have traveled with him through multiple nations and have encouraged saints worldwide. May this work continue.

Thank you David Witt for adding stories from your life time of world travels. Also thank you Bill Hickey and Tracy Drish for editing contributions.

Thanks to Sharri Payne and Michelle Rushworth for the hard work of transcribing and editing this material.

May all thanks be unto God: *And whatever you do in word or deed, do all in the Name of the Lord Jesus, giving thanks to God the Father through Him. (Colossians 3:17)*

Travis Hunt

TABLE OF CONTENTS

TRAVIS HUNT BIOGRAPHY

*T*ravis Hunt was called to be a pastor in 1997, while working as a corporate biologist. He answered the call and God took him to the town of his boyhood, Camas Valley, Oregon, where he now pastors a church as well as having planted another in a neighboring town.

He has traveled the globe, sharing the news of salvation and teaching discipleship. He has a passion for all to follow God. His dynamic style of sharing the Word stirs the soul and challenges all to step out into ministry.

He is married to his wife, Loriena, and together they have four children: Amanda, Theran, Jared and Daniel. They live on a farm and home-school their children.

M. PAULOSE BIOGRAPHY

*G*od called Pastor Moses Paulose into the ministry in 1966 when he was nineteen years old. He has faithfully served the Lord for more than forty years. He began as an itinerant evangelist until God called him through a vision to move to Rameswaram, South India and plant a work.

Through the preaching of the Gospel with miracles, signs and wonders following, the ministry has grown from one church in Rameswaram to hundreds in India and Asia. Pastor Paulose has impacted lives around the world by his godly character and powerful ministry.

DAVID WITT

*D*avid is the Founder and CEO of Spirit of Martyrdom ministries, International speaker and author, ordained Pastor and Associate Representative for The Voice of the Martyrs. He has traveled to 46 nations serving the persecuted and being inspired by the living martyrs of Christ.

I know of men who have made it their life's work to study the final words people say or write just before they leave this earth. Their thinking is that by the time a person gets to his or her final words, they no longer deal in the arena of the trivial but rather say what is truly on their heart. I've read their books and found many brilliant quotes from ordinary people as well as dignitaries.

Certainly we cannot put Jesus in a group of normal people who are facing their final moments on earth. None of His words were ever trivial, yet still I find it interesting that His final command to His followers is that they should go and make disciples of all the nations. Somehow those words of Jesus seem to carry extra weight since they are His final instructions for you and I as His followers.

Now at last there is a practical, simple yet challenging manual giving us step by step guidance as we seek to fulfill this great commission the Lord has given to us. I have had walls lined with Christian books in my library. Each of them were important in their own way and all of them worthy of a good read. But in all my years of ministry this is the first time I have found such a helpful guide book to navigate the trails of discipleship. Whether working with students, a congregation, or your own children, everyone can follow along, learn, understand and grasp the principles of discipleship so clearly laid out in these pages. May I suggest that before using this manual as a ministry to others, go through it with yourself in mind.

One of the reasons you will find this little manual so effective is the fact that it is chock full of Scripture. We can write volumes and speak great oratory but it's the Word of God that has the power to change lives. The Word alone has the ability to be the discerner of the thoughts and intents of the heart. And it is the Word that can convict, confirm and guide us into all truth.

Enjoy your journey to effective discipleship as you use this manual. May I close with one more little word of advice: Take your time; this is not a "summer read" where you will sit in the shade and read it from cover to cover. This is a manual, take it slowly and thoughtfully. Then you will be amazed at what the Lord can do in you and through you.

May the Lord richly bless you as you seek to be a more effective disciple.

Phil Evans,
Senior Pastor
Roseburg Christian Fellowship
(Calvary Chapel of Roseburg, Oregon, USA)

BELIEVERS AND DISCIPLES

The Command

n Matthew chapter 28, after showing Himself to His disciples for 40 days and just prior to His ascension into heaven, Jesus commands,

"Go therefore and make disciples of all the nations."

Or, literally, "Go! Disciple everywhere." His words...

"baptizing them in the Name of the Father and of the Son and of the Holy Spirit,"

clearly tell us that the first step to discipling must be evangelism. But, as wonderfully fulfilling as evangelism is, Jesus did not stop there. His unbroken sentence continues...

"teaching them to observe all things that I have commanded you; and lo, I am with you always, even to the end of the age."

For most, it is a struggle to grasp evangelizing the world. How much more inconceivable to consider discipling the world when two thirds of those living don't follow the Lord?

It's a command nonetheless; a command given to every single believer in Christ. Make disciples! So, what is a disciple?

The Greek word 'matheteuo' simply means "student or learner". My goal in discipling another is to teach them how to learn from Jesus Himself. But what did it mean to the Apostles standing on that mountain with Jesus? What is the Biblical definition of a disciple? What did Jesus ultimately mean? The Bible teaches a great deal on this subject and this book is going to explore seventeen biblical characteristics of a disciple.

There is an interesting Scripture in Isaiah chapter 8.

Bind up the testimony, Seal the law among my disciples. (Isaiah 8:16)

When we read the context, Isaiah is talking about God's judgment upon Israel because they have refused to follow Him and therefore they are about to suffer terrible consequences. So the Lord commands Isaiah to take His Word and give it to His disciples. The disciples are to protect or "seal" God's Word. Who was the Lord actually referring to? A six hundred year old mystery unveils itself...

> *And I will wait on the LORD, Who hides His face from the house of Jacob; And I will hope in Him. Here am I and the children whom the LORD has given me! We are for signs and wonders in Israel from the LORD of hosts, Who dwells in Mount Zion. (Isaiah 8:17-18)*

"*Here am I,*" Isaiah goes on to say. Here is who? According to Hebrews 2:13 this is a prophecy of Jesus Christ and His followers.

> *For it was fitting for Him, for whom are all things and by whom are all things, in bringing many sons to glory, to make the captain of their salvation perfect through sufferings (Jesus). For both He who sanctifies and those who are being sanctified are all of one, for which reason He is not ashamed to call them brethren, saying: "I will declare Your Name to My brethren; In the midst of the assembly I will sing praise to You." And again: "I will put My trust in Him." And again: "Here am I (Jesus) and the children whom God has given Me (disciples)."(Hebrews 2:10-13)*

So this is now a fulfilled prophecy concerning the followers of Jesus. God says, "Take the Word, seal it up and give it to my disciples." Don't you find it interesting that as followers of Jesus Christ we were even mentioned prior to our birth and pre-selected by God for such an amazing task? God looks to His disciples to seal His law.

Let's take a discipleship quiz: How many disciples were there? Twelve?

> *And He came down with them and stood on a level place with a crowd of His disciples... (Luke 6:17)*

How many are in a crowd? As you think about a crowd gathering, how many are in it?

> *Then the twelve summoned the multitude of the disciples (Acts 6:2)*

Now we have a multitude. Is a multitude bigger than a crowd? So, once again: How many disciples did Jesus have? Thousands. As Isaiah prophesied and Hebrews elaborated, they are the children that God has given to Jesus.

What qualified the original disciples? Did they come from the religious elite? Did they come from the seminaries? Did they come from the universities? Were they the Pharisees? Were they the Sadducees?

> *And Jesus, walking by the Sea of Galilee, saw two brothers, Simon called Peter, and Andrew his brother, casting a net into the sea; for they were fishermen. (Matthew 4:18)*

A disciple doesn't have to be a college graduate, or someone in "full-time" ministry. Look at the following verses.

> *Then He said to them, "Follow Me, and I will make you fishers of men." They immediately left their nets and followed Him. Going on from there, He saw two other brothers, James the son of Zebedee, and John his brother, in the boat with Zebedee their father, mending their nets. He called them, and immediately they left the boat and their father, and followed Him. (Matthew 4:20-22)*

How many fishermen do you know with a college degree? How many Bible studies do you think these men were leading? Are fishermen generally among the religious elite of high class society? When you think about fishermen, you think of a laborer, a gruff looking character with a wild beard and hardened hands. This is who Jesus Christ picked, rough, hard-working, common people.

We too often interpret this passage to read, "Follow Me, and I will send you to college." Or "Follow me and I will teach you Greek." Or "Follow me and I will train you in liturgy."

Do you think these unlearned and common men understood what was said to them? "I will make you fish for men!" He took their daily occupation and gave it a spiritual significance. Their knowledge about fishing would become God's blueprint for a

Temple greater than any that had ever been built.

> *Now, therefore, you are no longer strangers and*
> *foreigners, but fellow citizens with the saints and*
> *members of the household of God, having been built*
> *on the foundation of the apostles and prophets,*
> *Jesus Christ Himself being the chief cornerstone,*
> *in whom the whole building, being joined together,*
> *grows into a holy temple in the Lord, in whom you*
> *also are being built together for a dwelling place of*
> *God in the Spirit. (Ephesians 2:19-22)*

The invitation sounded so simple! Fishers of men. Dear
reader, the Bible teaches that discipleship is decidedly simple.
(Notice I didn't say, "easy.") The invitation includes all human
kind both elite and common.

What did these two groups of sweaty fishermen do after
they were called? They immediately followed. Immediately!
Which tells me that when God calls a disciple, don't linger. Come
quickly!

How could these common men possibly think they could
follow the Creator of the universe? They had never cast out a
demon before. They had never raised the dead. In fact, it is likely
that they had never done anything of significance up to that very
moment. They simply came because Jesus asked.

And when He had called His twelve disciples to Him, He
gave them power over unclean spirits, to cast them out, and to
heal all kinds of sickness and all kinds of disease. (Matthew 10:1)
It wasn't until after they came, that Jesus gave them their authority and power. Jesus said, "Okay, since you have followed me, I
will equip you." When God calls you, He equips you. The limit-
ing factor in discipleship is not the calling or even the equipping,
but the willingness to follow. God desires to bless His disciples
in incredible ways, when they come to Him. What if James and
John never left the boat? They could've said, "Wait a second,
I've never done that before." "I can't lead a Bible study. I can't
even read well." "I don't know how to evangelize. I'm not any
good at praying." But, the Lord knew all of this and just smiled
and said, "Perfect. Come and let God have the glory."

It wasn't just a men's club either:

At Joppa there was a certain disciple named Tabitha,

*which is translated Dorcas. This woman was full
of good works and charitable deeds which she did.
(Acts 9:36)*

So, there goes our religious myth. The disciples weren't twelve men, but a multitude of both men and women. And, don't think that disciple making stopped when the Lord departed. By the time Acts chapter 6 rolls around, Jesus is at the right hand of the Father in heaven. Yet, there was miraculous growth occurring in the early church, and Acts tells us how it was happening.

*The number of the disciples was multiplying...
(Acts 6:1)*

How? It wasn't the short sermons, awesome music and coffee bar. It wasn't the great seating and the perfectly set climate control. The church wasn't even located in a friendly neighborhood. But they were "multiplying"! HOW? Jesus had said, "Go make disciples" and they did. They didn't argue about where they would meet or any of the things that now swallow up a church's time and resources. They were reaching out to people and making disciples.

They gathered where they could and discipled. In fact, the New Testament speaks of many little house churches and the elders who were raised up to shepherd them. The Bible speaks nothing of giant cathedrals, or mega-churches. Now there is nothing inherently wrong with mega-churches or cathedrals as long as they're making disciples.

Before I go on, I want you to ponder two things. Are you a disciple? And secondly, are you making disciples? It is my hope that when you are done reading this book, all excuses will have been "sacrificed on the altar": "I don't know enough." "I'm too old." "I'm too young." "I'm married." "I'm single." The Master is offering you the ability to touch other people's lives with His love and power.

What if everyone who is saved took on one disciple? Within a year, we would have doubled in number. Within two years we would be quadrupled. Within three years there would be sixteen times as many of us. Imagine if we had sixteen times as many mature believers in the church. What would God do with that!

We so commonly refer to ourselves as "Christians" and yet

we may not even know what that means.

So it was that for a whole year they assembled with the church and taught a great many people. And the disciples were first called Christians in Antioch. (Acts 11:26)

What is a Christian? A Christian is a disciple. I might refer to myself as a Christian and attend a Church. I might be saved, but can I really be called a biblical Christian unless I am also a disciple? It does not say that the believers were called Christians, but the disciples.

The word "Christian" is only mentioned three times in the New Testament, but it has become the name we readily cling to as believers in Jesus. The amazing thing is that in the early church this was most likely a derogatory title.

What does King Agrippa say, when Paul gives his testimony?

You almost persuade me to become a Christian. (Acts 26:28)

Notice that Paul doesn't use this "title" in response.

I would to God that not only you, but also all who hear me today, might become both almost and altogether such as I am, except for these chains. (Acts 26:29)

When the early church was being persecuted, how does the Apostle Peter exhort them?

Yet if anyone suffers as a Christian, let him not be ashamed, but let him glorify God in this matter. (1 Peter 4:16).

If you suffer as a "Christian" don't be ashamed.

When I first realized that this word only occurred three times in the Bible, I was amazed. Since it was the term I grew up hearing, I thought that it must be used throughout the Bible. Jesus must have mentioned it hundreds of times. But He never even used the term once. In stark contrast to this, the Greek word for "disciple" occurs 260 times in the New Testament. Which do you think God wants us to be? A Christian? Or a Disciple?

These two words differ even in American society. If someone comes up to you and says, "Are you a Christian?" The great majority would say, "Yes." But, if someone asked, "Are you a disciple of Jesus Christ?" How would they respond? The latter word causes us to stop and think. It means a little more. There's a weight attached to it. Some sort of a responsibility.

Being a disciple is more than being a believer. Biblically, a believer simply comes to Jesus to receive but a disciple comes to Jesus to give everything away. It is the difference between stretching out an open hand and holding it up (to receive) or holding it down (to give).

Here are some Scriptures describing a believer…

For God so loved the world that He gave His only begotten Son, that whoever believes in Him should not perish but have everlasting life. (John 3:16)

How do you receive salvation? By being a disciple? No, by believing in the atonement of Jesus Christ on the cross. Period. That's grace. You are saved based on believing in the work of God, not your own. So, in this verse, a believer comes to receive eternal life.

When Jesus departed from there, two blind men followed Him, crying out and saying,

"Son of David, have mercy on us!" And when He had come into the house, the blind men came to Him. And Jesus said to them, "Do you believe that I am able to do this?" They said to Him, "Yes, Lord." (Matthew 9:27-28)

What does He ask them? "Do you believe…" The very next verse says that He healed them. So, we see in these verses that I can believe and receive eternal life and even healing.

Then one of the crowd answered and said, "Teacher, I brought You my son, who has a mute spirit. And wherever it seizes him, it throws him down; he foams at the mouth, gnashes his teeth, and becomes rigid. So I spoke to Your disciples, that they should cast it out, but they could not." He answered him and said, "O faithless generation, how long shall I be with you? How long shall I bear with you? Bring him to Me." Then they brought him to Him. And when

*he saw Him, immediately the spirit convulsed him,
and he fell on the ground and wallowed, foaming at
the mouth. So He asked his father, "How long has
this been happening to him?" And he said, "From
childhood. And often he has thrown him both into
the fire and into the water to destroy him. But if You
can do anything, have compassion on us and help
us." Jesus said to him, "If you can believe, all things
are possible to him who believes." Immediately the
father of the child cried out and said with tears,
"Lord, I believe; help my unbelief!" (Mark 9:17-24)*

All things are possible for him who believes...What is He
talking about? He was telling this man to believe that God could
do what he was asking. So, we have now been shown that if
we believe then God will save you, heal you and even remove a
demonic spirit from your life. If you believe, you shall receive.
That is a Biblical fact. We cannot even receive the Word of God
unless we believe.

*And when a great multitude had gathered, and
they had come to Him from every city, He spoke by
a parable: "A sower went out to sow his seed. And
as he sowed, some fell by the wayside; and it was
trampled down, and the birds of the air devoured
it. Some fell on rock; and as soon as it sprang up, it
withered away because it lacked moisture And some
fell among thorns, and the thorns sprang up with
it and choked it. But others fell on good ground,
sprang up, and yielded a crop a hundredfold." When
He had said these things He cried, "He who has ears
to hear, let him hear!... "Now the parable is this: The
seed is the word of God. Those by the wayside are
the ones who hear; then the devil comes and takes
away the word out of their hearts, lest they should
believe and be saved. But the ones on the rock are
those who, when they hear, receive the word with
joy; and these have no root, who believe for a while
and in time of temptation fall away. Now the ones
that fell among thorns are those who, when they
have heard, go out and are choked with cares, riches,
and pleasures of life, and bring no fruit to maturity.
But the ones that fell on the good ground are those*

who, having heard the word with a noble and good heart, keep it and bear fruit with patience."
(Luke 8:4-8, 11-15)

The ones that fell on the road were eaten and did not receive the Word of God because they never believed. If they would have believed, the Word would have gone in. Didn't believe; didn't receive. The second soil is actually referred to as a believer…who believe for a while, but, when the sun comes up their belief withers. They believed, and received, but the suffering was too much. The third soil also believed and received, but the cares of this world choked the fruit that their lives should've produced. Then there are the ones who have good ground and keep the Word of God (which the Lord referred to as a disciple in Isaiah 8:16). They work through the hard times and ultimately bear fruit.

So in this parable, we have three believers, but only one bears fruit: the disciple. What did Jesus say?

By this My Father is glorified, that you bear much fruit; so you will be My disciples. (John 15:8)

What is my point? My point is that a believer is different than a disciple. I do hope that you are all believers.

But without faith it is impossible to please Him, for he who comes to God must believe that He is, and that He is a rewarder of those who diligently seek Him. (Hebrews 11:6)

You must believe that God wants to give, that He answers prayer, and does good things for those who call upon Him. You've got to believe before you can even start your walk with the Lord. However, based on the parable in Luke, I am persuaded that you can be a believer and still bear no fruit. But like every plant, I believe there is a yearning within you for the fruit that you were designed to produce. For a believer, it is that desire to be alive with the Spirit of God and to walk in His Presence daily.

It is also important to note that Jesus Christ did not delegate His power and authority to the people He healed or those He fed or the ones who were forgiven of sin. When He told the paralytic that his sins were forgiven and that he should take up his bed and walk, it wasn't followed by, "Oh, by the way, you have the gift of healings now!" When Jesus told the woman that He wouldn't accuse her and that she should go and sin no more, He didn't end it with, "Now you have authority to cast out demons." He didn't raise the widow's son in Nain and then tell him to "Go and do likewise!"

Who did He give His authority, and power?

Then He called His twelve disciples together and gave them power and authority over all demons, and to cure diseases. He sent them to preach the kingdom of God and to heal the sick. (Luke 9:1-2)

He did not give His authority to the multitudes, nor the people He healed, but the disciples that followed Him.

Then the eleven disciples went away into Galilee, to the mountain which Jesus had appointed for them. When they saw Him, they worshiped Him; but some doubted. And Jesus came and spoke to them, saying, "All authority has been given to Me in heaven and on earth. Go therefore and make disciples of all the nations, baptizing them in the Name of the Father and of the Son and of the Holy Spirit, teaching them to observe all things that I have commanded you; and lo, I am with you always, even to the end of the age." Amen. (Matthew 28:16-20)

He takes all authority on earth: every single ounce of authority that has ever existed and gives it to them, so that they can make disciples for Him. This is the heart of His ministry on earth for us.

Many in the crowd never raised the dead. Many in the crowd never healed anyone. Many in the crowd did not do any of the great works the disciples did. Yet then Stephen comes along in the book of Acts and becomes a disciple, surrendering himself and taking the non-glamorous job of feeding elderly widows, what happens? The next thing you know he's not only giving out bread to the widows, but...

Stephen, full of faith and power, did great wonders and signs among the people. (Acts 6:8)

He became a disciple. This is what all of our hearts yearn for: to walk in the Presence and Power of our Lord Jesus. So, what is a disciple? Let's ask Jesus:

> *"Whoever does not bear his cross and come after Me cannot be My disciple. For which of you, intending to build a tower, does not sit down first and count the cost, whether he has enough to finish it --lest, after he has laid the foundation, and is not able to finish, all who see it begin to mock him, saying, 'This man began to build and was not able to finish.' Or what king, going to make war against another king, does not sit down first and consider whether he is able with ten thousand to meet him who comes against him with twenty thousand? Or else, while the other is still a great way off, he sends a delegation and asks conditions of peace. So likewise, whoever of you does not forsake all that he has cannot be My disciple. (Luke 14:27-33)*

✓ Did the believers hear these words? Yes. He is asking them to "count the cost" of becoming a disciple. Can you imagine starting a house and thinking, "Well, I don't know how much money I have. I'll just start it and maybe it'll be completed." Nobody does that. We count the cost and make sure that we can finish the project. This tells me that being a disciple is a calculated choice. I am not going to "fall into it" by accident one day.

Before I begin to disciple a person, I challenge them as Jesus did. A disciple will say, "I'll try" while those who are only believers will say, "What's in it for me?" A believer is there to receive, while a disciple is ready to "forsake all" and count himself last. Isn't this what Jesus just taught? So I'll say to them, "You've got to learn this or you've got to do that" or "You've got to start memorizing Scripture." And I'll give them assignments, not to lead them to salvation or even necessarily because it is super-spiritual, but because it causes them to "count the cost" before I begin. That's what Jesus taught about discipleship.

Do you think that when he said,

"You have to hate your father and mother..."

that He wanted you to go home and hate your father and mother? No. What was He doing? Laying out an enormous test and saying, "If you're willing to do this then you can be My disciple. And if you choose not to, then you are not My disciple." That's why He said,

"If anyone comes to Me and does not hate his father and mother, wife and children, brothers and sisters, yes, and his own life also, he cannot be My disciple." *(Luke 14:26)*

Then He said to another,

"Follow Me." But he said, "Lord, let me first go and bury my father." Jesus said to him, "Let the dead bury their own dead, but you go and preach the kingdom of God." (Luke 9:59-60)

Jesus isn't without compassion. The Bible says He has great compassion and that He loves every person. He wept at Lazarus' funeral. Jesus knew the suffering that this follower would have to go through in leaving his Dad. But He is telling him to count the cost. Does he love God more than his Dad? If he does, then he will become a disciple. If he doesn't then he will return home a believer in Jesus, yet with great emptiness inside.

So, before choosing to read the rest of this book, what will it cost you to become a disciple?

Whoever of you does not forsake all that he has cannot be My disciple. (Luke 14:33)

God loves us. He loves our family. He loves our children. He loves the people around us. But we've got to start discipleship by giving everything up. Then wherever the Lord leads will be full of His Presence. That's the first Biblical step of discipleship.

Do you want to be a disciple or a believer? The option is yours. Today, this very moment, God is asking you to count the cost and choose what you're willing to do. You might be thinking, "Can I do this?"

There is story of a man named Peter who fell and hit his head upon a rock. When he became conscience he had severe amnesia. His good friend Jonathan tried to help resuscitate his mind by showing him past photographs with friends and family and telling the stories. Peter did not recognize his friends and family in the pictures. Jonathan was exasperated and brought Peter to a mirror. Peter stared at the man in the mirror and then replied to Jonathan, "How can this man help me? He looks just as confused as me."

We need to remember that this is true for each of us as well. Much of the problem in Christianity throughout history has been people trying to make themselves better. But we need to remember that the Gospel never asks us to make better humans but rather to forsake all and follow Christ. Just remember, the only thing Jesus said was "follow Me". He, himself, did all of the transforming and shaping of them into His image. They were only fishermen remember. All we need to do today is step up and say to the Lord, "I choose to be a disciple!" As you watch, He will create a radical revolution in us and through us.

So, if you are willing to believe, receive and forsake all for Jesus, then step right up to chapter two and begin your journey into discipleship.

CHAPTER ONE REVIEW

i. *What is the difference between a believer and a disciple?*

ii. *How did you respond to this chapter? Sadness? Anger? Fear? What is God saying to you?*

iii. *What do you think keeps believers from becoming disciples?*

iv. *What area is Christ asking you to follow deeper? And what has been stopping you?*

v. *Are you willing to become a disciple today?*

vi. *What does Scripture tell us you gain when you give everything to Christ?*

vii. *Memorize Matthew 28:18-20*

*W*e have now learned that we cannot be a Biblical Christian unless we are first a disciple. In Acts 11:26, the disciples were first called Christians in Antioch, and yet, somehow we've taken the name Christian and forgotten the word disciple. We have also noted that there is a major difference between a believer and a disciple and that Jesus recognized this difference. He gave authority to His disciples. He taught His disciples in private settings when the crowds of believers were gone. He gave His disciples miraculous powers and He taught them His commands.

> *"Go therefore and make disciples of all the nations, baptizing them in the name of the Father and of the Son and of the Holy Spirit, teaching them to observe all things that I have commanded you; and lo, I am with you always, even to the end of the age. Amen."*
> *(Matthew 28:19-20)*

What are the things that He had "commanded them"? As we are discipling, what should we consider the most important? Jesus made it simple.

The first characteristic of a disciple is found in Mark 12:28-33.

> *"Then one of the scribes came, and having heard them reasoning together, perceiving that He had answered them well, asked Him, "Which is the first commandment of all?" Jesus answered him, "The first of all the commandments is: 'Hear, O Israel, the LORD our God, the LORD is one. And you shall love the LORD your God with all your heart, with all your soul, with all your mind, and with all your strength.' This is the first commandment. And the second, like it, is this: 'You shall love your neighbor as yourself.' There is no other commandment greater than these." So the scribe said to Him, "Well said, Teacher. You have spoken the truth, for there is one God, and there is no other but He. And to love Him*

*with all the heart, with all the understanding, with
all the soul, and with all the strength, and to love
one's neighbor as oneself, is more than all the whole
burnt offerings and sacrifices."*

What is the greatest command for a disciple? To love God.
However, He doesn't stop there, as we will see in a later chapter.
Loving your neighbor is linked to loving God (See 1 John 4:20)
Loving God is greater than all "burnt offerings and sacrifices".
It is the very foundation of being a disciple. Are you desperately
in love with God?

A story is told of an elder sage named David from India
who was known by his love for God. Many said that they could
feel the very Presence of God when they were with David. He
would often pray for great lengths of time causing many to seek
him for wisdom and to pray for their needs because, his prayer
had power. Yet, he was a humble man and with a smile would
always give God the glory and praise.

One day a younger man named Josiah sought the counsel of
the sage. Josiah asked, "Can you show me how to know God?"
"Follow me," said the mentor and led Josiah down into a lake to
where the water was above their waist. "If I you want to learn,
I must baptize you." He then dunked Josiah in the water and
held him under water with all his strength. To Josiah's surprise
the old sage did not lift him out of the water. Suddenly he was
desperate for air and fought gallantly to surface. He was met with
resistance as his new mentor held him fast under water. Now
in panic, he flailed to be released from the old man's death grip
but to no avail. His demise felt moments away. Convinced now
that this old sage was out of his mind and was trying to drown
him, he exerted all the strength he had left in his body and broke
to the surface. The sage no longer fought him as Josiah gasped
for air. After a few breaths Josiah yelled, "You tried to kill me!"
"No," replied the sage, "I am teaching you. If you want to be
a disciple of Christ you must desire Him as desperately as you
just desired to breathe."

This is one way to teach others how desperately we are to
love God, but perhaps there is an easier way.

We can teach how to love God with our minds (what we
meditate on) and with our strength (service), but rarely does it

seem that we take into account loving God with our heart. How do we train our kids to love their spouses? Mostly by example. We cannot say, "Do as I say and not as I do" and expect to have any success. Passionate love for God often comes during intimate times of prayer. So, if you are discipling someone, then you must have intimate times of prayer worked into your schedule. We should purpose not only to talk about God with them, but to get on our faces and adore Him together. The foundation of our discipleship must include these intimate times of singing and worship as well as adoring God (which differs from the "I need" prayer list).

Isn't it amazing? Loving God is the Lord's commanded foundation for being His disciple. And yet, in the discipleship courses that I've been through, this whole idea has become secondary. I have spent most of my discipleship time analyzing God (loving Him with my mind), but have overlooked loving Him with my heart. This type of wholehearted loving is what people are actually longing for. It is more attractive to people and to God than we could ever imagine!

With this first commandment of loving God in our minds, read Revelation 2 where Jesus is talking to the church gathered in Ephesus.

> *"These things says He who holds the seven stars in His right hand, who walks in the midst of the seven golden lampstands: 'I know your works, your labor, your patience, and that you cannot bear those who are evil. And you have tested those who say they are apostles and are not, and have found them liars; and you have persevered and have patience, and have labored for My name's sake and have not become weary.'" (Revelation 2:1-3)*

Now if we ended there, we would probably consider the church of Ephesus an excellent church- a church that is working hard. But what they have done, as we'll come to find out, is that they have traded their heartfelt love for religious service. They've exchanged their adoration for hard work. You come into their church and discover quickly that they have this Bible study, or that Bible study, counseling classes and marriage classes, but you don't find anyone loving God. They are serving God but not loving Him. Now consider Revelation 2:4 which says,

*"Nevertheless I have this against you, that you have
left your first love."*

What kind of a marriage do I have, if my wife and I are simply responsible for each other? Do you want to be in a marriage where you are just responsible? If we have an attitude that says "Well I'm supposed to feed you, so I'll feed you. I'm supposed to work for you, so I'll work for you...and we're supposed to hug regularly, and kiss twice a day. We've got a good marriage all planned out...this is great!" This would be missing the point of marriage and would only be serving each other out of duty. We need to be aware that we can be obedient and unfortunately still lack love.

Would you want a marriage like that? Neither does God. As a disciple, He wants you in love. It's the foundation for everything else, including repentance. Do you know why we repent? According to Romans 2:4, it is the goodness and love of God. It's the "goodness and kindness of God that leads men to repentance."

His love is the key to repentance. That's why people cry when they accept the Lord. They are receiving His love and can't believe it. They just can't believe the mercy and love of God.

Now, there are several things that can compete with our love for God. Revelation 2 just revealed to us that good works and service can overshadow love. Let me give an example: As a musician, I can reach a place – any of us can – during a time of worship and singing where it becomes too important to make the music just right. My focus becomes making sure the rhythm doesn't miss or that the guitar is in perfect tune. This is in fact, a very common struggle with musicians on worship teams. They lose the fact that they're worshipping and loving God. At that point God would have us pick up our guitar and smash it on the floor. Works can replace love. Don't let them.

What else can replace love? 1 John 2:15 gives us an answer.

*"Do not love the world or the things in the world.
If anyone loves the world, the love of the Father is
not in him."*

How do we love the world? In a word....Busyness! I'm not talking about Christian service: just busyness. We may say, "Well

I must work overtime because I have a new car payment. I have to do this because I own that. I have a house and a mortgage and health insurance." All of a sudden we become a full-time manager of the things of the world.

In an old legend, Jesus said to His faithful follower Gorun, "Go pitch a tent on Mount Carmel, and stay there for a time of meditation and prayer." Gorun did just as Jesus asked.

Then, one day Gorun went into the nearest village and asked, "Please give me a blanket. Rats have gnawed on my old one, and I can't sleep." The villagers gladly gave him a blanket, however Gorun began returning frequently because the same thing would happen again. Someone finally suggested, "We'll give you a cat to solve your problem for good."

After a few days, Gorun was back. "Could you please give me some milk for the cat?" Realizing the need would be ongoing, the villagers decided to give bless him with a cow. Later, Gorun returned again, exclaiming, "I need something to feed the cow." This time, the villagers gave him a plot of land. With so many responsibilities now, Gorun asked for workers for the land and materials to build houses for them and so on.

Years passed; finally Jesus went to see his beloved disciple. He was greeted by a fat man who asked, "What business brings you here sir? What would you like to buy?" Gorun, had become a rich businessman who didn't even recognize his beloved Master.

The moral of this story is that we must determine not to let anything supplant our love for God. The life of a disciple flows from the relationship we have with Christ. Let us remember what it is that Christ says.

> *"For what will it profit a man if he gains the whole world, and loses his own soul? Or what will a man give in exchange for his soul"? (Mark 8:36-37)*

It's never worth it to fill ourselves up with love for "things" rather than love for God.

So, not only can good works replace the love of God, but we see that the world can replace the love of God as well.

Peter is a wonderful example to teach us about the love God. What did Peter tell Jesus before He went to the cross? Before He was arrested: what did he say? Peter said – "If everybody else forsakes You, I will die with You." And he meant it! He was the one individual who pulled out his sword against an entire brigade and started lopping off ears. Peter had said (and meant) "I'm going to die with you Jesus. This isn't happening unless I'm dead too." That's devoted, isn't it? Very devoted!

But isn't it interesting, that in John 21, Jesus asked Peter the same question 3 times. "Do you love me, Peter?"

He didn't say, "Will you serve me Peter?" He didn't say, "Will you be the Apostle who starts the gentile church, Peter?" "Can you swing a sword, Peter?" He said, "Do you love me Peter?" And Peter answered, "Yes I love you." and Jesus said, "Okay, then feed my sheep."

You love me and that will be the reason that you feed my sheep. Don't feed my sheep without a deep love for Me.

Then He says, "Do you love me?" to Peter a second time, and Peter says, "You know I love you." "So okay, tend My flock." And then finally a third time He says, "Peter, do you love me?" Now what do you think this was doing to Peter? A third time, He inquires, "Do you love me?"

I would think that Peter's heart was grieved after this third time. Peter must have paused, and asked the question. "What is he asking? Do I really love Him?" All of a sudden it sank in: do I really love Him? And he said, "Yes." And Jesus said "Okay. Take care of the things that need to be taken care of."

Jesus made Peter really stop and answer the question, "Do you love Me?", and so I need to answer that same question myself. Do I really love God? Is my prayer life, Bible study and ministry based upon something else rather than a desperate love for God? Is my love for God faded or is it the very thing that opens my heart in the morning? When I wake up, do I wake up with a song of worship? Or do I sing a song of worship because in the Bible it says early in the morning my song shall rise to you, so I get up and "la...la...la". Or does my worship truly come from my heart?

Now it is your turn to ask, "Am I in love with God?" The very question Peter had to ponder three times, and the one that I now ask you. Are you in love with God?

Why did God come and walk in the garden with Adam? Do you think that the Garden of Eden really compared to heaven? Why then, would God come down, except to be with those He loves? Why did Jesus Christ come down? It is the same reason... to be with you! It is why He calls us His bride and why he calls us His friends. It is why He calls us His beloved. Imagine when Jesus said, "You call me Master and I am Master, but no longer. Now I call you friend."

Can you imagine what that sounded like? What would it have been like to have Jesus speak those words directly to you? Listen to His voice saying, "no longer are we Lord and servant, but friends." That is awesome! That is the soul purpose of His life on earth: what is yours?

Do me a favor. Tomorrow morning don't ask God for anything. Just get up and spend some time loving Him. You will walk out of the front door like a new person. You will smile from ear to ear. Herein lies the purpose of life.

CHAPTER TWO REVIEW

i.   *Luke 10:27 mentions four aspects of loving God. What are they and are you doing them?*

ii. *Is God more interested in your effort for Him or your intimacy with Him? Which do you focus on?*

iii. *What struck you the most in the story about Josiah's baptism by the sage David?*

iv. *Would you consider yourself "desperate" for God?*

v.   *Guron became "rich" but lost his relationship with Christ. Are there activities in your life that seem good but are distracting you from your "first love"?*

vi. *Meditate on Revelation 2:1-5*

vii. *Make a commitment to read God's word daily and focus upon His character. One good way is to read the book of Psalms out loud to Him. Change any words that are needed to make it a person-to-person conversation between you and the Lord.*

viii. *Make a habit of talking to God throughout your day about everything. He is always listening.*

ix. *Memorize Mark 12:30*

od placed great importance on loving others. If the great command is to love God, then according to Mark 12:28-33, the second greatest command is to love others. Love is the foundation on which everything else must be built. Without love - service, works, prayer, Bible study, tithing or church attendance are worthless. Let us look at this Scripture below and listen to the words of Jesus himself.

> *"Then one of the scribes came, and having heard them reasoning together, perceiving that He had answered them well, asked Him, "Which is the first commandment of all?"*
>
> *Jesus answered him, "The first of all the commandments is: 'Hear, O Israel, the LORD our God, the LORD is one. And you shall love the LORD your God with all your heart, with all your soul, with all your mind, and with all your strength.' This is the first commandment. And the second, like it, is this: 'You shall love your neighbor as yourself. There is no other commandment greater than these." So the scribe said to Him, "Well said, Teacher. You have spoken the truth, for there is one God, and there is no other but He. And to love Him with all the heart, with all the understanding, with all the soul, and with all the strength, and to love one's neighbor as oneself, is more than all the whole burnt offerings and sacrifices." (Matthew 12:28-33)*

So, what does this Scripture tell me? Simply, it tells me that the act of attending church without love for God or love for my neighbor is, in and of itself, absolutely worthless. Similarly, if I am giving thousands and thousands of dollars and do not love God or my neighbor, this too is worthless. The same applies to acts of service, Bible study, or anything else, because love must be the foundation: the root of everything (read 1 Corinthians 13:1-3).

The focus on love becomes clearer as we read John 13:34-

35 which says,

> *"A new commandment I give to you, that you love one another; as I have loved you, that you also love one another. By this all will know that you are My disciples, if you have love for one another."*

Read this Scripture again and listen carefully to what it says. What is it that lets others know we are His disciples? Clearly, it is by the love we have for one another! A true disciple of Christ should be recognized by his love for others. Is it possible to be a true believer, and still not have love for others? Have you ever met a bitter believer? Do you know someone who believes wholeheartedly in the atonement of Jesus Christ but is bitter through and through and has no love? This is not what God intended.

In India an evangelist named Samuel was entering a train station. It was hot and the thick smells of human bodies, grease, smoke, and rotting waste drifted in the air. In addition was the aroma of curry, coming from venders selling roasted lamb. Samuel had patiently endured one hour in line buying his ticket for his train that would leave in 15 minutes. As he descended the stairs to the rail platform, his eyes scanned the busy station. He spotted a vender selling chai tea fifty yards down the track towards his departing train. It was just the treat he hoped for before he boarded. It was then that Samuel's eyes landed halfway between him and the chai tea vender, to a boy of about twelve years old that was selling apples. Alone, this boy knelt next to his cart of apples. He was calling out to a sea of people, but was making no sales. Worse, the boy was obviously blind. In the hustle and bustle no one took notice as they walked by.

The boy was very skinny and Samuel could read a sense of desperation and loneliness on his face. The Holy Spirit transfixed Samuel's attention to this scene as he stopped for a moment with only five steps left to the bottom platform. Captivated, he watched the boy unsuccessful in selling an apple or even gaining anyone's attention. A large man was passing near the cart when his pant leg caught the corner and suddenly the cart tipped, scattering the apples across the floor. The large man gave no hesitation and walked on. The boy quickly tried to gather back his precious inventory as he felt the ground for apples but this was difficult as some apples rolled a good distance and were accidentally kicked by the moving mob. No one seemed to care.

Without hesitation, Samuel now moved quickly towards the boy as he negotiated the crowd. He joined the boy in picking up each apple and replacing them in the cart. This was not an easy job with the scattered fruit and the large crowd. After a few minutes the boy and Samuel collected the apples, which were now bruised and damaged. The Holy Spirit gave Samuel compassion. He asked, "How much for an apple?" "Ten cents," replied the boy. Samuel counted about 30 apples and then exclaimed, "Here is five dollars. I will buy them all. But I cannot take them with me so please give them away for me." It was then that Samuel heard the last announcement for boarding the train. As Samuel began to walk away the boy called out. "Excuse me sir, are you Jesus?"

In this story, the boy recognized Jesus by Samuel's act of love. Take inventory of your own life. Are you recognized as a disciple of Christ because of your acts of love? In 1 Thessalonians 3:12-13 we see that our love should both increase and abound.

"And may the Lord make you increase and abound in love to one another and to all, just as we do to you, so that He may establish your hearts blameless in holiness before our God and Father at the coming of our Lord Jesus Christ with all His saints."

I find it interesting that both "increase" and "abound" are mentioned. That is a double blessing. Don't just increase, but increase and abound in love to one another *and* to "all". Consider this word "all". Who can I leave out? Is there anyone "unlovable"? No, not Biblically. We are to love even those who seem unlovable, just as God does. How are we supposed to love them? In John 13:34-35 Jesus says,

"Love one another 'as I have loved you'."

So, now we know how to love one another - it is to be the same way Jesus loved His disciples. Did it mean that Jesus was always sweet like honey with them? No, that's not love. In fact, once He said to a disciple, "Get behind me Satan." This was a pretty harsh way to say, "You are out of line", but it was said out of love. Jesus expressed love in many ways, through correction as well as intimacy. Love doesn't always mean we just repeat –"Oh I love you, I love you." Sometimes it means we confront sin until it is corrected.

We have coined a phrase: "Tough love." It means doing what is right even though you know it is going to physically or emotionally hurt the person you love. It is the type of love that causes you to spank your child when he does what is wrong, knowing that in ten years his heart will have been trained to do what is right. A love that is tough looks past feelings to truth. Tough love is what Jesus had when he looked at the Scribes and Pharisees in essence he said, "Woe to you! You're going to hell." (Read Luke chapter 11 for more) Yet, Jesus looked upon those who were killing Him (including those same Scribes and Pharisees) and said

> *"Forgive them, they know not what they do."*
> *(Luke 23:34)*

He had love for them yet He had still spoken the truth.
The bitter agony in Psalm 41:9 is terrible.

> *"Even my own familiar friend in whom I trusted,*
> *who ate my bread, has lifted up his heel against me."*

This is a prophecy of David concerning Jesus' betrayal by someone He loved. The betrayal increases when Judas comes to Jesus and kisses Him. He said,

> *"Judas, are you betraying the Son of Man with a*
> *kiss?" Luke 22:48.*

That must have hurt more than we know, and is why I believe Judas killed himself. Judas knew that not only did he kill an innocent man, but he betrayed the One who loved him so dearly. That was by far the hardest thing to bear and it led him to suicide.

The Scriptures tell us that it is God who teaches us to truly love.

> *"But concerning brotherly love you have no need that*
> *I should write to you, for you yourselves are taught*
> *by God to love one another." (1 Thessalonians 4:9)*

Paul says, "I don't need to teach you. For you yourselves

are taught by God to love one another. If you are a disciple, you will have love for one another because it is His commandment.

"Love one another." (John 13:35)

All commands infer choice! I can choose to love or I can choose not to love.

> *You have heard that it was said, 'You shall love your neighbor and hate your enemy.' But I say to you, love your enemies, bless those who curse you, do good to those who hate you, and pray for those who spitefully use you and persecute you, that you may be sons of your Father in heaven; for He makes His sun rise on the evil and on the good, and sends rain on the just and on the unjust. For if you love those who love you, what reward have you? Do not even the tax collectors do the same? And if you greet your brethren only, what do you do more than others? Do not even the tax collectors do so? Therefore you shall be perfect, just as your Father in heaven is perfect. (Matthew 5:43-48)*

> *"But love your enemies, do good, and lend, hoping for nothing in return; and your reward will be great, and you will be sons of the Most High. For He is kind to the unthankful and evil. Therefore be merciful, just as your Father also is merciful." (Luke 6:35-36)*

Here we see that Jesus gives a reward for loving those formerly considered unlovable. Great will be your reward in heaven. But it's still a choice isn't it? You can't say – "God, I'll love him as soon as You give me love for him." First, you start loving him and then you will be given love for him. Sometimes the action precedes the emotion.

We are given some examples of how to love in Ephesians 5:2:

"And walk in love, as Christ also has loved us and given Himself for us..."

This is how we are to love each other – As Christ loved.

> *If you really fulfill the royal law according to the Scripture, "You shall love your neighbor as yourself," (James 2:8)*

Do you want to fulfill God's law to the greatest extent? Then, love one another. That makes it simple, doesn't it? "Where are all the rules?" the Pharisee asks. Love is the fulfillment of all the commandments. Mathew 5:43-48 (above) gives us some practical ways to express this love. Bless those who curse you. Pray for them. Do you want to love someone? Pray for them. Do well to those who hate you. Now that's a physical action. They hate you, so go mow their lawn. They hate you, so wash their car. They hate you, therefore help them out. Mend their fence: whatever. Help them! They hate you, leave money on their doorstep when they're in trouble and don't put your name on it. That's how you do something good for them.

Why does Jesus say to do this? In order that you may become sons of your Father in heaven. Because God gives everyone His blessings and we should too. If you love everybody then you'll be perfect. That's what Jesus just said. Just as your Father in heaven is perfect. Luke 10: 25-37 gives us even more practical ways to love through the parable we call 'The Good Samaritan':

> *"What must I do to inherit eternal life?" A lawyer said to him, and Jesus answered, "What is written in the law?" And he said, "To love God and your neighbor". Jesus replies, "That's right. Do that and you will live."*

But, then the man went a little further…"Who is my neighbor?" It is then that Jesus tells an interesting story.

> *"A certain man went down from Jerusalem to Jericho, and fell among thieves, who stripped him of his clothing, wounded him, and departed, leaving him half dead." (Luke 10:30)*

So, he's naked, wounded, bleeding and almost dead.

> *"Now by chance a certain priest came down that road. And when he saw him, he passed by on the other side." (Luke 10:31)*

I like how it says "now by chance". Ha! What a chance! God has set this priest up. Do not think that God doesn't purposely bring you into these types of situations. This priest has a hard heart. Let us consider 1John 3:17-18, which says,

"But whoever has this world's goods, and sees his brother in need, and shuts up his heart from him, how does the love of God abide in him? My little children let us not love in word or in tongue, but in deed and in truth."

If you see someone in need and don't meet it, how can you say, "I love them?" Or as one Christian brother became convinced, "Why would I pray to God for another's need, if I myself can supply it?" If someone has a need and I can supply it and am concerned enough to pray for their need, then why wouldn't God meet that need through me? It is this kind of thinking that has really affected my prayer life. When someone I know has a need, I should first really ask the question: "Should I meet it?" This shows true compassion. In the story of the Good Samaritan, the Levite was lacking this.

"Likewise a Levite, when he arrived at the place, came and looked, and passed by on the other side. But a certain Samaritan, as he journeyed, came where he was. And when he saw him, he had compassion." (Luke 10:32-33)

So here comes what they consider a "half-breed": half Jew, half Gentile - a Samaritan. Yet, we see that this Samaritan has love for this poor man.

"So he went to him and bandaged his wounds, pouring on oil and wine; and he set him on his own animal, brought him to an inn, and took care of him. The next day, when he departed, he took out two denarii, gave them to the innkeeper, and said to him, 'Take care of him; and whatever more you spend, when I come again, I will repay you.' (Luke 10:34-35).

This is an example of physical, practical love!

Think for a moment about the practicality of this. The Samaritan's promise to repay the innkeeper for this man's care was extremely risky. What if this man was a big eater? What if he were to need a doctor? What if he has fine taste in clothing? Too much thought about the details might have changed his mind. It can be risky to help people out. That's why Jesus said to give and don't expect anything in return. (Luke 6:35) Many times you will receive nothing but hurt in return for your help. So let us give, not with the intent to receive, but out of our love for Christ. Amen?

Perhaps loving others is simpler than we make it out to be. Practical loving means doing something good. Why do we make it more complicated than that? Do you want to change your community? Then, love one another. Love the people. Let them vandalize your car. Let them steal from you. Let them abuse you. Just love them. Perhaps then you will radically change the community, by the simple act of love.

In 1 John 3 and 4, John pleads with us to love. "I've got an old message." *"Love!"* (1 John 3:11) "I've got a commandment." *"Love!"* (1 John 3:23). Finally, in 1 John 4:21 he says,

"And this commandment we have from Him: that he who loves God must love his brother also."

You must love one another if you really love God. That is hard, because it is sometimes unenjoyable, but it is our choice.

Maybe you are asking the question...If a person really wrongs you, do I wait for the "ooey gooey" emotions to develop before I love them? The answer is no! It may take time for the emotions to arrive, but it does not take any time to love them, because it is your choice. Jesus did not have "ooey gooey" emotions when He hung on the cross and cried out to the Father to forgive them. He made a choice. It was a willful choice, with very few "love" feelings.

Love will eventually have emotions, but emotions are not love. We have felt pretty good about some things that we have not really loved. The reverse is true: we may have felt pretty bad about some things that we have truly loved. Can you imagine if your bride or your husband looked across the table and said, "I love you as long as I feel good about you?" Is that marriage going to last? First bad day, "boom", it's over. Instead we say, "I love you and therefore I choose you forever. Even when I don't like you and when you have done something wrong. I love you." It's a choice. It's an act. It's a willful decision.

i.   Why does God make love a choice?

ii.   Who is a "Good Samaritan" in your life? What did they do for you?

iii. The blind boy recognized Jesus in Samuel. Do others recognize Jesus loving them through you? How?

iv.   Why does God consider our service as worthless without love? Meditate on 1 Corinthians 13:1-3

v.   What is a bitter believer and how do you recognize them?

vi.   Is anything making you bitter?

vii. If so, can you find a time that Jesus experienced a similar hurt?

viii. Go to your knees and surrender the event, person and feelings that hurt you and built up bitterness.

ix.   Meditate on how Christ experienced pain and how He took it upon Himself to suffer for you because of love.

x.   Memorize John 13:34-35

> *Then Jesus said to His disciples, "If anyone desires to come after Me, let him deny himself, and take up his cross, and follow Me. (Matthew 16:24)*

*D*eny yourself" This is the defining line that separates believers and disciples, church goers and power filled people of God, starters and finishers of the faith. It is a non-optional decision if we are His disciple and the crossroad we must take if the rest of Christ's teachings are going to impact us. Without this chapter, the rest of the book is powerless.

What does it mean? What is the Scriptural definition of "deny"? Well, it happens to be the exact word used to describe what Peter did the night Jesus was captured in Gethsemane (Matthew 26:34). So, let's examine Peter's "denial" so that we can start with a definition.

When those warming themselves around the courtyard fire asked Peter if he was a follower of Jesus, what was his response?

> *"I do not know this Man of whom you speak!" (Mark 14:71)*

He claimed to have no concern for the Man and no attachment to what would happen to Him. Peter had "denied" Him. Are you willing to have this same attitude concerning yourself? That is the first step of discipleship.

Let Jesus be your example:

> *Let this mind be in you which was also in Christ Jesus, who, being in the form of God, did not consider it robbery to be equal with God. (Philippians 2:5-6)*

This particular verse in Philippians has given me a favorite illustration. Let us make an imaginary ladder. It will represent rank and authority and we will place Jesus at the very top since according to this Scripture, He was equal with God.

But, the passage in Philippians continues with a further description of Christ,

"But (he) made Himself of no reputation, taking the form of a bondservant, and coming in the likeness of men." (Philippians 2:7)

Jesus denied Himself! Who made Him of no reputation? The answer is, He personally chose it. Denying ourselves will never be a spiritual gift, but it is our own personal choice. Jesus made Himself nothing. The very same God who spoke, "Let there be light" also said, "Let Me be nothing". THINK ABOUT THAT FOR A MOMENT...

Now if the Lord Jesus started at the top of our imaginary ladder and chose to deny everything that He was, then where does that place Him? It places Him at the bottom of course. Dear reader, Scripture places Jesus below you. Jesus made Himself of NO reputation, while you at least have some reputation on the earth.

As unbelievable as this seems, look at the next verse:

And being found in appearance as a man, He humbled Himself and became obedient to the point of death. (Philippians 2:8)

Being the lowest living man wasn't enough. Jesus had such little concern and attachment for Himself that He chose to be less than nothing. He chose to die. Consider this my friend...Are you alive? Then you are greater than a dead man! This same God whom Peter calls the "Prince of life" (Acts 3:15) became less than those He gave life to. Who are we to boast of anything? Who are we to be concerned and attached to our own rights when our great God and Savior has done such a thing?

In the fourteenth chapter in Luke we are privileged to read a parable that Jesus told illustrating this point.

When you are invited by anyone to a wedding feast, do not sit down in the best place, lest one more honorable than you be invited by him; and he who invited you and him come and say to you, 'Give place to this man,' and then you begin with shame to take the lowest place. But when you are invited, go and sit down in the lowest place, so that when he who invited you comes he may say to you, 'Friend, go up higher.' Then you will have glory in the presence of those who sit at the table with you. For whoever exalts himself will be humbled, and he who humbles himself will be exalted. (Luke 14:7-11)

Picture the following scene for a minute. A person comes to dinner and sits in the place of honor next to the head of the table and begins feasting. Then suddenly, the person for whom that seat was actually reserved arrives. How embarrassing! It is much easier to sit in the lowest place and let the Master of the house invite you to a higher position. Jesus denied Himself and chose the lowest place in all of His creation and by doing so proved an unchanging principle of heaven.

For whoever exalts himself will be humbled, and he who humbles himself will be exalted. (Luke 14:11)

Hebrews reinforces this fact:

"[Look] unto Jesus, the author and finisher of our faith, who for the joy that was set before Him endured the cross, despising the shame, and has sat down at the right hand of the throne of God. (Hebrews 12:2)

Jesus 'despised' or literally 'set His mind against this' shame and humiliation. He knew about the cross. He chose it for Himself because of His love for you. When He came up from the water of His baptism, He looked to the cross. When He healed the ten lepers, and no one thanked Him, He looked to the cross. He always knew what awaited Him. The cross...that which is reserved for criminals. The cross...that terrible place of shame. He denied Himself and had no concern or attachment to His own life. And now, because of the aforementioned principle, He sits, exalted in the highest place of heaven.

Jesus not only told us we must deny ourselves, but He showed us what it would look like. He made it very clear that if we want to be something, then we must become nothing. This is of course, complete nonsense to the world around us, but not to those who look on from a heavenly perspective. The Lord knows that the door of earthly SHAME enters into the room of spiritual HONOR, while the door of earthly HONOR enters into the room of spiritual SHAME. Lack of perspective on this one issue has always held believers back and kept them from growing in their faith.

The ability to deny oneself is one of the first characteristics to look for in a believer. Simply ask the question, "Are they unconcerned and unattached to themselves?" If so, these are the ones whom God exalts. Soon they will be leading people to the Lord and saving souls! Their workplaces will be changed, their families will be transformed, and they will be walking in the power of God. Why? Because they are willing to deny themselves.

Don't be discouraged if you are struggling with this right now. Remember, the most common argument recorded among the disciples wasn't "Who brought the bread?" (They did argue about that once.) The most common argument was, "Who is the greatest?" We can picture Peter arguing about how he had walked on water, while John would argue that Jesus always referred to him as the disciple He loved. In fact, there are at least five separate incidents where the disciples argue among themselves about who is the greatest while in the very presence of the Servant of all. Let's briefly look at one of the most shameful of these incidents.

Now there was also a dispute among them, as to which of them should be considered the greatest. (Luke 22:24)

Can you imagine? Even we don't go this far. We may be arrogant at times, but we probably never have an open argument about how great we are compared to each other. Can you imagine that kind of an argument going on in the middle of your church? Can you imagine arguing like this in front of Jesus?

Jesus does not waste any time speaking the truth to them about who is actually the greatest.

And He said to them, "The kings of the Gentiles exercise lordship over them, and those who exercise authority over them are called 'benefactors.' (Luke 22:25)

'Benefactor' is not an insult; it simply meant that they were recognized as someone who had money and power.

But not so among you; on the contrary, he who is greatest among you - let him be as the younger, and he who governs as he who serves. (Luke 22:26)

Deny Yourself

The word for 'serves', can be translated 'errand boy'. If you want to be the greatest in the kingdom of heaven, Jesus says, don't be a 'benefactor', be an 'errand boy'.

For who is greater, he who sits at the table, or he who serves? Is it not he who sits at the table? Yet I am among you as the One who serves. (Luke 22:27)

When we enter a restaurant and sit down, we don't commend the waiter on how wonderful he is. No! We call him over and order our food. In the world's eyes the one who sits at the table and eats is always greater than the one who serves. In contrast, what are the facts of heaven? The greatest is actually the servant. Do not argue about who is the greatest. Deny yourself. Concern yourself with others and become great...like Jesus.

Now here is the most amazing part of the argument between the disciples: Do you know when they were arguing? Luke 22 reveals that they were actually arguing in front of Christ about their own greatness, while they were taking the last meal before the crucifixion...

He breaks the bread and says:

This is My body which is given for you; do this in remembrance of Me. (Luke 22:19)

He takes the wine and says:

This cup is the new covenant in My blood, which is shed for you. (Luke 22:20)

He shares the tragedy that lies ahead:

But behold, the hand of My betrayer is with Me on the table. And truly the Son of Man goes as it has been determined, but woe to that man by whom He is betrayed! (Luke 22:21-22)

And then a fear breaks out among them concerning who could be capable of such an act of treason:

Then they began to question among themselves, which of them it was who would do this thing. (Luke 22:23)

This soon turned into:

Now there was also a dispute among them, as to which of them should be considered the greatest. (Luke 22:24)

Now do you understand why, according to John, immediately following the supper, Jesus girded Himself with a cloth and began washing their feet? This is a good way to end an argument about greatness isn't it? Have you ever had anybody wash your feet? The first time someone washed my feet was in India. (It was utterly humbling, especially since the man who washed my feet only had one foot himself.) Do you know what happens when your feet are washed? You become aware of who you really are. By washing their feet, Jesus was awakening their conscience. Their feet were surely dusty and dirty, so while they were busy arguing about who was the greatest, He revealed His nature and took the lowest position in the house.

So when He had washed their feet, taken His garments, and sat down again, He said to them, "Do you know what I have done to you? You call me Teacher and Lord, and you say well, for so I am. If I then, your Lord and Teacher, have washed your feet, you also ought to wash one another's feet. For I have given you an example, that you should do as I have done to you. Most assuredly, I say to you, a servant is not greater than his master; nor is he who is sent greater than he who sent him. If you know these things, blessed are you if you do them. (John 13:12-17)

If you are not greater than your Master, then why should you strive to be? Deny yourself and wash feet. Hallelujah!

Let us look at another example from the lives of the disciples:

Then the mother of Zebedee's sons came to Him with her sons, kneeling down and asking something from Him. (Matthew 20:20)

Now you might do a little study on Matthew 27:56 and John 19:25 to discover that James and John's Mom was Jesus' Aunt. So, 'Auntie' comes asking for a favor.

And He said to her, "What do you wish?" She said

to Him, "Grant that these two sons of mine may sit, one on Your right hand and the other on the left, in Your kingdom." (Matthew 20:21)

Jesus, knowing who set this whole thing up, addresses James and John in verse 22. These two disciples were trying to manipulate Him to become great in heaven. They did not yet understand.

And when the ten heard it, they were greatly displeased with the two brothers. (Matthew 20:24)

I thoroughly believe that the others were angry, not because of James and John's ungodliness, but because each of them wanted that position of greatness for themselves. I only share these stories with you to encourage you that even the original disciples needed to learn how to deny themselves. It wasn't something that "came upon them".

In fact, Peter and John had their own personal rivalry for greatness. In John chapter 21, after Jesus questions Peter's love and restores him to leadership, he tells him about his death.

"Most assuredly, I say to you, when you were younger, you girded yourself and walked where you wished; but when you are old, you will stretch out your hands, and another will gird you and carry you where you do not wish." This He spoke, signifying by what death he would glorify God. And when He had spoken this, He said to him, "Follow Me. (John 21:18-19)

Peter is shocked! "I thought that I was going to lead and shepherd your people..."

Then Peter, turning around, saw the disciple whom Jesus loved (John)...Peter, seeing him, said to Jesus, "But Lord, what about this man? (John 21:20-21)

Even at that very moment, Peter was struggling with the rivalry for greatness between him and John. Denying himself at that moment would have been unnatural. "I want to know that at least John has to die too!" He hadn't learned yet.

Even on resurrection Sunday Peter and John were striving against each other for greatness. Mary Magdalene had just come

back from the empty tomb and told the disciples. Peter and John
are amazed, so:

*Peter therefore went out, and the other disciple
(John), and were going to the tomb. (John 20:3)*

Okay, they're going to check things out. Can't you see it?
First, they're walking along and then Peter's walking a little faster,
and pretty soon John is walking faster. Next thing you know,
they're both running! Now look what it says!

*So they both ran together, and the other disciple
outran Peter and came to the tomb first. (John 20:4)*

John just had to be first. It didn't matter that Peter was
huffing and puffing behind. "It's all about me!" Is John denying
himself? Well, while John is congratulating himself and catching
his breath:

*And he, stooping down and looking in, saw the linen
cloths lying there; yet he did not go in. (John 20:5)*

In second place, Peter shows up and shoves right past John,
standing at the entrance.

*Then Simon Peter came, following him, and went
into the tomb...Then the other disciple, who came
to the tomb first, went in also (John 20:6a, 8)*

Even on that marvelous morning, the two of them have a
foot race. How about you? Are you racing with others? Are you
concerned with putting others first and yourself last, or do you
strive to be greater than they? Do you serve tables or sit at them?
Yes, even the disciples understood this struggle. The good news is
that after they received the Spirit on Pentecost things did change.
They prayed together:

*Now Peter and John went up together to the temple
at the hour of prayer (Acts 3:1)*

They healed people together:

*the lame man who was healed held on to Peter and
John (Acts 3:11)*

They were placed in jail together:

they laid hands on them (Peter and John), and put them in custody until the next day (Acts 4:3)

They stood strong against persecution together:

But Peter and John answered and said to them, "Whether it is right in the sight of God to listen to you more than to God, you judge. (Acts 4:19)

They were even missionaries together:

Now when the Apostles who were at Jerusalem heard that Samaria had received the word of God, they sent Peter and John to them. (Acts 8:14)

What a relief to know that by the Spirit of God we can overcome this struggle.

Paul's own personal testimony and teaching reveals three specific areas where we can begin to focus on denying our selves.

Glory

Having risen up to Apostleship through the religious elite of his day, he might have become attached to prestige, but he didn't refer to himself as Reverend:

Paul, a bondservant of Jesus Christ (Romans 1:1)

He had been taught by Jesus to deny himself.

Though I also might have confidence in the flesh. If anyone else thinks he may have confidence in the flesh, I more so: circumcised the eighth day, of the stock of Israel, of the tribe of Benjamin, a Hebrew of the Hebrews; concerning the law, a Pharisee; concerning zeal, persecuting the church; concerning the righteousness which is in the law, blameless. But what things were gain to me, these I have counted loss for Christ. (Philippians 3:4-7)

Paul had a long list of reasons why his confidence could have been in the flesh, but his focus remained on Jesus instead. Paul even eventually became the most influential Apostle in the entire world, but he steadfastly remained unconcerned and unattached to his own glory.

For I am the least of the apostles, who am not worthy to be called an, because I persecuted the church of God. But by the grace of God I am what I am, and His grace toward me was not in vain; but I labored more abundantly than they all, yet not I, but the grace of God which was with me. Therefore, whether it was I or they, so we preach and so you believed. (1 Corinthians 15:9-11)

I love how he says, "Whether it was I or they". What he means is, "who cares!" Paul proclaims that it is truly unimportant who preaches, even if it was he who preached the most. It was by God's grace that they believed, and Paul was keenly aware of Who should receive all the glory. He has denied it for himself.

Personal Rights

Paul did an exemplary job in denying his successes. However, may I suggest that it may be a whole lot easier to deny our successes than to deny our personal rights? Not all of us have 'successful lives', but all of us believe we have 'personal rights'. In 1 Corinthians, Paul gives a long list of personal rights:

"Am I not an Apostle? Am I not free? Have I not seen Jesus Christ our Lord? Are you not my work in the Lord? If I am not an Apostle to others, yet doubtless I am to you. For you are the seal of my apostleship in the Lord." (1 Corinthians 9:1-2)

"Do we have no right to eat and drink? Do we have no right to take along a believing wife, as do also the other Apostles, the brothers of the Lord, and Cephas?" (1 Corinthians 9:4- 5)

"Who ever goes to war at his own expense? Who plants a vineyard and does not eat of its fruit? Or who tends a flock and does not drink of the milk of the flock?" (1 Corinthians 9:7)

"If we have sown spiritual things for you, is it a great thing if we reap your material things? If others are partakers of this right over you, are we not even more? Do you not know that those who minister the

*holy things eat of the things of the temple, and those
who serve at the altar partake of the offerings of the
altar? Even so the Lord has commanded that those
who preach the gospel should live from the gospel."*
(1 Corinthians 9:11, 12a, 13-14)

In these verses Paul loudly proclaims, "I've got rights!!!"

Amazingly however, Paul goes on to explain that as a disciple
he remains unconcerned and unattached to these rights.

*"But I have used none of these things...For if I
preach the gospel, I have nothing to boast of, for
necessity is laid upon me; yes, woe is me if I do
not preach the gospel! For if I do this willingly,
I have a reward; but if against my will, I have
been entrusted with a stewardship. What is my
reward then? That when I preach the gospel, I
may present the gospel of Christ without charge,
that I may not abuse my authority in the gospel."*
(1 Corinthians 9:15a, 16-18)

Paul even preached this:

*"For we do not preach ourselves, but Christ Jesus
the Lord, and ourselves your bondservants for Jesus'
sake." (2 Corinthians 4:5)*

The writings of Paul reveal to us that denying ourselves not
only includes our glory and our rights, but even goes as far as
our own personal liberties.

*"For you, brethren, have been called to liberty; only
do not use liberty as an opportunity for the flesh, but
through love serve one another." (Galatians 5:13)*

Let us look at the following example in Paul's letter to
Corinth. Many of the local butchers in the Roman culture were
supplied from the sacrifices of the pagan temples. In fact, much
of the meat for any particular city would have been slain in a
temple prior to being hauled to the butcher. This troubled some
Christians during Paul's time who felt that they would be par-
taking of a sacrifice to an idol if they ate this meat. Paul was
completely convinced that he had the personal freedom to eat

any meat, as long as he avoided asking questions about its origin:

*"Eat whatever is sold in the meat market,
asking no questions for conscience' sake; for
"the earth is the LORD'S, and all its fullness."
(1 Corinthians 10:25-26)*

Did Paul have the personal liberty to eat this meat, regardless of where it was killed? Yes, but a disciple is even willing to deny personal liberty.

*"Therefore, if food makes my brother stumble, I
will never again eat meat, lest I make my brother
stumble." (1 Corinthians 8:13)*

So, whether it be glory, rights or liberties, we have been called by Jesus to deny ourselves and follow Him. This is the path of biblical discipleship and according to Christ, a life choice we must make if we are going to grow in Him.

Let me end with a modern example. Consider the story of Richard Wurmbrand, a pastor in Romania during the communist regime, who was persecuted and imprisoned for 14 years due to his faith. One day as his Christian cellmate was singing praises to God, he was caught by the guards and received the strict punishment of standing in the snow overnight just outside the window of the cell he and Richard had been sharing. There was now a barred window separating the two Christians, one in the snow and the other in the cell.

Richard was looking on with compassion at his friend who was shivering in the exposed cold. His roommate's clothes were tattered and worn and the only protection from the harsh blowing wind was a thin long sleeved shirt. Richard could see that the freezing cold was brutal to his skin and it wasn't long before he made a personal decision that could cost him his own life.

Although it was extremely cold inside the cell where Richard was standing, he had greater concern for his brother than himself. He had recently been given a sweater to wear during his cold winter in prison, so when the guards were not looking, he took off his warm sweater and shoved it through the bars to his friend outside. The guards would surely punish him for what he had done, but he was willing to take that chance.

Not only did Richard risk punishment, but he also sacrificed his own warmth for another. Later, this brother in Christ shared how the warmth of Richard's personal sacrifice helped him survive more than the sweater itself. Richard Wurmbrand chose to deny himself, and this sacrificial act of love sustained his friend's body and soul from death through that long night. This is the same Richard Wurmbrand whom God later raised up to found the organization "Voice of the Martyrs", which is still aiding hundreds of thousands of suffering believers across the world today.

"If anyone desires to come after Me, let him deny himself"

CHAPTER FOUR REVIEW

i.   Define "deny" in your own words.

ii. Which of the three "denials" that Paul spoke about is most difficult for you?

iii. Does it discourage or encourage you that the disciples struggled with this step?

iv. Richard Wurmbrand denied his own comfort for another. In what ways has the Holy Spirit led you to deny yourself for others?

v.   Think of an area in your life where you need to deny yourself. Surrender this to the Lord and do not be discouraged, but if needed, surrender it a hundred times a day until God has give you victory.

vi. Memorize Luke 9:23

TAKE UP THE CROSS

Then Jesus said to His disciples, "If anyone desires to come after Me, let him deny himself, and take up his cross, and follow Me." (Matthew 16:24)

"And he who does not take his cross and follow after Me is not worthy of Me." (Matthew 10:38)

"Whoever desires to come after Me, let him deny himself, and take up his cross, and follow Me." (Mark 8:34)

"Whoever does not bear his cross and come after Me cannot be My disciple." (Luke 14:27)

*J*esus didn't make this statement just once, but four times. "Unless you bear your cross and come after Me you cannot be My disciple." That tells me two things: First, I cannot be His disciple unless this is true in my life, and second, I cannot say I have discipled another, unless it is true in their life. With these statements from Jesus, my 'cross' becomes an essential requirement for discipleship and perhaps the hardest to receive. As we talk about this in the next two chapters, each of us will have our 'cross' laid before us and will make a decision about what we are willing to do.

So, what does it really mean to "take up your cross"? Those listening to the words of Jesus understood that He was referring to their death. To take up a cross meant to receive the death penalty, fully knowing it would mean suffering. Although God surely does not require everyone to physically die for Him, He does ask us to be willing to suffer for our faith in Him. When we become a disciple of Christ we must have an attitude that accepts personal suffering as something that glorifies our Savior. Our hearts need to develop a willingness to suffer as we follow our Lord. A true disciple is agreeable to follow Christ, whatever the cost!

There is a story told of two twins in China named Gao and Ching. Unfortunately, as the twins grew older their paths went in separate directions. Ching chose the life of drugs, immorality and worldly pleasures. In contrast, Gao became a loving disciple of Jesus. Knowing that his Ching had chosen a life of destruction, Gao prayed for his brother and witnessed the love of Jesus to him whenever he was able.

One late night Ching ran into the home of Gao. Ching shaking with fear and with blood on his shirt cried out, "I've killed a man and now the police are chasing me." Without hesitation, Gao instructed his brother to change clothes with him. Moments later, when the police arrived they arrested Gao for murder, and left Ching free . At the trial Gao pleaded guilty and was sentenced to death. On the day of his execution he was able to speak to his brother Ching. Out of deep love he said, "I have bought your life; follow Christ and I will see you in heaven."

Most of us will never be placed in such an extreme situation as Gao and Ching's, but each of us will have to make personal choices about our willingness to suffer. In fact, it is generally acceptable for most people to take great measures in avoiding suffering. We avoid dentists or strenuous exercise or myriads of other situations. As humans, we don't like suffering. We even buy items to aid us in our battle against suffering: heated blankets, shoe inserts, soft shirts. Many think the ultimate goal of life is to reach a place where there is no suffering of any kind. No wonder we are surprised when Christ asks us, "Will you suffer for Me?"

From the moment Jesus spoke these words until today, people have had to choose whether they would deny themselves and take up their cross for Him or avoid the suffering and not be His disciple. This is in fact, a choice God's people have been making for ages. Hebrews 11:24-27 says that Moses dealt with this exact issue.

> *By faith Moses, when he became of age, refused to be called the son of Pharaoh's daughter, choosing rather to suffer affliction with the people of God than to enjoy the passing pleasures of sin, esteeming the reproach of Christ greater riches than the treasures in Egypt; for he looked to the reward. By faith he forsook Egypt, not fearing the wrath of the king; for he endured as seeing Him who is invisible.*

Moses didn't accidentally pick up his 'cross'; he made a choice. He chose to refuse being called the son of Pharoah's daughter, which would have allowed him to enjoy the passing pleasures of life and instead he willingly accepted suffering for following His God. Let us remember that 'to refuse' something means to forcefully push it away. Refusing is much more forceful than forgetting or disregarding. Moses said in essence, I have an opportunity to take what the world is offering, but I refuse it and choose "to suffer affliction with the people of God, rather than to enjoy the passing pleasure of sin." In this we can see that Moses took up his 'cross'.

We must, however, be careful not to misapply Christ's teaching about the cross. It is foolish to seek ways to harm ourselves for the sake of God. We shouldn't purposely stir up a riot so that we can be beaten or spit upon. This is not the cross, this is stupidity. A dear friend of mine who has been beaten near to death several times for His faith in Christ can be heard saying, "Some people are beaten for Jesus and others for foolishness." Let us be sure to understand that taking up our cross doesn't mean recklessly looking for suffering, but instead it is our refusal of this world and our choosing of Christ above all things; above our husband, our wife, our job, and ultimately above our own life.

Again Moses esteemed the reproach or shame of Christ as greater than all the treasures in Egypt. Pharaoh owned everything and Moses looked at it and determined that it was nothing compared to what awaited him if he chose the Lord. This is paralleled in Matthew when Christ asks, "What if you gained the whole world and lost your soul?" (Matthew 16:26) The truth is that if you gained all the dollars, yen, rupees, gold, diamonds, companies, servants, retirement, and all the yachts but lost your soul, YOU WERE CHEATED! Moses wisely looked to better rewards than these when he took up his cross saying, "I am not going to be a child of Pharaoh. I could be a king or a prince, but instead I choose to be a slave for the Lord!" David said,

> *For a day in Your courts is better than a thousand. I would rather be a doorkeeper in the house of my God than dwell in the tents of wickedness. (Psalms 84:10)*

Jesus Himself, willingly chose to suffer and now asks us to join Him.

Therefore Jesus also, that He might sanctify the people with His own blood, suffered outside the gate. Therefore let us go forth to Him, outside the camp, bearing His reproach. (Hebrews 13:12-13)

Jesus Christ died outside the city of Jerusalem, where the Levitical law said the sin offering was to be taken. Therefore, by being killed outside the city, He fulfilled the requirements of God's law and personally bore our shame, 'outside the camp'. To follow him as a disciple then, we must go to Him 'outside the camp', even though we know that shame awaits us as we follow Him. The author of Hebrews makes it very clear that disciples are willing to "bear" the consequences of following Him.

Within the church, there may be some that believe that if you are a disciple of Jesus Christ you do not have to suffer. They may believe that there should not be pain or suffering in the life of a believer. Jesus' own words openly contradict this teaching.

"Behold, I send you out as sheep in the midst of wolves. Therefore be wise as serpents and harmless as doves. But beware of men, for they will deliver you up to councils and scourge you in their synagogues." *(Matthew 10: 16-17)*

Let us consider what this means. Pretend that you are now a sheep going into the midst of a wolf pack. A sheep in those circumstances doesn't say, "Woopee, woopee, woopee!" does he? And the wolf doesn't say, "Oh it's so nice to see you Mr. Sheep. I was hoping you would come to dinner." On the contrary, if you stick a sheep in the midst of a pack of wolves, it will be torn limb from limb. As Christians we must accept that we will be persecuted in this world for His Name's sake.

"And you will be hated by all for My name's sake. But he who endures to the end will be saved." *(Matthew 10:22)*

What else does Scripture have to say about this topic?

"When they persecute you in this city, flee to another. For assuredly, I say to you, you will not have gone through the cities of Israel before the Son of Man comes. A disciple is not above his teacher, nor a servant above his master. It is enough for a disciple

*that he be like his teacher, and a servant like his master. If they have called the master of the house Beelzebub, how much more will they call those of his household! Therefore do not fear them."
(Matthew 10:23-26a)*

Consider what this is saying. If they call Jesus Beelzebub, or literally, Lord of the flies or Satan, how much more will they call His followers? "If they treated Me badly then they will treat you badly." He gives us His own life as an example of how the world will treat us. You can look at Jesus' life and know exactly how others are going to respond to your faith (more in the next chapter).

Listen to Paul's writing.

*But you have carefully followed my doctrine, manner of life, purpose, faith, longsuffering, love, perseverance, persecutions, afflictions, which happened to me at Antioch, at Iconium, at Lystra--what persecutions I endured. And out of them all the Lord delivered me. Yes, and all who desire to live godly in Christ Jesus will suffer persecution.
(2 Timothy 3:10-12)*

According to Paul, if we do not suffer persecution, then we are not living godly in Christ Jesus. I didn't say it: Paul did.

When Paul was initially called by Jesus Christ into ministry, God sent Ananias. (Acts 9) When Ananias was told by the Lord to lay hands on Paul, he responded in essence, "Oh, but Jesus, this guy came all the way from Jerusalem to throw us into jail and kill us." And Jesus replies,

"For I will show him how many things he must suffer for My name's sake." (Acts 9:16)

Clearly, when Jesus called Paul, He shared the same things He had shared with the other Apostles. Paul would be sent like a sheep among wolves and he would be beaten and scourged. The very same religious leaders who had authorized Paul's campaign against the Christians would now believe that they were doing God a favor by killing him. When Jesus instructed the Apostles He made the call to suffering clear! Not surprisingly, the moment he called Paul, He was taught the same thing. In fact, a great deal of the Lord's teaching was about this very topic, and yet it now amazes me how the topic is avoided at all costs in the church today. Instead, we are told: "Name it and claim it" or "You should never be sick or ever suffer." This is a false teaching, because our Lord could definitely 'name it and claim it', yet He chose to suffer at the hands of His enemies.

> *For what credit is it if, when you are beaten for your faults, you take it patiently? But when you do good and suffer, if you take it patiently, this is commendable before God. For to this you were called, because Christ also suffered for us, leaving us an example, that you should follow His steps. (1 Peter 2:20-21)*

Not only did Jesus teach us about suffering, we have been "called" to it just like the Apostles were. Even when we are doing good we need to expect suffering. This may be a strong teaching, but as a disciple it cannot be denied that He has called us to the cross. We either follow or don't.

However, at this point, we must also note that there is a place of suffering that Jesus has not called us to. A place where we cannot follow His steps. You see, there were two parts to Jesus' suffering. There was the suffering that occurred as a man from His birth until the last prayer in the garden of Gethsemane and then there was His suffering under God's wrath against sin.

Jesus identified the differences of these two sufferings;

> *"And do not fear those who kill the body but cannot kill the soul* (the first suffering). *But rather fear Him who is able to destroy both soul and body in hell."* (the second suffering)*" (Matthew 10:28)*

The Lord is not calling us to take part in suffering under His wrath against sin.

> *For God did not appoint us to wrath, but to obtain salvation through our Lord Jesus Christ. (1 Thessalonians 5:9)*

Praise God! We shall not taste eternal torment. We shall never feel the wrath of God upon our sin and thankfully, won't ever have to embrace this second kind of suffering. When Jesus said, "it is finished" (John 19:30) from the cross, it was truly finished. None of God's wrath for our sin will come upon us. This suffering was for Him and Him alone. Hebrews 1:3 says, by Himself [He] purged our sins..

Why is this so important? One of the reasons we need to be clear on this topic is because some may teach a doctrine called "the doctrine of blood atonement". This is something that is actually taught in the Church of Latter Day Saints (the Mormon Church). They teach that there are some sins that Christ's blood will not cover and that the blood of the offender must cover themselves with their own suffering. This is not true. We need to know that the Bible teaches that we will not touch the atonement of Jesus Christ's suffering.

> *But we see Jesus, who was made a little lower than the angels, for the suffering of death crowned with glory and honor, that He, by the grace of God, might taste death for everyone. (Hebrews 2:9)*

Let us not forget that Christ died for all of us!

> *For all have sinned and fall short of the glory of God, being justified freely by His grace through the redemption that is in Christ Jesus, whom God set forth as a propitiation by His blood, through faith, to demonstrate His righteousness, because in His forbearance God had passed over the sins that were previously committed, to demonstrate at the present time His righteousness, that He might be just and the justifier of the one who has faith in Jesus. (Romans 3: 23-26)*

He is first 'Just', in that our sins are punished, but He is also 'The Justifier' of us, because our debt is now over and He is our "propitiation." This is a beautiful word, "propitiation". What does it mean?

When a space shuttle flies into outer space, it is propelled by a rocket. After it has encircled the earth and returns to the atmosphere, what happens? Lots of sparks and lots of heat! Now if a meteorite or "falling star" enters the atmosphere like this, what happens? It burns up. Why doesn't the space shuttle burn up when it re-enters this same atmosphere? It is because there is a ceramic heat shield on the front known as the 'Propitiatory

Shield'.

Now we understand the word "propitiation". When you and I stand in the Presence of God Almighty, we have 'Propitiatory Shield' through our Beloved Jesus Christ. God has said that no man can see Him and live, but we will stand in the Presence of God with the shield of Jesus surrounding us. When the fire of judgment and wrath against our sin is poured out, it never touches us because it strikes Him. We will never suffer under God's wrath. That is the propitiation of Jesus Christ. Hallelujah!

Now that you know what propitiation is, share this wonderful message with others, so that they might step behind that same shield when they meet God as well. No one will want to be outside the 'Propitiatory Shield'.

At this point, I hope that what Jesus means by the "cross" is becoming clearer. We are not being called to suffer under God's wrath but we do need to be prepared for suffering as we follow Christ through this world.

In the next chapter we will look at twelve specific examples of suffering that Jesus experienced prior to Gethsemane and we will see how they relate to our lives today.

i. What is your view of suffering?

ii. Can we live a godly life without suffering? Why or why not?

iii. Do you consider suffering for Christ a greater reward than the comforts of this world?

iv. How was Christ's suffering after Gethsemane different than His suffering before?

v. Gao exchanged his identity for Ching's. In what ways can you relate to this story?

vi. Describe what it means to be "willing" to suffer for following Jesus.

vii. Have you ever heard a "no suffering" gospel? How would Jesus respond to this?

viii. Memorize 1 Peter 2:21

THE CROSSES WE BEAR

efore we continue our discussion about suffering, I want to look at Hebrews 2:18 so that we will not become overwhelmed.

For in that He Himself has suffered, being tempted, He is able to aid those who are tempted. (Hebrews 2:18)

As we begin to understand the suffering of a disciple, we need to know that the Lord Jesus will be with us in it. He will never leave us nor forsake us and will always aid us.

God is our refuge and strength, a very present help in trouble. (Psalms 46:1)

We discussed Christ's suffering under the wrath of God last chapter and found that we will never share in that suffering. But now we begin to look at suffering that Jesus received by the hands of the world and Satan, and recognize that it will be the same for us.

A disciple is not above his teacher, nor a servant above his master. It is enough for a disciple that he be like his teacher, and a servant like his master. If they have called the master of the house Beelzebub, how much more will they call those of his household!" (Matthew 10:24-25)

One day brother David Witt was visiting a church in Southern Sudan. The floors were dirt and had mounds of dark earth for pews. The walls were made out of mud bricks with high windows to protect from stray bullets in case of an attack from the Islamic ruled government. As they praised the Lord in song he looked over the congregation. Here he was in fellowship with a mass of beautiful Sudanese men, women and children. These disciples were full of tales of persecution, beatings, imprisonments and lost loved ones. Scars marked many of their bodies, testifying to their faith.

But it was not the physical scars that held David's attention.

His great inspiration was the sea of handmade wooden crosses, which were held above the heads of each believer. Some held their cross high, while others swayed theirs to the music. It was a dramatic picture. They had each experienced their own personal suffering and had received its mark. But God had lavished them with love. Instead of despising the cross, they loved the cross and worshiped with joy, hope and boldness in the Holy Spirit. One pastor shared that despite the cross of suffering, his network of churches had grown in attendance by two thousand percent. Another pastor shared that "suffering was a gift from God. Not because God likes suffering but He likes what it produces: disciples."

As I talk about Christ's suffering I feel the need to make one important note. Nine of the twelve points we will cover entail *internal and emotional* suffering rather than physical. Since I am an American, I recognize how little I physically suffer for the Lord. But when I realized how often the Lord had suffered emotionally, I began to understand that as I have followed Jesus, I have frequently taken up my own cross, just like my Savior.

Rejection

Jesus Christ was rejected by men. John 1:11 literally says, "He came to His own possessions and His own people would not receive Him." He came to those He had made and owned and yet His people would not receive Him. He was rejected! But, He knew that was going to happen.

> *"Have you never read in the Scriptures: 'The stone which the builders rejected Has become the chief cornerstone. This was the LORD'S doing, and it is marvelous in our eyes'?" (Matthew 21:42)*

Was Jesus Christ a man? Yes, He was both completely a man and still fully God. Do you think that as a man, it hurt when He reached out to those He loved and they rejected Him? Didn't He openly weep over Jerusalem? How about you? What do you weep over? Have you ever felt alone? Have you ever felt everyone you love has alienated you because you're a Christian? Perhaps it is comforting to know that Christ felt that way.

When He preached His very first sermon in the town of

Nazareth, the crowds didn't shout for joy. No, instead, they tried to take Him out on a hill and kill Him. The very first sermon He ever preached turned into a violent riot. There was an immediate rejection. There wasn't any waiting around. The fellowship meal had to wait; they must first throw Jesus over the hill. Now some of us have experienced this type of immediate rejection as we too were sharing the Gospel.

One of my Christian brothers recently shared the Gospel with a lady who was serving ice cream. She was telling us how good the ice cream was, and so he said, "Well, have you tasted Jesus? For it says, 'Taste and see that the Lord is good.'" She responded, "What?!" and he answered, "You know: Christianity. Jesus." She turned around and walked away. He was immediately rejected.

There are those that may not reject the message of Jesus so abruptly, but rather slowly decide that they are not interested in what is being shared. We may refer to this type of rejection as a person's heart growing hard. Even though they first may be interested in the message, they begin to display an attitude of annoyance and become disagreeable. Jesus experienced this rejection from those he taught as well. Although this type of rejection always starts with complaining, it does not often end there.

Complaining Against

The Jews then complained about Him, because He said, "I am the bread which came down from heaven." (John 6: 41)

Let us consider what happened. Jesus said something they did not agree with and they began complaining. Has this ever happened to you? Those who are listening to you suddenly start murmuring and complaining, saying something like, "He's always talking about this Jesus. I'm getting sick of this. I don't even want to invite him over any more. In fact, I am completely tired of hearing his incessant talk about being born again."

Complaining: that is the first part. They complained at His teaching. Isn't it interesting, when Jesus knew His disciples complained, He said to them, "Does this offend you?" (John 6:61) Keep in mind that at this time it wasn't the Jewish leaders or the crowds of followers that had begun complaining against him, but His own disciples! This is one of the most painful types of rejection. It really hurts when someone that you have poured yourself into and tried and tried to help begins grumbling and griping about what you've done for them. We know that Christ not only did the best He could, He did the best, period, and yet they still complained. I can think of several people that I have dug out of a ditch, poured my life into, and then they turned on me. It hurts.

Paul had a similar thing happen to him when Demas left him at the very end of his life. He said, "Demas has forsaken me, having loved this present world." (2 Timothy 4:10) A few years earlier Paul had called Demas his "fellow laborer" (Philemon 1:24), but now he had forsaken him.

So, after Jesus had poured Himself into His disciples day after day, they complained against Him. He walks up to them and overhears their murmuring and griping. In contrast to immediate rejection, complaining is the beginning of a much slower rejection. Just keep sharing and you too will experience complaining, but it often doesn't end there either.

Quarreling

> *The Jews therefore quarreled among themselves, saying, "How can this Man give us His flesh to eat?" (John 6:52)*

The complaining didn't end; it simply led to quarreling. They went from, "I don't like this teaching" to "Hey, I'm starting to get mad about this." And then all of a sudden, the arguing begins. They may not even be fighting directly with you: they may be fighting with another person over what you have said, but the slow rejection is building. This slow rejection doesn't stop at arguing…

Griping

> *Therefore many of His disciples, when they heard this, said, "This is a hard saying; who can understand it?" (John 6:60)*

If you are truly following Christ, people will sometimes feel that you push them too far.

"You're overboard. You want me to do what? You want me to leave the woman I'm living with and move out because we're not married? Look, we've been together for 15 years, man."

"Hey, I'm sorry. Being with a woman outside of marriage is called fornication and it's a sin."

"You're ridiculous. You push me too far."

Or

"You want me to stop doing what? Look, I've been doing this with my taxes since you were 'this high', kid, and you know what? I'm comfortable with it. It's not a sin to me."

"Well, it says in Romans, render taxes to those whom taxes are due."

"You push me too far."

It may start with some of your relatives saying, "Ahhh, I don't like this", and then pretty soon they are arguing about it and the next thing is, "Fine, fine, have your religion. But, don't go overboard."

Believe it or not, you are now walking in the way of the cross. As you watch the slow rejection building, you are moving into Christ's suffering. People rejected Christ when He pushed them too far and they will you also. Guess what happens next? Where does the complaining, quarreling and griping lead?

Desertion/Abandonment

From that time many of His disciples went back and walked with Him no more. (John 6:66)

MANY! Not some. Many of the disciples went back and –underline it – "walked with Him no more." They didn't get angry and then come back later. They never returned. They said something like, "Oh yeah, I've heard that Jesus teach. I used to be one of His followers, but I grew out of it."

I had somebody say this once about a teaching I had done. "I've heard that Travis teach and I think he goes too far. I think he's a jerk." They started to call me names. "I don't agree with his interpretation." (This really meant they don't agree that sin is sin, and righteousness is righteousness.) "Yeah, I don't agree with it. In fact, I am never going back to that church." These are real statements that were made because I was teaching the Bible.

I had never attacked them. In fact, one of the people I'm thinking of, I barely even know. But somehow they are sure that I personally attacked them and they're never coming back. Yet I don't even know them.

If that should happen to you, just realize it is the way of the cross. In fact, expect it to happen to you if you desire to follow Christ with your whole heart. There will always be people who say, "I'm never talking to you again." Keep in mind that this is not because you have done what was wrong, but because you have done what was right.

The Bible has an interesting way of describing our effect on those around us. We are an aroma in everyone's nostrils.

> *For we are to God the fragrance of Christ among those who are being saved and among those who are perishing. To the one we are the aroma of death leading to death, and to the other the aroma of life leading to life. And who is sufficient for these things? (2 Corinthians 2:15-16)*

It should not be surprising then that some people will blossom and grow when the Word of God is shared with them, and others turn and spit when taught the same information. Have you experienced this? Do you know what that was? It was your cross.

Hatred

Let us go to a little stronger word. There is a word in my family that my children are not even allowed to say. They are not allowed to "hate" things or people. I feel that it is too strong a word to use for little children. Listen to what Jesus says...

> *The world cannot hate you, but it hates Me because I testify of it that its works are evil. (John 7:7)*

The world did not just have 'poor feelings' toward Jesus, but outright hatred! Why does the world hate Jesus? He testifies that what it is doing is wicked. How then do you think the world is going to respond if we obey Ephesians 5:11?

And have no fellowship with the unfruitful works of darkness, but rather expose them". (Ephesians 5:11)

To clarify, this does not mean our job is to run around and point at everyone's sin. Instead, it means my life is to be so truthful that when people talk to me I just simply speak about the truth. I should not seek them out to beat them over the head with their sin, but I also should not shrink away from it. If it's true, it's true. If it's sin, it's sin. If it's wrong, it's wrong.

It's hard not to waver, because most people are not going to accept the truth according to Jesus. His way is too narrow and too difficult for them.

Because narrow is the gate and difficult is the way which leads to life, and there are few who find it. (Matthew 7:14)

In fact, those who refuse God often hate any sign of holiness. If Jesus would have simply said, "God loves you, God loves you, God loves you", nobody would have hated him. Instead, He spoke the truth about sin, and declared holiness. He drew a line and all of a sudden we are either in agreement or in disagreement, right?

The life of a disciple is like that.

If the world hates you, you know that it hated Me before it hated you. If you were of the world, the world would love its own. Yet because you are not of the world, but I chose you out of the world, therefore the world hates you. (John 15:18-19)

I cannot tell you how many times I have been mocked about how little I allow my children to watch TV. I'm not telling others what they can watch. I'm not going to their house and saying you can't let your children watch that. I'm simply saying that my children are not allowed to watch certain sinful things that are on TV. As a result, I am persecuted. All of a sudden, people hate me, simply because I have spoken about sin and have chosen to live a holy life.

For we have spent enough of our past lifetime in doing the will of the Gentiles--when we walked in lewdness, lusts, drunkenness, revelries, drinking

parties, and abominable idolatries. In regard to
these, they think it strange that you do not run with
them in the same flood of dissipation, speaking evil
of you. (1 Peter 4:3-4)

Just the fact that you are not a drunk anymore will make
them hate you. You don't have to say a single word, but they
will suddenly turn on you and start talking negatively about you.
This is just like they did to Jesus.

Insults

Blessed are you when they revile and persecute you,
and say all kinds of evil against you falsely for My
sake. (Matthew 5:11)

Oh, yes, they insulted Jesus.

The people answered and said, "You have a demon."
(John 7:20a)

Then the Jews answered and said to Him, "Do we
not say rightly that You are a Samaritan and have
a demon?" (John 8:48)

Then the Jews said to Him, "Now we know that You
have a demon!" (John 8:52a)

I have actually had somebody say that to me. "You're possessed." I've had others yell out that I was a false prophet. Don't
worry: they called Jesus a sinner.

So they again called the man who was blind, and
said to him, "Give God the glory! We know that
this Man is a sinner." (John 9:24)

Ever hear that? "Oh, I know the real them. They're a hypocrite. They're a sinner."

Are people so offended by your faith that they want to dig
up dirt on you? Good. Blessed are you when you are suffering
for Christ's sake. It's a good thing when they do that: not a bad
thing. This is because you have been called to suffer as Christ did.

But when His own people heard about this, they went out to lay hold of Him, for they said, "He is out of His mind." (Mark 3:21)

Jesus' own family called Him crazy. His very own family! Simply because He was serving God above His own hunger. This is exactly what my family did to me when I quit my job and became a minister. My Dad told me I was insane and self-centered. He insulted me. My father is my very best friend and his insult hurt me more than I can share. The shame that I felt from him was one of my greatest obstacles in becoming a minister. But I picked up my cross and followed Jesus anyway. Praise the Lord, because my Dad is now saved and thanks me for taking up that cross!

You see, I willingly chose to suffer. My Dad had never said anything against me before. It didn't matter what I wanted to do. He always wanted me to do the best that I could. It didn't matter if it was sports or college. So, you can imagine what it felt like to have my Dad say, "You are a self-centered fool." It tore my heart out and hurt me terribly. Yet, it is assuring to know that Christ went through even deeper suffering than this.

Anger

If a man receives circumcision on the Sabbath, so that the law of Moses should not be broken, are you angry with Me because I made a man completely well on the Sabbath? (John 7:23)

I refer to this particular type of anger: as 'illogical anger' because it is irrational. If a man can be circumcised on the Sabbath so that the Law of Moses is not broken, then becoming angry with a person who heals someone on the Sabbath is illogical. It just doesn't make sense.

Have you ever experienced or witnessed illogical anger? My friend was recently fired from his job after 20 years of faithful service, because a new manager was continually getting angry at him. The new manager had rejected Christianity and did not appreciate the faith of my friend. The manager often became illogically angry at him, even to the point of mistakenly blowing up at him about things or projects he wasn't even involved in. My friend was suffering persecution indeed. Whether our aggressors understand it or not, illogical anger is often simply a response to Jesus. When you have been treated unjustly and your circumstances appear illogical, you may be suffering persecution without realizing it.

Arrest

> *Therefore they sought to take Him; but no one laid a hand on Him, because His hour had not yet come. (John 7:30)*

Right now, in Eritrea, Africa, there are hundreds of Christians in jail. There are Christians in jail for their faith in China, North Korea, and in India. Right now there is a man I know in India who is in jail and on trial for being a follower of Jesus Christ.

Are you ready to do that? What happens if they come in and say you can no longer worship Jesus Christ? What will you say? Are you determined to worship your God no matter what the consequences may be? This is the cross that Jesus told us about. Decide now, because you must be willing to take up that cross if you are going to be a disciple of Jesus Christ.

Division

Jesus caused division among many people.

> *So there was a division among the people because of Him. (John 7:43) Therefore there was a division again among the Jews because of these sayings. (John 10:19)*

Jesus told us that our own families would become increasingly difficult to live in after becoming a disciple. In fact, He said,

> *"A man's enemies will be those of his own household." (Matthew 10:36)*

The rejection of our own families is probably the hardest persecution one can suffer in the United States. Our families probably won't kill us, but there is a very real possibility they won't talk to us again. Again, that is a cross.

The Greek word schism, used in John 7:43 that speaks of division, is the same word that you would use to describe tearing a book in half. That is what happened in my life and that is a good description of what it feels like inside you when your family rejects you.

> *Do not think that I came to bring peace on earth. I did not come to bring peace but a sword. For I have come to 'set a man against his father, a daughter against her mother, and a daughter-in-law against her mother-in-law'; and 'a man's enemies will be those of his own household.' (Matthew 10:34-36)*

For most of us, the bonds we have formed with our families are the strongest we will ever have. However, at some point in our lives, we may be asked to make a choice that could destroy these bonds. We should be prepared to choose our relationship with Jesus over the relationships we have with any other, including those we are closest with, like our parents and/or children. We have to be willing to walk in a way of division if God is calling us to it.

> *He who loves father or mother more than Me is not worthy of Me. And he who loves son or daughter more than Me is not worthy of Me. (Matthew 10:35)*

Dear reader, if you are walking in the hatred of your relatives at this very moment, let me tell you: blessed are you of God. He will carry you through this, and bless you in amazing ways and the Spirit of God will rest upon you. Be encouraged by the following words:

> *If you are reproached for the name of Christ, blessed are you, for the Spirit of glory and of God rests upon you. On their part He is blasphemed, but on your part He is glorified. (1 Peter 4:14)*

You don't have to give in: you can walk through their hatred, knowing that it is simply your cross. Then on that day you stand before our great Savior you will be able to say, "I took my cross for you Lord. I don't care what they said about me Lord: even my Mom and my Dad; they forsook me Lord, but I believed on

You and I carried my cross."

So now let's move away from the internal emotional suffering of the cross to the physical sufferings that may happen.

Murder

Who plotted Jesus' murder? Was it not the religious leaders of the day? In fact, eventually the religious leaders of that time would also kill the prophets and Apostles Jesus sent.

> *Therefore, indeed, I send you prophets, wise men, and scribes: some of them you will kill and crucify, and some of them you will scourge in your synagogues and persecute from city to city. (Matthew 23:34)*

Jesus told His disciples then and now, to expect suffering at the hands of those who claim they serve the Lord.

> *These things I have spoken to you, that you should not be made to stumble. They will put you out of the synagogues; yes, the time is coming that whoever kills you will think that he offers God service. (John 16:1-2)*

Now this is always happening. It happened during the Spanish inquisition where the Catholic Church killed thousands of Christians and thought they were doing service to God. Even today, I have a dear missionary friend in Mexico whom the Catholic Church stirred up hatred against. They aided the drug lords in capturing and imprisoning him, but by the grace of God, he wasn't murdered. However, they did deport him and drive him from the area. And yet, this persecution came from the very heart of the supposed Christian church.

They tried to kill Jesus.

> *Did not Moses give you the law, yet none of you keeps the law? Why do you seek to kill Me? (John 7:19)*

> *Now some of them from Jerusalem said, "Is this not He whom they seek to kill?" (John 7:25)*

Even the crowds knew about the murder plot. It seemed to be public knowledge, so, it was obviously not a secret that the Pharisees and Scribes were seeking to kill Jesus for religious reasons. Everybody knew.

Sometimes the murderous plots were pre-meditated, but at other times they occurred spontaneously. They would become suddenly overwhelmed by their zeal and try to kill him.

So all those in the synagogue, when they heard these things, were filled with wrath, and rose up and thrust Him out of the city; and they led Him to the brow of the hill on which their city was built, that they might throw Him down over the cliff. (Luke 4:28-29)

Jesus' teaching was so difficult to receive and the Spirit's Presence so strong upon Him that even when He was just sitting in the temple, they would become overwhelmed by murderous hatred.

Then they took up stones to throw at Him; but Jesus hid Himself and went out of the temple, going through the midst of them, and so passed by. (John 8:59)

Who was behind all of this murderous plotting? The established religious leaders! It has always been that way for the disciples of Jesus, just as He foretold. Who killed Stephen in Acts 7? The religious leaders! Later, others even took an oath to God that they wouldn't eat or drink again until they had killed Paul in Acts 23:14.

Peter was beaten. John was beaten. And they rejoiced because as disciples, they knew that this was their cross.

So they departed from the presence of the council, rejoicing that they were counted worthy to suffer shame for His name. (Acts 5:41)

They rejoiced for being allowed to suffer for His Name. They knew when Christ arose and went to heaven that it was now their turn to suffer. And they carried their cross, considering it joy to do this for Jesus.

According to Peter, suffering is simply a willingness to follow Jesus.

For to this you were called, because Christ also
suffered for us, leaving us an example, that you
should follow His steps. (1 Peter 2:21)

Don't be discouraged. In the Scriptures we always see suffering side by side with the glory of God. Like Siamese twins: wherever there is suffering for Jesus, you will find the glory of the Lord. Pay attention the next time you see the word "suffering" and see if the word "glory" isn't near it. Let us look at several examples.

Ought not the Christ to have suffered these things
and to enter into His glory? (Luke 24:26)

But he, being full of the Holy Spirit, gazed into
heaven and saw the glory of God, and Jesus standing
at the right hand of God...and they cast him out of
the city and stoned him. (Acts 7:55, 58)

For I consider that the sufferings of this present time
are not worthy to be compared with the glory which
shall be revealed in us. (Romans 8:18)

For our light affliction, which is but for a moment,
is working for us a far more exceeding and eternal
weight of glory. (2 Corinthians 4:14)

But we see Jesus, who was made a little lower than
the angels, for the suffering of death crowned with
glory and honor, that He, by the grace of God,
might taste death for everyone. For it was fitting for
Him, for whom are all things and by whom are all
things, in bringing many sons to glory, to make the
captain of their salvation perfect through sufferings.
(Hebrews 2:9-10)

But rejoice to the extent that you partake of Christ's
sufferings, that when His glory is revealed, you
may also be glad with exceeding joy. If you are
reproached for the name of Christ, blessed are you,
for the Spirit of glory and of God rests upon you.
On their part He is blasphemed, but on your part
He is glorified. (1 Peter 4:13-14)

> *The elders who are among you I exhort, I who am*
> *a fellow elder and a witness of the sufferings of*
> *Christ, and also a partaker of the glory that will be*
> *revealed. (1 Peter 5:1)*

The Scriptures are replete with examples of the glory of God being shared with those who suffer with Him. Our suffering, our cross is not insignificant. It is rewarded. Often I hear from the persecuted believers, "Where there is a cross there is a crown of glory. Where there is a crucifixion there is a resurrection." We do not seek suffering. We seek Jesus. If we want to be like Jesus then He must give us a cross.

Dear reader, the only place we can store up glory for God is here and now, while we are still alive. After I am dead, my glory for God is full. Whatever I have, I have. That is it for all eternity. You honor and praise God with what you have: there is no avenue to gain more. What an awesome opportunity lies before us today!

> *For to you it has been granted on behalf of Christ,*
> *not only to believe in Him, but also to suffer for His*
> *sake, having the same conflict which you saw in me*
> *and now hear is in me. (Philippians 1:29-30)*

This is a statement only a disciple can receive. We have been granted two things: to believe and to suffer because of our belief. Listen to the Apostle Paul's view on suffering:

> *Therefore I take pleasure in infirmities, in reproaches,*
> *in needs, in persecutions, in distresses, for Christ's*
> *sake. For when I am weak, then I am strong.*
> *(2 Corinthians 12:10)*

> *I now rejoice in my sufferings for you, and fill up*
> *in my flesh what is lacking in the afflictions of*
> *Christ, for the sake of His body, which is the church.*
> *(Colossians 1:24)*

Paul never said he enjoyed suffering, (as if anyone could), but instead that he rejoiced in the suffering, knowing that the followers of Christ were strengthened and receiving eternal life. Paul was himself a living example of how the suffering of Stephen had brought eternal life to a persecutor.

We are hard pressed on every side, yet not crushed;
we are perplexed, but not in despair; persecuted,
but not forsaken; struck down, but not destroyed--
always carrying about in the body the dying of
the Lord Jesus, that the life of Jesus also may be
manifested in our body. For we who live are always
delivered to death for Jesus' sake, that the life of
Jesus also may be manifested in our mortal flesh.
So then death is working in us, but life in you.
(2 Corinthians 4:8-12)

A disciple loves God and others so deeply that he is willing
to trade his life for the salvation of others. Do you remember
Gao and Ching from the last chapter? I can only think of what
Paul said when he was in prison under a Roman guard.

But I want you to know, brethren, that the things
which happened to me have actually turned out for
the furtherance of the gospel, so that it has become
evident to the whole palace guard, and to all the rest,
that my chains are in Christ. (Philippians 1:12-13)

We find him rejoicing because he is able to share the Gospel
with the Roman soldiers guarding him, and as they change shifts,
he begins anew with the fresh soldiers. Paul was able to speak
with the entire palace guard about Jesus. And he rejoiced!

This way of thinking is contrary to the natural world. The
world says: don't suffer. Stay healthy. Make sure that you protect
yourself from disease, malnutrition and physical ailment. Paul
says "follow whole-heartedly after God". Peter says, "walk in
his footsteps and if you are granted to suffer for Jesus Christ,
rejoice because it is bringing life to others and glory to God."

This isn't taught in many Bible colleges or seminaries and
unfortunately it isn't taught from most church pulpits. Even
though Jesus specifically said:

And whoever does not bear his cross and come after
Me cannot be My disciple. (Luke 14:27)

Listen to Paul's resumé:

But in all things we commend ourselves as ministers
of God: in much patience, in tribulations, in

needs, in distresses, in stripes, in imprisonments, in tumults, in labors, in sleeplessness, in fastings; by purity, by knowledge, by longsuffering, by kindness, by the Holy Spirit, by sincere love, by the word of truth, by the power of God, by the armor of righteousness on the right hand and on the left, by honor and dishonor, by evil report and good report; as deceivers, and yet true; as unknown, and yet well known; as dying, and behold we live; as chastened, and yet not killed; as sorrowful, yet always rejoicing; as poor, yet making many rich; as having nothing, and yet possessing all things. (2 Corinthians 6:4-10)

ETERNITY

These things I have spoken to you, that in Me you may have peace. In the world you will have tribulation; but be of good cheer, I have overcome the world. (John 16:33)

Jesus says the world is a terrible place, but cheer up! Consider when Paul had been seized in Jerusalem and was hauled up the Antonio Fortress steps and thrown in prison. In his mind he must have been struggling with, "Oh, oh, oh. What did I do wrong? If I just would have tried something else, the Jews might have believed." I'm sure that Paul was depressed at how things had turned out, but Jesus appears to him and says: "Cheer up! Cheer up: it's okay. This suffering you are experiencing is for Me and for the salvation of others. Cheer up! You're going to Rome!"

But the following night the Lord stood by him and said, "Be of good cheer, Paul; for as you have testified for Me in Jerusalem, so you must also bear witness at Rome." (Acts 23:11)

When in the midst of our suffering, the Lord Himself will say, "Cheer up. Things are going good. I have overcome the world." Perhaps the Lord is speaking those very words to you right now as you read this.

Jesus said... These things I have spoken to you, that

*My joy may remain in you, and that your joy may
be full. (John 15:11)*

Jesus, will come during times of suffering and will bring you
joy. In every situation, He is with you.

*For He Himself has said, "I will never leave you nor
forsake you." So we may boldly say: "The LORD
is my helper; I will not fear. What can man do to
me?" (Hebrews 13:5-6)*

If you will stop and meditate on the words that you have just
read, no matter what happens to you, you can agree with Paul.

*For I consider that the sufferings of this present time
are not worthy to be compared with the glory which
shall be revealed in us. (Romans 8:18)*

Jesus is looking into eternity right now and makes a guarantee.

*Blessed are you when men hate you, and when they
exclude you, and revile you, and cast out your name
as evil, for the Son of Man's sake. Rejoice in that day
and leap for joy! For indeed your reward is great in
heaven, for in like manner their fathers did to the
prophets. (Luke 6:22-23)*

Just so that we can gain a full appreciation for what our
Lord has just said, please put this book down and jump up and
down as high as you can, "leaping for joy"...That is how great
your reward is in heaven when you take up the cross.

Paul was blessed to actually receive a vision of heaven which
he records in 2 Corinthians 12:4 and it transformed his attitude
towards suffering. Sure, he had suffered...

*in stripes above measure, in prisons more frequently,
in deaths often. From the Jews five times I received
forty stripes minus one. Three times I was beaten
with rods; once I was stoned; three times I was
shipwrecked; a night and a day I have been in the
deep; in journeys often, in perils of waters, in perils
of robbers, in perils of my own countrymen, in perils
of the Gentiles, in perils in the city, in perils in the
wilderness, in perils in the sea, in perils among false
brethren; in weariness and toil, in sleeplessness*

often, in hunger and thirst, in fastings often, in cold and nakedness. (2 Corinthians 11:23b-27)

But, he had also seen the other side and wrote...

Therefore we do not lose heart. Even though our outward man is perishing, yet the inward man is being renewed day by day. For our light affliction, which is but for a moment, is working for us a far more exceeding and eternal weight of glory, while we do not look at the things which are seen, but at the things which are not seen. For the things which are seen are temporary, but the things which are not seen are eternal. (2 Corinthians 4:16-18)

Paul tells us the key to rejoicing in our times of suffering is to not look at the things which are seen, but at the things which are not seen. Jesus has promised eternal blessings and Paul was allowed to see them. If we can trust Jesus' words and Paul's vision, then in light of our promised rewards, our suffering and even our death becomes a light affliction. Remember that our reward is far more exceeding, and eternal! In other words, it's not only bigger, it's bigger FOREVER!

i.   *Christ was rejected by so many, even His own family, friends and disciples; what is it about Christ that people rejected? What physical, emotional or mental suffering have you experienced? Can you find a similar experience in Christ's life?*

ii.   *Looking back at a previous cross you have had to bear, are you rejoicing in it? Why or why not?*

iii.   *How can you find joy during a time of suffering?*

iv.   *Reflect on the persecuted Christians of Sudan. Why do you think the cross gave them such hope?*

v.   *How has your view of the cross changed as you have read these last two chapters?*

vi.   *Exercise your faith and thank the Lord right now for the suffering you have endured, trusting that God has greater glory awaiting you.*

vii.   *Memorize Romans 8:18*

A Mind To Serve

A disciple is not above his teacher, nor a servant above his master. It is enough for a disciple that he be like his teacher, and a servant like his master. (Matthew 10:24-25a)

For even the Son of Man did not come to be served, but to serve, and to give His life a ransom for many. (Mark 10:45)

That word 'serve' is 'diakonos' or 'waiter'. We refer to those in the church who care for physical needs as 'deacons' from this very same word. Now if Jesus was a Servant, then what attitude should we have as a disciple? Jesus tells us in Luke that every human has a master.

No servant can serve two masters; for either he will hate the one and love the other, or else he will be loyal to the one and despise the other. You cannot serve God and mammon. (Luke 16:13)

There are many believers who have a conflict raging within them. They wish to serve Jesus AND the world, but cannot seem to do either. They have too much of the world to be happy in Christ and too much of Christ to be happy in the world.

And whatever you do, do it heartily, as to the Lord and not to men. (Colossians 3:23)

I love that word heartily: 'ex psuche' - out of your soul. This is one of those words that we cannot grasp easily. Do "whatever you do" from your very soul, with passion! WHATEVER! This doesn't say, "If you're preaching" or "If you're praying", but WHATEVER YOU DO!

And whatever you do, do it heartily; out of your soul. As unto the Lord and not to men. Knowing that from the Lord you will receive the reward of the inheritance; for you serve the Lord Christ. (Colossians 3:23-24)

Kelso is a 70-year-old Colombian servant of Christ. Colombia is not an easy country to serve the Lord in, being one of the most violent nations on earth. The civil war between the communist based guerillas and the democratic controlled government has lasted over 40 years. The communist guerillas believe that there is no god and so their violence has spilled over into attacks against Christians. They have destroyed and shut down many churches in the remote areas. In the midst of all the violence raging across the land, Kelso for years has preached the gospel to those same communist soldiers.

In 2005 the Holy Spirit spoke to Kelso that he should take a boat downriver to an area which up until then had never received any gospel literature. Through prayer, God confirmed his feeling by taking him to Jesus' words, "Go and make disciples." He knew God was calling him to "GO", but he admits that God did not tell him if he was coming back. All he was sure of is "GO." Along with him, he took four other faithful servants of Christ who were also willing to risk their lives. During the first week they distributed Bibles and Christian literature all along the river. One lady danced with joy when she met Kelso on the beach. She had heard the gospel being preached on the radio and had been praying for two years that someone would bring her a Bible. After the first week Kelso and the team were taken hostage by the communist soldiers.

Now their ministry of service was to the guerilla soldiers themselves. As hostages of Jesus they looked for opportunities to "show" His love. At one point the camp became very low on food. Kelso, who is a very good fisherman, told one of the communist officers a few tricks about fishing and offered a special hook that he had made. He then suggested a place along the river and told the officer that he would pray. The officer went to fish and Kelso gathered the team together to pray. Kelso prayed, "Lord, bless this officer with a catch that not only feeds the whole camp but also feeds us."(The team was also very hungry from lack of food.) The officer ended up catching a cat fish which weighed over 100 pounds. It was the biggest catch the camp had ever seen. Everyone ate and there were even some leftovers that were given to the poor villagers in the area.

As Kelso served these soldiers, God worked many miracles.

Part of their lack of food was from an extended drought. Kelso told some of the leaders that he would begin praying for rain. That same day a downpour filled and even overfilled their reservoirs of water. As their imprisonment continued, Kelso and the team gained more and more favor with the soldiers. After 57 days of captivity they were finally released and allowed to return home. Because they had chosen to never stop serving, God never stopped blessing.

Who are we really serving throughout our day? We are to serve Jesus Christ at our desk, when we are bathing our child, at our mill, in our car, when we are cooking. We don't serve a company or an employer; we are ALWAYS serving Jesus.

You may have forgotten who you serve, but the Lord hasn't. Often, God will remind me, "It's for Me Travis." And those moments change my whole attitude. This recently happened when I had spent an entire day digging a deep ditch for an electrical cable. The next day, while I was absent, the electric company arrived and determined that my ditch would be better if I moved it about 6 feet uphill. An entire day's work for 6 feet! That evening, I went to bed with a very bad attitude. Through the night, the Lord spoke to my heart, that He had orchestrated every day of my life, and if I had to re-dig the ditch, it would be for Him. That morning, I awoke with great joy. (This is the most wonderful part of the story) When I arrived at the worksite, my friend happened to be there and he just happened to have a ditch-digging machine. Within 2 hours, the work was done. How foolish it was to forget whom I actually served.

God desires for us to remember that everything we do is counted as service to Him. Listen to this:

> *If anyone serves Me, let him follow Me; and where I am, there My servant will be also. If anyone serves Me, him My Father will honor. (John 12:26)*

Put your occupation in the blank.

If anyone serves me [as a_____], let him follow Me and where I am there my servant will be also. If anyone serves Me [as a_____], him my Father will honor.

If I am a disciple of Jesus Christ, whatever I do has spiritual implications. Think of all the years we've traded off; not realizing that we were serving the Lord in our occupation, in our hobbies, in our life, and that we will actually be receiving honor from God the Father in doing so. Even if all we ever do is shift gears and drive a truck. If it's for the Lord then there should be a lot of smiling truck drivers.

Did you know that there are no less than eight parables where Jesus Christ calls us a servant? It was one of His favorite names describing a disciple. Eight parables!

Matthew chapter 18: The parable of the servant who was forgiven a great debt by the king - and then, wouldn't forgive his fellow servant who owed him money.

Matthew chapter 20: Where a group of servants went to work in a vineyard. Some of them came in early and worked all day long and some of them came in right before the end, but they all received the same wage.

Matthew chapter 25: Where a group of servants have been given money. He wanted them to do business until the Master returned. The only one who received rebuke was the servant who did nothing.

Mark chapter 13: Where the servants who were waiting for their Master forgot to watch and pray. Falling asleep, their Master returned suddenly.

Luke 12:35: Another group of servants, but this time they didn't fall asleep while their Master was away. They waited a long time; past the first, second, and third watch of the night and then the Master showed up suddenly. What does our Lord say to these servants?

> *Blessed are those servants whom the master, when he comes, will find watching. Assuredly, I say to you that he will gird himself and have them sit down to eat, and will come and serve them. (Luke 12:36-37)*

If you are serving Christ, then when He comes, this will be His response to you. The rewards and blessings that the Lord God has prepared for those who serve Him aren't comprehensible.

Luke 12: There is an evil servant who doesn't think that his Master is returning, so he begins to act wickedly and is caught by the His sudden reappearance.

Luke 17: (This is one of my favorites, because of its context.) Jesus has just told them that if someone "sins against you seven times in a day, and seven times in a day returns, saying, 'I repent,' you must forgive him." Now that is hard!! If you sin against me even three times in a day, I will probably run out of forgiveness. That is exactly what the disciples thought too, so they respond,

> *"Increase our faith." So the Lord said, "If you have faith as a mustard seed, you can say to this mulberry tree, 'Be pulled up by the roots and be planted in the sea,' and it would obey you." (Luke 17:5-6)*

In other words, you don't need more faith to forgive someone seven times in a day: you have plenty of it already. What you need is a servant attitude! And then He gave the eighth parable of a servant.

> *And which of you, having a servant plowing or tending sheep, will say to him when he has come in from the field, 'Come at once and sit down to eat'? But will he not rather say to him, 'Prepare something for my supper, and gird yourself and serve me till I have eaten and drunk, and afterward you will eat and drink?' (Luke 17:7-8)*

Can you imagine a wealthy master coming home and when he saw that his servant looked tired, gave him the rest of the night off? Show me a workplace like that! Employers hardly ever even thank their servants, do they? When was the last time your employer thanked you for the task he paid you to do?

> *So likewise you, when you have done all those things which you are commanded, say, 'We are unprofitable servants. We have done what was our duty to do.' (Luke 17:10)*

A true servant knows the Master's commands are to be followed, regardless of how he feels. The word 'unprofitable' doesn't mean useless, it simply means that the task wasn't that big. And the word 'duty' means 'we owe it to the Master'. Dear reader, whatever you or I do for the Lord cannot even compare to what the Lord has given us. We owe it to our Master. If He says forgive seven times, we don't need more faith; we need a servant minded heart.

For though I am free from all men, I have made myself a servant to all, that I might win the more. (1 Corinthians 9:19)

Paul's number one evangelism tool was serving others. Heaven is filled with those whom Paul served. He not only lived it: he preached it from the pulpit.

For we do not preach ourselves, but Christ Jesus the Lord, and ourselves your bondservants for Jesus' sake. (2 Corinthians 4:5)

Can you imagine any pastor standing and offering to be your slave? That was how Paul preached! "Call me anytime day or night: I'm your slave." A true servant's heart comes from a true love for others.

And He said to them, "The kings of the Gentiles exercise lordship over them, and those who exercise authority over them are called 'benefactors.' But not so among you; on the contrary, he who is greatest among you, let him be as the younger, and he who governs as he who serves. For who is greater, he who sits at the table, or he who serves? Is it not he who sits at the table? Yet I am among you as the One who serves. (Luke 22:25-27)

Listen carefully now. The Kingdom of God should not look like a corporation. Those who are given the greatest authority must be the ones who serve the most. Do not select a spiritual leader who refuses to be a servant.

A disciple should not be serving for earthly reimbursement. Look at the following verses:

But Jesus called them to Himself and said, "You know that the rulers of the Gentiles lord it over them, and those who are great exercise authority over them. Yet it shall not be so among you; but whoever desires to become great among you, let him be your servant (deacon). (Matthew 20:25-26)

According to their culture the servant or deacon was a paid employee. So, Jesus tells them that the "great ones" in the kingdom of heaven are like paid employees, but then He goes further.

And whoever desires to be first among you, let him be your slave. (Matthew 20:27)

The word slave is 'doulos', and it means a servant without pay. A slave! In other words, if you want to be great in heaven, then have the attitude of an employee, but if you want to be number one in heaven, then have the attitude of a slave.

Jesus said in Matthew chapter 6, not to desire reimbursement from the world. In fact, He rebuked the Pharisees who did all of their religious practices just to receive some earthly reward, thereby forfeiting the spiritual rewards.

Take heed that you do not do your charitable deeds before men, to be seen by them. Otherwise you have no reward from your Father in heaven. Therefore, when you do a charitable deed, do not sound a trumpet before you as the hypocrites do in the synagogues and in the streets, that they may have glory from men. Assuredly, I say to you, they have their reward. (Matthew 6:1-2)

Seven separate times the New Testament refers to Jesus, the Apostles and various church leaders as bondservants. A bondservant in the Old Testament had an option. He was an Israelite slave who had been freed. At his release:

[I]f the servant plainly says, 'I love my master, my wife, and my children; I will not go out free,' then his master shall bring him to the judges. He shall also bring him to the door, or to the doorpost, and his master shall pierce his ear with an awl; and he shall serve him forever. (Exodus 21:5-6)

They would then take his ear, pierce it and put an earring in it. This meant that he had chosen to serve his master forever. This is the word chosen by Paul and Peter to describe themselves.

Paul, a bondservant of Jesus Christ. (Romans 1:1)

Simon Peter, a bondservant and apostle of Jesus Christ. (2 Peter 1:1)

Is this your attitude? Do you have a mind to serve?

In the Gospel of Mark, the author records an important additional word...

And whoever of you desires to be first shall be slave of all. (Mark 10:44)

This means not just the ones you feel like serving. It means that if you choose to be a slave to Jesus, then you have that attitude with everyone. When you are standing in line, and see someone who needs help, serve them!

And the King (Jesus) *will answer and say to them, 'Assuredly, I say to you, inasmuch as you did it to one of the least of these My brethren, you did it to Me.' (Matthew 25:40)*

This world has enough leaders. This world has enough ambitious people. The kingdom of God is going to be full of slaves who willingly and happily served each other.

There is the story of a Rabbi who had a vision of Heaven and Hell. He went to Hell and was surprised to see a beautiful large banquet of food. But the people looked terrible. They were gaunt and starving, although there was food everywhere. When he looked more closely he found that each of them had their arms in splints and were unable to feed themselves. Therefore, they could only look at the delicious food.

Then, he was transported to Heaven and strangely enough, it looked exactly like Hell. There was all the food and people and even the arm splints, yet everybody was happy, full and satisfied. He didn't understand it until he looked more closely. The person on one side of the table would stick his fork into the food and feed the individual opposite him, while the other did the same thing. They were just feasting.

So, the rabbi returned to Hell and there he proclaimed that they didn't have to starve anymore. He told the man at one end of the table, "All you must do is feed that man opposite you and I'm sure he will also feed you." The man's response to this idea of serving someone else was, "He's never done anything for me. Why would I give him the pleasure? I'm not serving him."

i.   *What does it mean to be a servant?*

ii.   *What do all of the servants have in common from the 8 parables?*

iii. *What challenges did the servants face in the 8 parables?*

iv. *When a Christian suffers for Christ what does it mean that we are only doing our "duty"?*

v.   *Kelso served his enemies. How can you serve your enemies?*

vi. *How does Christ being a servant allow Him to relate to all people in society?*

vii. *Have you chosen to be a servant of Christ? How about a servant of others?*

viii. *Search your heart about how willing you are to be a servant in Christ's kingdom. Now dedicate yourself daily to becoming a true bondservant for Christ.*

ix. *Memorize Matthew 20:26-28*

A WITNESS OF JESUS

e are now living in the generation after Billy Graham. His generation is nearly over. The generation of evangelism with huge crusades in large stadiums. Crusade type evangelism is still being conducted in Africa and Asia but there are not many in America. However, we need not be discouraged because God's original plan for evangelism was never based upon large crusades, but upon each disciple personally witnessing.

I'd like to start in Mark 16 where Jesus is about to ascend to His Father in heaven. Since you are now reading this book nearly two thousand years later, you have hindsight and know that He is going to be gone a very long time. So, this is His final command prior to leaving for several thousand years.

And He said to them, "Go into all the world and preach the gospel to every creature." (Mark 16:15)

The word 'creature' denotes that everywhere on the planet where there is life, this message must also then go. In other words, if there is a village with only five people in it, "Go!" and "Preach!" One village, one family, one person...Go to all creation.

First, we must "Go!"

Now if I told you right this moment, "go!" I would then be expecting something, wouldn't I? If you just sat there, I would think that there was some sort of communication problem. The common every day definition of "Go" is: Leave where you are. Evangelism is hard for that very reason. We each desire to be left alone so that we can live our lives in the places we are comfortable and with the people we know. I love evangelism, but do you know what happens when I witness to someone right here in my own town? My heart races, I sweat, I fear failure. Evangelism is not easy. We are going up against the gates of hell to release a prisoner and we fear failure.

An airplane pilot once asked an evangelist, "Why can't we simply learn to evangelize by taking a class and learning a technique?" (Many have taken this approach). The evangelist responded to the man, "Well, you're a pilot. Why don't we just take out pilots, give them 100 hours of classroom time, and send them on their way?"

Would you fly in an airplane where the pilot had never been in the cockpit? He may know all of the math. He might be able to chart his course and work his computer. But, what if he'd never felt the throttle, and never adjusted the flaps, and never landed a real airplane? But, hey, he had hundreds and hundreds of hours of training in the classroom. Would you go? Not me!

There are a myriad of ways to reach "every creature", but each one takes a measure of personal sacrifice. Whether, it be the Christian taxi cab driver in the Muslim nation who puts his Bible in the back seat, hoping his passengers will mention it and open up an opportunity for him to share his testimony, or the team of traveling Korean barbers who offer cheap haircuts in the various villages, hoping to exchange their skill for 20 minutes in which they can share the Gospel with each customer while cutting his hair.

The key to evangelism isn't training its "Go!"ing. Not having a good technique is no excuse. I know one man who has led hundreds to the Lord. Would you like to know his technique? Here it is. He walks up to them and asks, "So, are you a Christian?"

I know another man who has a thriving prison ministry. Would you like to know his technique? He enters the prison grounds and sits at one of the benches and begins praying for someone to sit beside him. Both of these techniques work well, as long as they have the "Go!" in them. Neither technique works very well, if these two men never leave their houses.

So, first of all it has to be a purposeful choice to "Go!" Then Jesus added a second command. "Preach!" Now, that does not mean we need to find a church and a pulpit. Jesus used neither of these. The word 'kerusso' means 'to proclaim.' It is what a herald would do centuries back. They would herald what was happening in the city, or they would herald that someone important was coming. The herald would often have a trumpet. What was so important about the heralder? Height? Eye color? No! What was important was whether the message was clearly heard. He didn't force people to listen; he simply made sure they could.

Guess how the disciples responded to Jesus' final words?

> *And they went out and preached everywhere,*
> *the Lord working with them and confirming the*
> *word through the accompanying signs. Amen.*
> *(Mark 16:20)*

They went! That's what it says. They went - and what did they do? They proclaimed! And where did they go? Everywhere! They stopped at every village, shoe shop and bus station and made sure everyone heard. What did they herald? Did they stop someone on the road and say, "May I talk to you about doctrine?" Ha! That's a great witnessing technique isn't it? Or maybe they said, "I'd like to talk to you about whether or not you think it is transubstantiation when you take communion." Probably not!

Acts 1:8 gives us insight into what they were proclaiming.

> *But you shall receive power when the Holy Spirit*
> *has come upon you; and you shall be witnesses to*
> *Me. (Acts 1:8)*

Literally it reads in the Greek, "You shall be to me, witnesses." Let me ask you what it means to witness. Is this referring to doctrine or theology? The power that the Holy Spirit gives us is to witness about the existence and reality of Jesus. That's exactly what they understood it meant. Your goal is not to describe the doctrinal minutia of your church; your goal is to proclaim that you know Jesus!

Someone must tell them about the Lord, because they don't know Him.

> *And these things they will do to you because they*
> *have not known the Father nor Me. (John 16:3)*

> *And the glory which You gave Me I have given them,*
> *that they may be one just as We are one: I in them,*
> *and You in Me; that they may be made perfect in*
> *one, and that the world may know that You have*
> *sent Me, and have loved them as You have loved*
> *Me. (John 17:22-23)*

Evangelism is not trying to convince someone that they need to change their life, but instead, that they need to know the Lord.

> *And this is eternal life, that they may know You,*

*the only true God, and Jesus Christ whom You have
sent. (John 17:3)*

If I can convince you who Jesus is, then you will want to
know if what He says is right or wrong. One man in Mongolia,
who became a follower of Jesus, continued to beat his wife when
he was angry, because that's what he had been taught. However,
when he found out that the Lord wanted him to be tender to
his wife and treat her with love, he responded, "I have never
known how to live my life before, because no one has taught
me." Knowing Jesus is leading him to know right and wrong.
Without Jesus, we only have religious laws and moral codes.

In Acts 2:32 Peter proclaims to the crowd!

*"This Jesus God has raised up, of which we are all
witnesses."*

Witnessing what you know about Jesus is called a testimony.

And they overcame him (the enemy) *by the blood
of the Lamb and by the word of their testimony,
(Revelation 12:11)*

I can prove to you that I know the Lord God, by describing
how He changed my life. I can tell you what I was like before I
met Him and then I can share about how I met Him and how
He has changed me. Every Christian already possesses this evangelism tool. Everyone who is born again has a testimony. And
that's what people need to hear. Yelling and arguing about false
gods and doctrine is not the witnessing Jesus was speaking about.

*How then shall they call on Him in whom they have
not believed? And how shall they believe in Him of
whom they have not heard? (Romans 10:14a)*

Salvation comes from calling on Him, not calling on His
teachings! Believing on Him, not His doctrine! How can they
believe on Him, whom they have never met or heard about? Do
not think that the world knows the Son of God. I have stood face
to face with a man and asked if he would like to hear about Jesus
Christ. And he responded, "I don't know Jesus Christ. Maybe
he's in the next village." That's what he said to me. How will he
ever be saved, if I don't tell him who Jesus is?

And how shall they hear without a preacher? (Romans 10:14b)

God has given you what the world is starving for: the knowledge of Him. The world has been led to believe that we have a different religion. They believe that we are simply devoted to our religion. What they don't know is that we actually know the living God and His Son the resurrected Jesus. You see we're supposed to be witnesses to Jesus. And here's what we're supposed to witness:

And how shall they preach unless they are sent? As it is written: "How beautiful are the feet of those who preach the gospel of peace, who bring glad tidings of good things!" (Romans 10:15)

How beautiful are the feet of those who- 'who evangelize peace' and 'good things.' We bring the good news of peace! Share the testimony of how you personally found peace!

Peace I leave with you, My peace I give to you; not as the world gives do I give to you. Let not your heart be troubled, neither let it be afraid. (John 14:27)

What was John the evangelist's ministry? (Otherwise known as John the Baptist)

And you, child, will be called the prophet of the Highest; For you will go before the face of the Lord to prepare His ways, to give knowledge of salvation to His people by the remission of their sins, through the tender mercy of our God, With which the Dayspring from on high has visited us; To give light to those who sit in darkness and the shadow of death, To guide our feet into the way of peace. (Luke 1:76-79)

How much training do you need to tell people what God has done for you? I'm going to give three examples of evangelism in the New Testament.

THE INSANE MAN, THE IMMORAL WOMAN and THE INSOLENT MURDERER

The Insane Man

Let me set the scene. Jesus is in a boat headed over to the land of Gadara, the Gadarenes. And, if you read the Scriptures correctly, you can prove from the other accounts of this event that they would have landed in the dark of night. As they disembark, a naked demon possessed man runs at them screaming. At this point, if I were with the disciples, I would quickly get back in the boat.

The man falls down in front of Jesus and cries out, "What do you want with us? Did you come to destroy us?" And Jesus responds, "Be quiet. What's your name?" The demons answer, "Legion, because we are many." They plead with Him not to send them away, but into a herd of swine instead. They possess the pigs and around 2,000 hogs die as they plummet off of the cliffs. Try to grasp what a powerful stronghold these demons must've had on this man's mind and body. In fact, the villagers used to shackle him, but he would just break the shackles and then run around the tombs cutting himself. Nobody wanted to deal with this insane man. He had quite a reputation. But, Jesus saves him! Hallelujah!

Well, the people who were herding the pigs freak out and run back home to tell the city something like this: "This guy landed on the shores and I'm sure he's in partnership with Legion because suddenly all of our pigs ran off the cliff!" So, the villagers gather together in a mob and head towards the shore. They see the demon possessed man wearing clothes and in his right mind and sitting at the feet of this man (whom we know to be Jesus) Mark 5:17 says:

Then they began to plead with Him to depart from their region.

"Please go away; please go away!" they cry.

And when He got into the boat, he who had been demon-possessed begged Him that he might be with Him. (Mark 5:18)

"Let me go with you Jesus! Please! They hate me," was what this man was saying.

> *However, Jesus did not permit him, but said to him,*
> *"Go home to your friends, and tell them what great*
> *things the Lord has done for you, and how He has*
> *had compassion on you." (Mark 5:19)*

And Jesus said to him, "Go!" Now that sounds familiar doesn't it? Go home to your friends. (I bet the list wasn't very long. How many friends can a demonized insane man who terrorizes the community have?) "And tell" again, very familiar words, the "Great things the Lord has done for you." Jesus said, "Go!" and "Preach!" What were they to preach? The message was the "Good news of peace" and "good things!"

That's it! Did He send him to Biblical seminary? No! Did He send them through a training course? No! He said, "Go tell them what God has done for you and how He has had compassion on you." And so what did he do?

> *And he departed and began to proclaim in Decapolis*
> *all that Jesus had done for him; and all marveled.*
> *(Mark 5:20)*

He departed - which means, he understood the "Go!" part. Then the Scriptures say he began to proclaim all that Jesus had done for him." Decapolis means 10 cities, so you might say; he went on a 10 city preaching tour.

Now, how much time had he spent with Jesus? Six hours at the absolute most. Do you think he knew as much as the Apostles? Do you think he had accurate doctrine? No way! In six hours? So he went and told them something like this: "I was insane and everyone was afraid of me, until I met Jesus and He gave me such incredible peace. Would you like to know Him?"

What was their response? Were they interested in knowing the real and living God? It says they all marveled. So, now what happens when Jesus returns to the area? The very next time Jesus shows up to Gadara is in Mark 6:53. Here it's called by its other name "the land of Gennesaret", but you can look on your map: it's the same place as Gadara and Decapolis. So Jesus lands on the shoreline where they had pleaded with Him to leave...

> *When they had crossed over, they came to the land*
> *of Gennesaret and anchored there. And when*
> *they came out of the boat, immediately the people*

recognized Him. (Mark 6:53-54)

How? If you look that word up in Greek, it doesn't mean that he was familiar to their eyes, but that they knew Him in their mind. "Hey! You're Jesus, aren't you?" They recognized Him, but how? Because, one insane man had been traveling around telling them, "This Jesus, He delivered me. Wow, I'm at peace!" It was simply his personal testimony!

That's all he did was tell his personal testimony. And guess what they did?

> *[They] ran through that whole surrounding region, and began to carry about on beds those who were sick to wherever they heard He was. Wherever He entered into villages, cities, or in the country, they laid the sick in the marketplaces, and begged Him that they might just touch the hem of His garment. And as many as touched Him were made well. (Mark 6:55-56)*

They 'begged' to touch Him. This is the exact word used in Mark 5:17, when they 'begged' that He would leave them. What caused the change? One man with a testimony!

1 Peter 2:12 says something very interesting.

> *[Have] your conduct honorable among the Gentiles, that when they speak against you as evildoers, they may, by your good works which they observe, glorify God in the day of visitation. (1 Peter 2:12)*

What does that mean? It means that when you share the Gospel you are preparing the hearts of people around you for the day when they will be visited by God. So that they will recognize Him, the same way that the land of Gennesaret did. The only other time this phrase is used, 'the day of visitation' is in Luke 19:44 when Jesus weeps because Jerusalem didn't know Him at the 'time of their visitation.' Live your life in such a way that when God visits the people around you, they recognize Him, because of your testimony. So, the insane man was a 10 city success.

The Immoral Woman

Most everyone knows the story of John chapter four. Jesus is in Samaria and He is sitting at a well while His disciples go to get some food. As He's sitting there a woman shows up at an unusual hour to draw water. We find out later that she is not exactly a well-respected woman in the town. Jesus asks, "Can I have some water?" And she basically answers like this, "Are you talking to me? You're a Jew and I'm a Samaritan; why are you talking to me?"

In kindness Jesus doesn't become angry but says, "Well, I'll tell you that if you knew who I was, you'd ask for some water from me and I'd give you the water that has life." She responds, "Oh, I want that water!" (Everyone is looking for peace). So, He tells her to go get her husband. She replies, "Uh, I don't have a husband." "Oh, that's right. You've had five husbands and the man you are now living with is not your husband." She just had an encounter with God didn't she? Immediately she responds with her religious beliefs. "Hey, I perceive you're a prophet. So, where do you think we should worship God? Here or in Jerusalem?" He tells her that people everywhere need to worship in truth, not in a specific location.

At this point His disciples come, and they marvel that He talked with a woman; yet no one said, "What do You seek?" or, "Why are You talking with her?"

The woman then left her waterpot, went her way into the city, and said to the men, "Come, see a Man who told me all things that I ever did. Could this be the Christ?" (John 4:28-29)

Now in my Bible I circled the word 'went' because that's what the Lord commanded us to do and that's what the insane man did, and that is what she is now doing. And then what did she do? She proclaimed her personal encounter with Jesus. She shared her 30 minute testimony, not her doctrinal discussion about where they should worship. She must've been running through the town very excited since she didn't even take her water pots with her. "Hey! Hey! Hey! There's a man out there who told me everything that I ever did! Is it possible that He is the Christ?" It's amazing! She wasn't even sure yet, but she is already witnessing. "Hey, I've met Jesus! I think He might be the Savior!" Has she received any evangelism training?

Let's follow the narrative,

then they went out of the city and came to Him. (John 4:30)

And many of the Samaritans of that city believed in Him because of the word of the woman who testified, "He told me all that I ever did." (John 4:39)

And many more believed because of His own word: (John 4:41)

Now after they met Jesus themselves, they had their own personal testimony to share, rather than the woman's.

Then they said to the woman, "Now we believe, not because of what you said, for we ourselves have heard Him and we know that this is indeed the Christ, the Savior of the world. (John 4:42)

Here we have an entire town of fully capable evangelists.

The insane man proclaimed his testimony: Did it work? Yes.

The Immoral woman proclaimed her little testimony: Did it work? Yes.

What has Jesus told us? You shall be witnesses to Me.

The Insolent Murderer

Who is the insolent murderer of Scripture? It is the Apostle Paul himself. He was a part of murdering Stephen and even refers to himself in 1Timothy 1:13 as an insolent man. Insolent means disrespectful.

Did Paul have a day of visitation with the Lord? Oh yes! We know the story in the book of Acts, chapter nine. He is on his way to capture, and perhaps kill the Christians in Damascus, when all of a sudden a light surrounds him. Next thing he knows, he's lying on the ground and hearing voices from the sky. Everyone around him is in fear and he ends up blind. Ananias, a disciple of Jesus, lays hands on him and he is saved and receives his sight.

He then is baptized and "Goes!" and "Proclaims!"

What did he preach at that point? "Watch out for bright lights!?"

> *Immediately he preached the Christ in the synagogues, that "He is the Son of God." (Acts 9:20)*

Jesus is the Christ and the Son of God! How did he suddenly know this? He had met Him. I'm sure that Paul shared again and again what happened on the way to Damascus. In fact, we not only have his conversion experience recorded here, but we also have it repeated two more times within the same book of Acts. In three different locations in the book of Acts, you can read how Paul met Jesus. With so much scholarly learning and training, why did he keep going back to his testimony? Because it is what we have been called to proclaim, and it is absolutely effective.

But what if people don't get saved? Whose fault is that?

All that you have been asked to do is share your witness.

> *"No one can come to Me unless the Father who sent Me draws him." (John 6:44a)*

There are those times when we get shaken and discouraged. When Paul went to Corinth, in Acts 18, and witnessed in the synagogue, they still rejected him, and in the days ahead, he must have been discouraged that so many had refused salvation. Therefore, the Lord Jesus comes to him at night:

> *Now the Lord spoke to Paul in the night by a vision, "Do not be afraid, but speak, and do not keep silent; for I am with you, and no one will attack you to hurt you; for I have many people in this city." (Acts 18:9-10)*

So if Jesus had to tell Paul, "Don't fear," what does that mean? It means Paul the Apostle was afraid. And what did Jesus tell him? "Keep speaking!" At this point, if Paul would have kept silent, it would have been sin. When the Lord says, "Don't be silent" and you're silent, that's a sin right? When the Lord says, "Go and preach" and you don't go and preach, that's a sin right? Are you going and proclaiming?

Let me paraphrase on this Scripture, "You keep speaking and I'll keep saving." And that's what Jesus says to each of us.

"You keep speaking and I'll keep saving." It's as simple as that!

Paul experienced another big failure after his return to Jerusalem. A riot started in the Temple and the Roman centurion has to save Paul's life. While he's taking Paul to the fortress, Paul asks for permission to speak to the raging crowd. The commander gives permission and when Paul steps up, what does he begin to share? His personal testimony! The crowd falls silent. He may have had as many as a thousand or two thousand people before him. It's a perfect amphitheater. Everything is going excellent until he says, "The Lord sent me to the gentiles." And then the crowd blows up! The commander, not knowing the language Paul was speaking takes him to the prison to beat him until he can find out what happened. It all centered on that one word Paul used; 'Gentiles.' Everything was going fine until that word came out. They were all listening about how he had met the Messiah. Then he had to use that word!

Have you ever wished you hadn't said something? He could have said "God fearing non-Jews"...anything besides Gentiles! Do you think Paul is discouraged? Jesus comes to him again.

> *But the following night the Lord stood by him and said, "Be of good cheer, Paul; for as you have testified for Me in Jerusalem, so you must also bear witness at Rome." (Acts 23:11)*

He doesn't say, "You have failed, Paul. You shouldn't have said, 'Gentiles!'" Instead, He commends him for sharing his witness. He commends him for sharing his personal testimony. In fact, he tells Paul that he wants him to share it again; only this time in Rome.

The book of Acts ends in a very interesting way. Paul ends up in a rented house where he is witnessing to everyone. Nobody enters his doors or has dinner with him without hearing about Jesus. Once, from a jail cell, Paul wrote:

> *But I want you to know, brethren, that the things which happened to me have actually turned out for the furtherance of the gospel, so that it has become evident to the whole palace guard, and to all the rest, that my chains are in Christ; and most of the brethren in the Lord, having become confident by my chains, are much more bold to speak the word*

without fear.(Philippians 1:12-14)

For I am not ashamed of the gospel of Christ, for it is the power of God to salvation for everyone who believes, for the Jew first and also for the Greek. (Romans 1:16)

I am not ashamed, Paul would say,

[N]ecessity is laid upon me; yes, woe is me if I do not preach the gospel! (1 Corinthians 9:16)

Has God entrusted the angels to share the Gospel? No! Cornelius was told by an angel to get Peter, so that he might hear the Gospel. God has entrusted it with us. If you are a disciple of Jesus Christ, then the necessity of sharing the Gospel is laid upon you as well. Go! Proclaim the Good News of Peace and Good Things!

Romans 10:13-15

For "whoever calls on the name of the LORD shall be saved." How then shall they call on Him in whom they have not believed? And how shall they believe in Him of whom they have not heard?

And how shall they hear without a preacher?

And how shall they preach unless they are sent?

As it is written: "How beautiful are the feet of those

who preach the gospel of peace, Who bring glad tidings of good things!"

i. *What are we supposed to witness?*

ii. *Explain the day of visitation.*

iii. *The taxi cab driver and Korean barbers used their occupation to present the Gospel. In what ways does your occupation present opportunities to share the Gospel with others?*

iv. *How is the Gospel beautiful?*

v. *How much training is necessary for evangelism?*

vi. *When we are commanded by Jesus in Mark 16:15 to go to every creature, what does that mean?*

vii. *Practice your personal testimony until you are comfortable giving it in 5 minutes.*

viii. *Memorize Romans 10:13-15*

HUMBLENESS

he key verse for this characteristic is from Matthew.

Then Jesus called a little child to Him, set him in the midst of them, and said, "Assuredly I say to you, unless you are converted and become as little children you will by no means enter the kingdom of heaven." (Matthew 18:2-4)

What does that mean? Spiritually, it means pride is too big to fit through the door into heaven. You can't walk in through those gates as a powerful, important person: you have to enter as a 'little' person. You have to be 'nothing' to enter.

Therefore, whoever humbles himself as this little child is the greatest in the kingdom of heaven. (Matthew 18:4)

In what way is a child humble? Have you ever watched a little two or three year old child in the backseat? Do they get tense while mom and dad are driving? Do they stress because mom and dad drive poorly? No. Instead, they have total trust. They know when they get into that seat that they will also get out when it is the right time. They have no worries about being hurt.

When a child comes to you and says, "Mommy, daddy, I'm hungry." They have already recognized that they aren't able to feed themselves! So, to get food they must first become humble beggars who trust that their asking will be enough.

There is a Scripture that says,

"Without Me you can do nothing." (John 15:5)

Nothing is a rather extreme word isn't it? Recently someone told me, "I'll never fall into a particular sin. I've beaten it." In fact, he told me he had beaten alcohol. "I beat alcohol in my own strength." That is dangerous.

Therefore let him who thinks he stands take heed lest he fall. (1 Corinthians 10:12)

I talked to him about the power of Satan. He responded,

"Satan is not going to get me." I said, "You don't understand who Satan is. Can you kill 185,000 men in one night?" (2 Kings 19:35) He said "No". I told him, "An angel did. Perhaps not even a high-ranking angel, yet Satan was a high-ranking angel. Do you think you can still beat him?"

Pride is very dangerous. There are warnings of pride in Proverbs.

> *Pride goes before destruction and a haughty spirit before a fall. It is better to be of a humble spirit with the lowly than to divide the spoil with the proud. (Proverbs 16:18-19)*

There is also a warning in 1 Peter.

> *God resists the proud, but gives grace to the humble. (1 Peter 5:5)*

Now, I don't want God standing in my way to stop me, but would rather have His grace picking me up when I stumble and fall, wouldn't you?

There is not just a warning for pride, but the promise of a reward for humility.

> *Thus says the high and lofty one, who inhabits eternity, whose name is holy. I dwell in the high and holy place with him who has a contrite and humble spirit. (Isaiah 57:15)*

What is the reward of a humble spirit? Humility brings access to the One who created all things. Just like Jesus said, "We must become like children" and then we will have access to the kingdom of heaven. When we are proud, that access is resisted, closed.

There is another reward mentioned in Luke chapter 14.

> *He told a parable to those who were invited when he noted how they chose the best places, saying to them: 'when you are invited by anyone to a wedding feast, do not sit down in the best place lest one more honorable than you be invited by him, and he who invited you and him come and say to you, 'give place to this man' and you begin with shame to take the lowest place. But when you are invited go and*

sit down in the lowest place, so that when he who invited you comes he may say to you, 'friend, go up higher'. Then you will have glory in the presence of those who sit at the table with you. For, whoever exalts himself will be humbled. (Luke 14:7-11)

God will bring the proud down, and the humble up. He is revealing that, in His kingdom, if you go to a dinner and sit at the place of importance because you think you are important, then you need to expect that God will pluck you from that place of pride and put you in the place of the least. God will also reseat the one who did not feel worthy to the seat of importance at His table. This is a promise of God. So we can choose to go higher by living lower or go lower by living higher. Start at the head and you will end up at the tail, or choose the tail and you'll be at the head. Where will you sit?

Jesus gives us a living example of this promise.

Let this mind be in you which was also in Christ Jesus, who, being in the form of God, did not consider it robbery to be equal with God, but made Himself of no reputation, taking the form of a bondservant, and coming in the likeness of men. And being found in appearance as a man, He humbled Himself and became obedient to the point of death, even the death of the cross. (Philippians 2:5-8)

Who humbled Him? He humbled himself. Even to the point of death, even the death of the cross. Then it goes on to say,

Therefore God also has highly exalted Him and given Him the name which is above every name, that at the name of Jesus every knee should bow, of those in heaven, and of those on earth, and of those under the earth, and that every tongue should confess that Jesus Christ is Lord, to the glory of God the Father. (Philippians 2:9-11)

There is the promise fulfilled! Humble yourself and God will exalt you. Jesus humbled Himself to the lowest degree and, therefore, God exalted Him to the highest degree. At the Name of Jesus, every single knee, believer and nonbeliever, will bow.

Every tongue will confess Jesus Christ is Lord. Even the demons and angels! That is about as high as you can get.

So, what does humility look like? There are two characteristics that we should focus on. Number one is submission and number two is having a teachable spirit.

Submission

A current manual of Psychology stated, "The trait of submission requires adopting a weak stance. This is the dependant person. The basis is "I'm not OK, but you are OK", so there is the weakness. This is an emotionally unstable introversion." In other words the world says that submission to others means we are not mentally healthy. This is in direct conflict with the Word of God!

> *There is a way that seems right to a man, but its end is the way of death. (Proverbs 14:12)*

> *Beware lest anyone cheat you through philosophy and empty deceit, according to the tradition of men, according to the basic principles of the world, and not according to Christ. (Colossians 2:8)*

The Biblical word submission is 'hupotasso' which means 'under orders' and is a military word that describes an officer and a soldier. The soldier is 'under orders' from the general. The Lord very clearly instructs us that there are seven different authorities that we need to submit to.

1) God

> *Therefore submit to God. Resist the devil and he will flee from you. (James 4:7)*

Therefore, whatever the Lord declares, obey. I spoke to a man yesterday who was against spanking his children, and he is a Christian! I told him that he needed to obey whatever God says, regardless of his opinion. He struggled with that, so I said, "You need to find out what God says about the discipline of a child." I didn't tell him what to do; I simply asked him if he was willing to obey what God says. I left him troubled, because he had already determined in his mind what he was willing to do and was now realizing that he might be in rebellion to God.

What if you have been committing adultery but are unaware that adultery is sin? While you are reading God's Word you come to a Scripture which states 'don't commit adultery'. What are you going to do? When the Lord reveals His will to you, if you obey then you are in submission to God. James tells us that if we are willing to do this, then we will have power to resist the devil and he will flee.

Submission to God must be first and most important in your life. If any of the following authorities we will study command you to not submit to God's authority don't obey them. Submission to God is above all others.

> *But Peter and the other apostles answered and said:*
> *"We ought to obey God rather than men. (Acts 5:29)*

Again, if any authority directs you to do something that is contrary to God then don't submit to them: submit to God. But, if they are not telling you to do something ungodly then submit to them.

2) *Your husbands*

1 Peter 3:1-2 says that wives are to submit to their husbands.

> *Wives, likewise, be submissive (hupotasso) to your*
> *own husbands, that even if some do not obey the*
> *word they, without a word, may be won by the*
> *conduct of their wives when they observe your chaste*
> *conduct accompanied by fear.*

Let me clarify what this does not say. It does not say women submit to men. It says wives submit to your own husbands. Please remember this. Put yourself under the authority of your own husband, who is the head of your house.

> *For the husband is head of the wife, as also Christ*
> *is head of the church; and He is the Savior of the*
> *body. (Ephesians 5:23)*

Ephesians also says that the way a wife submits to her

husband is a mirror image of how she submits to God, because, as God watches her submission to the husband, He counts it as submission to Him.

> *Wives, submit to your own husbands, as to the Lord.*
> *(Ephesians 5:22)*

If you are rebellious to your husband you are rebellious to God.

3) *Parents*

After writing about the roles of husbands and wives in Ephesians 5, Paul speaks to the children. Ephesians chapter 6:1 should be familiar to you. I make my children memorize it, so that they know that it is the Lord's will to submit to their mother and me, rather than a principle that I have created.

> *Children, obey your parents in the Lord, for this is*
> *right. "Honor your father and your mother," which*
> *is the first commandment with a promise, "that it*
> *may be well with you and you may live long on the*
> *earth." (Ephesians 6:1-3)*

Let's look at an amazing example of this. In Luke 2, a 12-year-old Jesus stayed behind in Jerusalem to worship, while his parents headed home. They were unaware that He was not with their caravan until that evening. After three days Jesus was discovered in the Temple. When they finally found Him His mother said,

> *"Son, why have You done this to us? Look, your*
> *father and I have sought You anxiously." And He*
> *said to them, "Why did you seek Me? Did you not*
> *know that I must be about My Father's business?"*
> *(Luke 2:49)*

At that point in time, He was under the authority of Who? Father God. "I am about my Father God's business." As if Jesus was saying: "I knew you had left, and I remained in the Temple because God wanted me here." This wasn't rebellion but submission in its correct order. How do I know? Look at the following verses.

> *Then He went down with them and came to Nazareth, and was subject to them, but His mother kept all these things in her heart. And Jesus increased in wisdom and stature, and in favor with God and men. (Luke 2:51-52)*

The young Jesus knew how to hear His Father God's will, and He knew how to be subject (hupotasso) to His human parents.

Perhaps you think that you are more spiritual than your parents and therefore can refuse to submit to them. Try being the Son of God who had flawed, human parents saying, "We think this is best for you Jesus": all the time knowing Father God's perfect will. Yet as a child is to submit to their parents, the Lord Jesus Himself submitted. How much more should we? According to Paul, one of the perilous consequences of rising ungodliness is that more will be *"disobedient to parents"* (2 Timothy 3:2)

How long does submission or obedience to my parents last? At what point am I not required to submit? Remember the spheres of authority: God, then husband (if married), and then parents. But ALWAYS, God first. Before asking what my husband or my parents command, I should know what God says through His Word. However, at marriage, according to the creation principle found in Genesis 2:24 and repeated by the Lord three times in the New Testament (Matthew 19:5, Mark 10:7, and Ephesians 5:31), when you are married God places the marriage authority above the parental authority.

4) Church leadership

1 Timothy says we are to submit to the leadership of the church.

> *Let the elders who rule well be counted worthy of double honor, especially those who labor in the word and doctrine. (1 Timothy 5:17)*

Let the elders who rule well. The word there for 'rule' is literally 'stand in front.' Let the elders who stand in front of the line be counted worthy of double honor, especially those who labor in the Word and doctrine. In other words, submit to them.

I urge you, brethren--you know the household of Stephanas, that it is the firstfruits of Achaia, and that they have devoted themselves to the ministry of the saints--that you also submit to such, and to everyone who works and labors with us. (1 Corinthians 16:15-16)

Paul pleads with the church of Corinth to submit to those who have been placed in leadership over them.

Obey those who rule over you, and be submissive, for they watch out for your souls, as those who must give account. Let them do so with joy and not with grief, for that would be unprofitable for you. (Hebrews 13:17)

Submit to the teachers and leaders in the church. 'Obey' literally means 'yield in agreement'. It means that if you have a different opinion than the church leader, *yield*. When you are driving a car and come to a 'yield' sign, what does it mean? It does not matter who was there first. It is your responsibility to let them lead the way. Yield unless it is unbiblical or ungodly. Let them lead, or as the Lord wrote, it will be *unprofitable for you*, because they 'watch out for my soul'. It is the picture of someone guarding a treasure through the night. They are protecting my soul and will deliver the record of what they have done to the Chief Shepherd Jesus.

The elders who are among you I exhort, I who am a fellow elder and a witness of the sufferings of Christ, and also a partaker of the glory that will be revealed: Shepherd the flock of God which is among you, serving as overseers, not by compulsion but willingly, not for dishonest gain but eagerly; nor as being lords over those entrusted to you, but being examples to the flock; and when the Chief Shepherd appears, you will receive the crown of glory that does not fade away. (1 Peter 5:1-4)

As an elder, teacher and shepherd of the church of Jesus, I am going to stand before Him and give account of those I oversee. I will give account of how I helped them spiritually or hindered them for my own benefit. How I responded when they were brokenhearted or in sin. Did I use them or serve them for the Lord? (Ezekiel 34) When people determine in their hearts, "I'm not going to obey the leaders of the church." These people are in rebellion to God not the leadership.

> *And the LORD said to Samuel, "Heed the voice of the people in all that they say to you; for they have not rejected you, but they have rejected Me, that I should not reign over them." (1 Samuel 8:7)*

Elders are very accountable to God! Let them oversee you *"with joy and not with grief."* This is a serious thing.

5) Elderly

> *You shall rise before the gray headed and honor the presence of an old man and fear your God. I am the Lord. (Leviticus 19:32)*

> *Likewise, you younger people be submissive to your elders. Yes, all of you, be submissive to one another and be clothed in humility because God resists the proud and gives grace to the humble. (1 Peter 5:5-6)*

These references are not talking about church leadership, but simply older individuals. Young people submit yourselves to your elders. Gray hair is an honor according to the Bible (if found in righteousness, Proverbs 16:31). Submit to the gray headed out of respect for God. Respect for elders used to be prevalent across the world. When they speak to you, respect them. If they direct you to do something evil, then submit to God.

6) Government

> *Let every soul be subject to the governing authorities. For there is no authority except from God, and the authorities that exist are appointed by God. Therefore whoever resists the authority resists the ordinance of God, and those who resist will bring judgment on themselves. (Romans 13:1-2)*

Therefore submit yourselves to every ordinance of man for the Lord's sake, whether to the king as supreme, or to governors, as to those who are sent by him for the punishment of evildoers and for the praise of those who do good. For this is the will of God, that by doing good you may put to silence the ignorance of foolish men--as free, yet not using liberty as a cloak for vice, but as bondservants of God. (1 Peter 2:13-16)

Let every soul be 'under orders', to the governing authorities. For, there is no authority except that which has been ordained by God. And the authorities that are over you are set in order by God. If we serve our countries for the Lord's sake, we will put to silence the ignorance of those who speak against us and the Lord.

Do you feel that since you are a Christian, the laws of the land don't apply to you? Are you rebellious to the law and the government? Are you rebellious to the nation that God placed you in?

And He has made from one blood every nation of men to dwell on all the face of the earth, and has determined their preappointed times and the boundaries of their dwellings, (Acts 17:26)

Okay, let's put it in the simplest of terms. What if your country is ungodly? The book of Daniel proves that God will honor submission even to an ungodly government. God put Nebuchadnezzar in a place of authority over Daniel, and Daniel was a faithful follower of God AND a faithful citizen who completely changed two world empires through his humility and submission. If the government is corrupt, obey them. As long as they are not telling you to disobey God, obey them. This passage in Romans was written during the time of Caesar Nero, who was murdering Christians. Yet Paul was still instructing believers to submit to Nero, because his authority was from God.

What did Jesus say to the Roman governor Pontius Pilate when Pilate was ordering His execution?

Then Pilate said to Him, "Are You not speaking to me? Do You not know that I have power to crucify You, and power to release You?" Jesus answered,

"You could have no power at all against Me unless it had been given you from above. (John 19:10-11a)

7) *Employers*

Servants, be submissive to your masters with all fear, not only to the good and gentle, but also to the harsh. (1 Peter 2:18)

The word used for 'servants' is 'oiketes' which refers to a paid employee. In other words, this Scripture applies to every occupation regardless of whether your boss is 'good and gentle' or 'harsh'.

Exhort bondservants to be obedient to their own masters, to be well pleasing in all things, not answering back, not pilfering, but showing all good fidelity, that they may adorn the doctrine of God our Savior in all things. (Titus 2:9-10)

The best employee of any business should be a Christian, regardless of the character of the employer. They shouldn't be disrespectful to their employer in conversation or by taking what they feel they deserve from their employer. They should be faithful employees rather than looking to leave.

Teachable Spirit

We have learned that humility means we are to be submissive to the authorities God has placed over us, but it also means that we must have a teachable spirit in our relationship with all people.

The word 'teachable' doesn't occur in the Bible, but is a word that fitly describes an attitude of humility towards learning. Jesus has called us to make disciples. The word disciple means 'learners' or 'students.' To be a student we must be humble enough to be taught.

Do you see a man wise in his own eyes? There is more hope for a fool than for him. (Proverbs 26:12)

Let no one deceive himself. If anyone among you

*seems to be wise in this age, let him become a fool
that he may become wise. (1 Corinthians 3:18)*

A disciple or learner must by necessity have a teachable
spirit and be able to learn in all situations and from all people.

Let me give you an example. There is a command in Matthew 18 about what to do when someone sins against you. You
are to go and speak to him privately. Jesus tells us that you can
win your brother in that way.

*Moreover if your brother sins against you, go and
tell him his fault between you and him alone.
If he hears you, you have gained your brother.
(Matthew 18:15)*

James tells us that this approach makes it the easier for a
brother or sister to grow.

*Now the fruit of righteousness is sown in peace by
those who make peace. (James 3:18)*

While this is the way we need to approach others, a disciple
must be humble and teachable enough to receive correction in
any form. My example is from Matthew 16:23. After Peter tells
Jesus that He can't go to the cross, the Lord responds to him in
the presence of all the other disciples, *"Get behind Me, Satan!"*
How hard would that be to receive? My pride would have a hard
time receiving such public rebuke. He could have said "bad boy"
or "you are making a mistake." But, *"Get behind Me, Satan"* is
as hard a rebuke as anyone can give, and it was in the presence
of all. Would you receive this lesson?

If we are humble disciples then we cannot respond to correction with pride, but need to be willing to 'learn' no matter how
public our lessons are. Besides, leaders aren't to receive private
rebukes, because they have such a great responsibility before
the people. Peter was the leader of the disciples and if he was
in sin, Jesus knew that it would greatly harm the work of God.
When a leader is in sin, they must be humble enough to receive
public correction.

*Do not receive an accusation against an elder except
from two or three witnesses. Those who are sinning
rebuke in the presence of all, that the rest also may*

fear. (1 Timothy 5:19-20)

If I am an elder in the Ephesian church who is sinning, then Timothy is supposed to rebuke me in public, so that the other elders would be terrified. This will quickly reveal whether I am a disciple with a teachable spirit or not. There is another Scripture in Galatians 6:1 that also commands us to rebuke gently.

Brethren, if a man is overtaken in any trespass, you who are spiritual restore such a one in a spirit of gentleness. (Galatians 6:1)

So when a believer falls into sin, not only are we supposed to go to them privately, but we are to go to them gently.

However, what if someone comes to you and is not gentle? Will you still be teachable? In Matthew chapter 23 Jesus reveals a long list of woes to the Scribes and the Pharisees.

"But woe to you, scribes and Pharisees, hypocrites... you travel land and sea to win one proselyte, and when he is won, you make him twice as much a son of hell as yourselves. Woe to you, blind guides...Fools and blind...For you are like whitewashed tombs which indeed appear beautiful outwardly, but inside are full of dead men's bones and all uncleanness...Serpents, brood of vipers! How can you escape the condemnation of hell?" (Matthew 23:13-33 excerpts)

Jesus said that publicly and harshly. Would you be teachable in that situation? Some must have been, because many priests became followers of Christ after the resurrection.

Then the word of God spread, and the number of the disciples multiplied greatly in Jerusalem, and a great many of the priests were obedient to the faith. (Acts 6:7)

Paul the Apostle was also a Pharisee. He may have very well been listening to this rebuke. Aren't you glad that he was teachable? What if these priests had hardened their hearts and said, "He can't talk to me this way!" To be a disciple we must have a spirit that can be rebuked *openly and publicly*. In another instance (Acts 15:36-40) a debate breaks out between the two missionary Apostles, Paul and Barnabas, about a young man named Mark, who had abandoned them on their first missionary trip after experiencing some hardships. Paul says, "Let's begin another journey." Barnabas responds, "Let's take Mark." Paul responds, "We're not taking Mark, he is unreliable!" Barnabas becomes angry and they end up in a quarrel.

> *Then after some days Paul said to Barnabas, "Let us now go back and visit our brethren in every city where we have preached the word of the Lord, and see how they are doing." Now Barnabas was determined to take with them John called Mark. But Paul insisted that they should not take with them the one who had departed from them in Pamphylia, and had not gone with them to the work. Then the contention became so sharp that they parted from one another. And so Barnabas took Mark and sailed to Cyprus; but Paul chose Silas and departed...* (Acts 15:36-40)

How would you like to be Mark? It is the Apostle Paul who is refusing to work with you because of your past failures. How would you like to be in the other room listening to them argue about whether or not you are reliable enough to even go on this trip because you abandoned them last time? If you were Mark, would you be 'teachable' enough to recover from such a statement? He could have taken Paul's criticism terribly hard and in fact, he probably found it difficult not to. However, Mark was a true disciple and willing to learn in all situations. At the end of Paul's life, Paul says, "I am about to die. Timothy, get Mark and bring him here. I need him"

> *Only Luke is with me. Get Mark and bring him with you, for he is useful to me for ministry.* (2 Timothy 4:11)

Mark didn't quit. He may have failed once, but, as a disciple, he kept growing and learning. He was openly shamed because of his failures, but he kept learning. And at the very end, the same Paul who refused to rely on him was able to say; "I need him with me because I can count on him." Mark had a teachable spirit. By the way, who do you think wrote the Gospel according to Mark? Aren't you glad he was teachable?

Here is a different example from Galatians. This is a very interesting story about another rebuke from Paul.

> *Now when Peter had come to Antioch, I withstood him to his face, because he was to be blamed; for before certain men came from James, he would eat with the Gentiles; but when they came, he withdrew and separated himself, fearing those who were of the circumcision. And the rest of the Jews also played the hypocrite with him, so that even Barnabas was carried away with their hypocrisy. But when I saw that they were not straightforward about the truth of the gospel, I said to Peter before them all, "If you, being a Jew, live in the manner of Gentiles and not as the Jews, why do you compel Gentiles to live as Jews? (Galatians 2:11-14)*

Paul refers to this encounter as opposing Peter "*to his face*". What do you think that means? How about the words "*before them all*"? This was a hard and public rebuke! Peter had been eating pork and living like a gentile among the gentile believers. His kosher diet had been set aside to honor his fellow non-Jewish believers. But, when the Jewish believers showed up, he pretended that eating like a gentile would defile him. So Paul literally gets in his face. Paul's rebuke was neither private, nor gentle. How did Peter respond? Did he harbor bitterness? I don't think so, because prior to Peter's martyrdom, he commends Paul's wisdom and letters and refers to him as a "beloved brother."

> *And consider that the longsuffering of our Lord is salvation--as also our beloved brother Paul, according to the wisdom given to him, has written to you, as also in all his epistles, speaking in them of these things.. (2 Peter 3:15-16)*

To be humble then we must not only be submitted to the authorities God has given; we must also be teachable in all circumstances.

I am going to close this characteristic with some examples of how Jesus was teachable. There is a reference to Him in Isaiah:

> *The Lord GOD has given Me The tongue of the learned, That I should know how to speak a word*

*in season to him who is weary. He awakens Me
morning by morning, He awakens My ear to hear
as the learned. The Lord GOD has opened My
ear; And I was not rebellious, nor did I turn away.
(Isaiah 50:4-5)*

The Lord opened my ear and I didn't turn away. In other
words, Father God said, "I want this to be done." And Jesus
always said, "Okay."

*"I gave My back to those who struck Me, and My
cheeks to those who plucked out the beard; I did not
hide My face from shame and spitting." (Isaiah 50:6)*

Jesus was even willing to submit Himself to suffering at the
government's hands. There is an amazing cross-reference to this
Scripture in Hebrews:

*"though he was a son, yet he learned obedience by
the things which he suffered." (Hebrews 5:8)*

Jesus Christ submitted Himself to the government, even
though it meant suffering. How much humility do you and I
have compared to that? How teachable was He?

*I can of Myself do nothing. As I hear, I judge; and
My judgment is righteous, because I do not seek My
own will but the will of the Father who sent Me.
(John 5:30)*

"I only do what My Father teaches me to do." Jesus was not
a *free thinker*, which is a term often used in Singapore and Asia
and has been spreading across the United States. It simply means
those who are *unteachable*. Jesus was a completely submissive
teachable Follower. He completely submitted to the Father and
as His disciples we are to be like Him.

*Then He said to another, "Follow Me." But he said,
"Lord, let me first go and bury my father." Jesus said
to him, "Let the dead bury their own dead, but you
go and preach the kingdom of God." (Luke 9:59-60)*

Did this man? We don't know: it doesn't say. The real question is, will you?

> *He who has My commandments and keeps them, it
> is he who loves Me. And he who loves Me will be
> loved by My Father, and I will love him and manifest
> Myself to him. (John 14:21)*

He who is teachable by Me, will see more of Me.

> *He who believes in the Son has everlasting life; and
> he who does not believe the Son shall not see life,
> but the wrath of God abides on him (John 3:36)*

A disciple cannot say, "This is my boss, but I don't obey
him." "This is my husband, but I don't follow him." "This is my
church, but I don't submit to the leadership." "This is my nation,
but I don't follow what they say." Because what they are really
saying is, "This is my God and I am not going to obey Him."

I want to close with one more example. In John chapter
six, Jesus refers to Himself as the "Bread of life" and that those
present "have to eat this bread to have eternal life."

> *Therefore many of His disciples, when they
> heard this, said, "This is a hard saying; who can
> understand it?" (John 6:60)*

Or, literally, "I can't listen to this. It's too hard." As a disciple
of the Lord, we will sometimes receive rebuke or a teaching that
is "too hard". I have had people say to me after I have shared
from the Scriptures, "Your message troubled me." My response
to them is, "Was there anything I said which was not true?"
If there wasn't, then it means they are simply trying to decide
whether they are teachable.

John 6 goes on to say:

> *When Jesus knew in Himself that His disciples
> complained about this, He said to them, "Does
> this offend you? What then if you should see the
> Son of Man ascend where He was before? It is
> the Spirit who gives life; the flesh profits nothing.
> (John 6:60-63)*

It is like He is saying, "You think it is hard for Me to be the
bread of life? What if you watch Me ascend into heaven?" He
helps them understand His teaching by informing them, "It is

the Spirit who gives life, and the flesh profits nothing." They're not supposed to literally eat Him. This was a spiritual teaching.

> *The words that I speak to you are spirit, and they are life. "But there are some of you who do not believe." For Jesus knew from the beginning who they were who did not believe, and who would betray Him. And He said, "Therefore I have said to you that no one can come to Me unless it has been granted to him by My Father." From that time many of His disciples went back and walked with Him no more. (John 6:64-66)*

Never again. Why? They did not have a teachable spirit.

> *Then Jesus said to the twelve, "Do you also want to go away?" (John 6:67)*

Even though I don't think Peter enjoyed the thought of eating Jesus and probably didn't fully understand what was being taught, he was a true disciple and remained teachable.

> *But, Simon Peter answered Him, "Lord, to whom shall we go? You have the words of eternal life. (John 6:68)*

In other words, "Lord, I am submitted to your teaching, even if it is hard."

i.   What does God say He will resist and what does "resist" mean?

ii.   Name a Bible character in the Old Testament who exhibited humbleness. How?

iii.   God's Word tells us that being submissive is "being under orders;" are you awaiting your orders? How?

iv.   Name the 7 spheres of authority in the Scriptures.

v.   In what ways has God blessed you through humility and obedience?

vi.   What does it mean to have a teachable spirit?

vii.   We must be willing to receive rebuke from anyone, but how do we test it, to see if it is from God?

viii.   Memorize Isaiah 57:15

I want to talk about hard work and how it fits into discipleship. I will first draw from the Old Testament stories, which, according to Paul *became our examples.* (1 Corinthians 10:6a) In fact, it has been said that the Old Testament is a physical representation of the New Testament spiritual truths. For example, it says in Ephesians 6 that our warfare is not against flesh and blood, but in the Old Testament, king David's warfare was flesh and blood. Our New Testament war is spiritual and his Old Testament war was physical. You can look at the Old Testament and see spiritual truths that are taught all the way through the New Testament.

With this in mind, we know that God established king David over a *physical kingdom.*

> *David knew that the Lord had established him as king over Israel and that he had exalted his kingdom for the sake of his people, Israel. (2 Samuel 5:12)*

It was a real physical location.

How about the New Testament kingdom? Is God's kingdom still a physical location?

> *Jesus answered, "My kingdom is not of this world. If My kingdom were of this world, My servants would fight, so that I should not be delivered to the Jews; but now My kingdom is not from here." (John 18:36)*

When they came to Jesus and asked, "Are you the one bringing in the kingdom? Where is the kingdom of God?" In Luke chapter 17 He responds,

> *Now when He was asked by the Pharisees when the kingdom of God would come, He answered them and said, "The kingdom of God does not come with observation; nor will they say, 'See here!' or 'See there!' For indeed, the kingdom of God is within you." (Luke 17:20-21)*

Literally, it's in your midst. The kingdom of God exists inside you at this very moment. It is in your heart where God has total sovereignty. In the Old Testament, it was a physical kingdom; in the New Testament it is a spiritual kingdom. In the Old Testament it was David who was God's appointed king. Who is the King over God's kingdom now? The Son of David!

> *"What do you think about the Christ? Whose Son is He?" They said to Him, "The Son of David." He said to them, "How then does David in the Spirit call Him 'Lord,' saying: 'The LORD said to my Lord, "Sit at My right hand, Till I make Your enemies Your footstool."' (Matthew 22:41-42)*

If David calls him Lord, how can He be his Son except that Jesus, the Son of David is the root and the offspring of David? (Revelation 22:6) The One who made David became David's Son. So now David's Son (Jesus) sits over a spiritual kingdom, just like David sat over a physical kingdom.

What do we know about God's kingdom? There is a famous verse in Isaiah that people memorize.

> *For unto us a Child is born, unto us a Son is given; And the government will be upon His shoulder. And His name will be called Wonderful, Counselor, Mighty God, Everlasting Father, Prince of Peace. Of the increase of His government and peace there will be no end, upon the throne of David and over His kingdom, to order it and establish it with judgment and justice from that time forward, even forever. The zeal of the LORD of hosts will perform this. (Isaiah 9:6-7)*

The increase of His government is what I want to focus on in this chapter. How does the kingdom of God increase? It says here in Isaiah 9:7 that the increase will never end once the kingdom has been established. Jesus told us in Luke 17 that it was established during His day. From that day forward, how has the kingdom of God increased?

We find our answer through the Old Testament examples of David's kingdom. How did the kingdom of David increase? Did David make a wish and suddenly there was an increase of his kingdom? No, it increased by hard work and warfare. And it wasn't just David alone. David was the leader and the king, but others followed him into battle. The Old Testament kingdom was expanded by the king's efforts and those who followed him. It was a work of God through some very unusual people.

This is who David's mighty men were:

> *David therefore departed from there and escaped to the cave of Adullam. And when his brothers and all his father's house heard it, they went down there to him. And everyone who was in distress, everyone who was in debt, and everyone who was discontented gathered to him. So he became captain over them. And there were about four hundred men with him. (1 Samuel 22:1-2)*

The distressed, the impoverished, the disgruntled. These are not the people you would normally enlist in your army! But, they came to the king and were transformed. Who are those who come to the Son of David and establish His kingdom?

> *For you see your calling, brethren, that not many wise according to the flesh, not many mighty, not many noble, are called. But God has chosen the foolish things of the world to put to shame the wise, and God has chosen the weak things of the world to put to shame the things which are mighty; and the base things of the world and the things which are despised God has chosen, and the things which are not, to bring to nothing the things that are, that no flesh should glory in His presence. (1 Corinthians 1:26-29)*

Looks like the same group of people who gathered to David! God had chosen David to be king. No one else did. God has chosen Jesus to be King and has sent out an invitation to bring in any who will come. But for some reason, the mighty and noble refuse.

> *Then he said to his servants, 'The wedding is ready, but those who were invited were not worthy. Therefore go into the highways, and as many as you find, invite to the wedding.' So those*

*servants went out into the highways and gathered
together all whom they found, both bad and good.
And the wedding hall was filled with guests.
(Matthew 22:8-10)*

The kingdom of God is filled with those who are not mighty
or wise or even good by the world's standards, but they all recognize their King, the Lord Jesus.

How did David's disgruntled and impoverished castoffs
become the mighty men who expanded his kingdom?

Through hard work.

*Now these are they that came to David to Ziklag,
while he yet kept himself close because of Saul the
son of Kish: and they were among the mighty men,
helpers of the war. They were armed with bows, and
could use both the right hand and the left in hurling
stones and shooting arrows out of a bow, even of
Saul's brethren of Benjamin. (1 Chronicles 12:1-2)*

Who throws as well right handed as they do left? It takes a
great deal of effort and exercise to throw as strong with your left
hand as your right. It does not come by sitting around, but by
hard work instead. During David's time, there were no tanks or
guns: the men had to be the weapons. They each had to swing the
sword or shield or rock. If they were wounded, then the weapon
was lost. So if their right arm was wounded and they could still
throw with their left, then they were mighty.

My dear friend pastor M. Paulose continually urges me, "To
learn everything I can learn." As an example, I play guitar: not
because I have a passion to play guitar, but because it is a good
tool. I have been able to evangelize all over the world, simply
because I sit down and play guitar. If you can learn a foreign
language, learn it! If you have the ability to learn a trade that
might be useful for missionary work, learn it! "Learn to sling with
the right hand and the left," my friend would say. Is this what
the New Testament says about our Lord's spiritual kingdom?

*For though I am free from all men, I have made
myself a servant to all, that I might win the more;
and to the Jews I became as a Jew, that I might
win Jews; to those who are under the law, as under*

*the law, that I might win those who are under the
law; to those who are without law, as without law
(not being without law toward God, but under law
toward Christ), that I might win those who are
without law; to the weak I became as weak, that I
might win the weak. I have become all things to all
men, that I might by all means save some. Now this
I do for the gospel's sake, that I may be partaker of
it with you.(1 Corinthians 9:19-23)*

Spiritually, Paul adapted to every audience, every ethnic
group, and every culture for the purpose of expanding the kingdom. You might even be able to say he could sling with the right
hand and the left. If Paul was in a Jewish group he was Jewish. If
Paul was in a Gentile group he was Gentile. If Paul was among
philosophers in Athens, he became a philosopher. Paul worked
hard to expand the Lord's kingdom.

Paul is the one who wrote:

*How then shall they call on Him in whom they
have not believed? And how shall they believe in
Him of whom they have not heard? And how shall
they hear without a preacher? And how shall they
preach unless they are sent? As it is written: "How
beautiful are the feet of those who preach the gospel
of peace, who bring glad tidings of good things!"
(Romans 10:14-15)*

He also wrote:

*Preach the word! Be ready in season and out
of season. Convince, rebuke, exhort, with all
longsuffering and teaching. (2 Timothy 4:2)*

A disciple must be willing to work hard. In 1 Chronicles 12:8
it says that David's men were able to use the shield and the spear
and they ran as swift as gazelles. I ran track. But I never looked
like a gazelle. Yet I trained very hard. Sometimes I would train so
hard that I would vomit during practice, just so I could run faster.
How hard would you train if your speed would win a war and
the lives of your family? You would train hard, wouldn't you?

*Do you not know that those who run in a race
all run, but one receives the prize? Run in such a*

*way that you may obtain it. And everyone who
competes for the prize is temperate in all things.
(1 Corinthians 9:24)*

An athlete's whole life is focused on winning the prize. For
an Olympic gymnast their training starts about age five. Then,
ten years later they may be capable of competing in the Olympics. Ten years! Do you know how hard it is to be a disciplined
five-year-old? But they do it, and they are tremendous when you
watch them. Paul says that's the attitude of a disciple.

*Now they do it to obtain a perishable crown, but
we for an imperishable crown. Therefore I run
thus: not with uncertainty. Thus I fight: not as one
who beats the air. But I discipline my body and
bring it into subjection, lest, when I have preached
to others, I myself should become disqualified.
(1 Corinthians 9:25-27)*

Can you imagine saying:

*For I am the least of the apostles, who am
not worthy to be called an apostle, because I
persecuted the church of God. But by the grace of
God I am what I am, and His grace toward me
was not in vain; but I labored more abundantly
than they all, yet not I, but the grace of God
which was with me. (1 Corinthians 15:9-10)
(Also Colossians 1:29, 1 Thessalonians 2:9 and
1Timothy 4:10)*

Can you imagine being able to say, "I labor more abundantly
than every preacher in my country. Every missionary, every
evangelist: I labor harder." Paul wrote that by the Holy Spirit.
He 'labored', which means he was hard working. He slung with
both the right hand and the left hand and ran like a gazelle, and
handled the spear for his King. That is the life of a disciple:

*Therefore, my beloved brethren, be steadfast,
immovable, always abounding in the work of the
Lord, knowing that your labor is not in vain in the
Lord. (1 Corinthians 15:58)*

In the Old Testament, David's mighty men wouldn't give up

because they reflected their leader.

> *These are the names of the mighty men whom David had: Josheb-Basshebeth the Tachmonite, chief among the captains. He was called Adino the Eznite, because he had killed eight hundred men at one time. And after him was Eleazar the son of Dodo, the Ahohite, one of the three mighty men with David when they defied the Philistines who were gathered there for battle, and the men of Israel had retreated. He arose and attacked the Philistines until his hand was weary, and his hand stuck to the sword. (2 Samuel 23:8-10a)*

His hand was so tired that it cramped up and they couldn't get it to release the sword. But he just kept swinging! This wasn't fun: it was painful. But he never gave up and...

> *The LORD brought about a great victory that day. (2 Samuel 23:10b)*

Did you see that? Eleazar wielded the sword, but the Lord won the battle. Did it cost Eleazar anything? It said he was weary. How did God bring expansion to David's kingdom? Eleazar's hard work! He didn't stand back and say, "Get them Lord!" He did what he could before the Lord.

> *And after him was Shammah the son of Agee the Hararite. The Philistines had gathered together into a troop where there was a piece of ground full of lentils. Then the people fled from the Philistines. But he stationed himself in the middle of the field, defended it, and killed the Philistines. And the LORD brought about a great victory. (2 Samuel 23:11-12)*

He stationed himself. What does that mean? He purposefully placed himself against an entire army in a field of lentils. And so the Lord brought about a great victory. There it is again. Who defeated them? Shammah did. But, whose victory was it really?

*For the eyes of the LORD run to and fro throughout
the whole earth, to show Himself strong on
behalf of those whose heart is loyal to Him.
(2 Chronicles 16:9)*

On behalf of those in His kingdom who will labor like Paul.
On behalf of him who will be so tired his hand will stick to the
sword of the Spirit, which is the Word of God (Ephesians 6:17).
He will show Himself strong on behalf of any who would purposely resist the enemy (James 4:7). Shammah became a mighty
man of the king because he worked hard.

*Then three of the thirty chief men went down at
harvest time and came to David at the cave of
Adullam. And the troop of Philistines encamped
in the Valley of Rephaim. David was then in the
stronghold, and the garrison of the Philistines was
then in Bethlehem. And David said with longing,
"Oh, that someone would give me a drink of the
water from the well of Bethlehem, which is by the
gate!" So the three mighty men broke through the
camp of the Philistines. (2 Samuel 23:13-16)*

Three men, because they loved the king so much. How about
you? Are you willing to make such a great sacrifice, simply for
the love of your King?

*So the three mighty men broke through the camp
of the Philistines, drew water from the well of
Bethlehem that was by the gate, and took it and
brought it to David. Nevertheless he would not
drink it, but poured it out to the LORD." And he
said, "Far be it from me, O LORD, that I should
do this! Is this not the blood of the men who went
in jeopardy of their lives?" Therefore he would not
drink it. These things were done by the three mighty
men. Now Abishai the brother of Joab, the son of
Zeruiah, was chief of another three. He lifted his
spear against three hundred men, killed them, and
won a name among these three. Was he not the most
honored of three? Therefore he became their captain.
However, he did not attain to the first three. Benaiah
was the son of Jehoiada, the son of a valiant man*

from Kabzeel, who had done many deeds. He had killed two lion-like heroes of Moab. He also had gone down and killed a lion in the midst of a pit on a snowy day. (2 Samuel 23:16-20)

Do you think that was a purposed choice? There is a lion in the pit down below. You have the choice to throw a spear or jump down and kill it by hand. He jumped in.

And he killed an Egyptian, a spectacular man. The Egyptian had a spear in his hand; so he went down to him with a staff, wrested the spear out of the Egyptian's hand, and killed him with his own spear. These things Benaiah the son of Jehoiada did, and won a name among three mighty men. He was more honored than the thirty, but he did not attain to the first three. And David appointed him over his guard. (2 Samuel 23:21-23)

They simply reflected their king. David killed a lion (1 Samuel 17:34-35), so his men wanted to kill a lion. David killed a giant with no weapons (1 Samuel 17:43), so his men wanted to kill a giant with no weapons. David, killed ten thousands (1 Samuel 18:7), so they killed eight hundred in one shot, or three hundred in another. They'd fight until they couldn't move any-more. They reflected their king. They reflected the tenacity of their king. David led them by example. The kingdom was established because the head of the kingdom set the example. He didn't sit in his chair and send orders. He fought beside them.

How hardworking is our King? Look at a normal 'working day' for Jesus:

Then they went into Capernaum, and immediately on the Sabbath He entered the synagogue and taught. And they were astonished at His teaching. (Mark 1:21-22)

Jesus gets up on Saturday and enters the synagogue and teaches the early morning church service. And they were aston-ished at His teaching, for He taught them as one having authority, and not as the scribes.

Now there was a man in their synagogue with

*an unclean spirit. And he cried out, saying, "Let
us alone! What have we to do with You, Jesus of
Nazareth? Did You come to destroy us? I know who
You are--the Holy One of God!" But Jesus rebuked
him, saying, "Be quiet, and come out of him!" And
when the unclean spirit had convulsed him and
cried out with a loud voice, he came out of him.
Then they were all amazed, so that they questioned
among themselves, saying, "What is this? What new
doctrine is this? For with authority He commands
even the unclean spirits, and they obey Him." And
immediately His fame spread throughout all the
region around Galilee. (Mark 1:22-28)*

Now, that is a very emotional and eventful church service!
He's teaching as well as casting out demons; people are amazed
and in awe. So, what does he do after returning home?

*Now as soon as they had come out of the synagogue,
they entered the house of Simon and Andrew, with
James and John. But Simon's wife's mother lay sick
with a fever, and they told Him about her at once.
So He came and took her by the hand and lifted
her up, and immediately the fever left her. And she
served them. (Mark 1:29-31)*

He comes home from church and begins ministering to Peter's
mother-in-law by healing her.

*At evening, when the sun had set, they brought to
Him all who were sick and those who were demon-
possessed. And the whole city was gathered together
at the door. (Mark 1:32-33)*

"At evening", meant that the Sabbath was now over and
people could freely move about. Well, where did everyone go? To
Jesus' house. Do you think he is tired yet? He taught at church,
cast out demons, healed the sick mother-in-law and now when
evening has come, and instead of resting, the whole city gathers
at his door.

*Then He healed many who were sick with various
diseases, and cast out many demons; and He did
not allow the demons to speak, because they knew*

Him. (Mark 1:34)

How long would it take to cast out all the demons and heal all the sick in the town of Capernaum? Finally, Jesus must have gone to bed. Did He sleep in?

> *Now in the morning, having risen a long while before daylight, He went out and departed to a solitary place; and there He prayed. (Mark 1:35)*

I am thinking that He may have had only a few hours of sleep at this point.

> *And Simon and those who were with Him searched for Him. When they found Him, they said to Him, "Everyone is looking for You." But He said to them, "Let us go into the next towns, that I may preach there also, because for this purpose I have come forth." And He was preaching in their synagogues throughout all Galilee, and casting out demons. (Mark 1:36-39)*

That's a day in the life of Jesus, our King. Jesus once became so exhausted that He fell asleep in a boat that was being swamped by waves. The waves were crashing over and yet Jesus kept sleeping. I believe our Lord was often tired.

Another glimpse into how hard our King works is from Mark.

> *Then the apostles gathered to Jesus and told Him all things, both what they had done and what they had taught. (Mark 6:30)*

At this point, John the Baptist (Jesus' cousin) has just been killed. This overwhelms Him, but His disciples have just returned from their first missionary trip and are very excited. However, there are so many who want help that none of them can even eat a meal.

> *And He said to them, "Come aside by yourselves to a deserted place and rest a while." For there were many coming and going, and they did not even have time to eat. (Mark 6:31)*

So they haven't eaten yet and file into a boat to find a quiet place.

> *So they departed to a deserted place in the boat by themselves. But the multitudes saw them departing, and many knew Him and ran there on foot from all the cities. They arrived before them and came together to Him. (Mark 6:32-33)*

Have they eaten? Have they rested? Our Lord still hasn't had a chance to even mourn the death of His own beloved cousin.

> *And Jesus, when He came out, saw a great multitude and was moved with compassion for them, because they were like sheep not having a shepherd. So He began to teach them many things. (Mark 6:34)*

He didn't selfishly send them away, even though they are tired and hungry and He is full of sorrow for John the Baptist.

> *When the day was now far spent His disciples came to Him and said, "This is a deserted place, and already the hour is late."Send them away, that they may go into the surrounding country and villages and buy themselves bread; for they have nothing to eat. (Mark 6:35-36)*

The day is over and they still haven't rested or eaten! Now, I believe at this point the apostles have double motives: "Let the people eat…and perhaps we could eat as well."

> *But He answered and said to them, "You give them something to eat." And they said to Him, "Shall we go and buy two hundred denarii worth of bread and give them something to eat?" But He said to them, "How many loaves do you have?" (Mark 6:37-38)*

You know the miraculous story. Jesus Himself eventually feeds five thousand men and their families. My Lord Jesus put people above His own hunger, above His own sleep, above His own comfort and even above His sorrow! Our King is the hardest working man that ever walked the face of the earth. Amen!

Here is another example. Jesus stops at a well in Samaria and His disciples go to buy food. While they are gone, a woman comes to the well and Jesus ministers to her. Her spiritual life becomes the most important thing in His day. When the disciples finally return:

> *...His disciples urged Him, saying, "Rabbi, eat."*
> *But He said to them, "I have food to eat of which*
> *you do not know." (John 4:31-32)*

When was the last time you were so wrapped up in the Lord's work that you skipped a meal? Two? Three? When was the last time you completely forgot to eat for a whole day, because there were so many people who needed ministering? How hardworking is our King? If David's kingdom was expanded by the hard work of the king and his followers, how about the Son of David's kingdom?

I want to close with a final example of a disciple of Jesus. Paul!

> *Imitate me, just as I also imitate Christ. (1*
> *Corinthians 11:1)*

Paul was talking about hard work when he penned these words. In Hebrews there is a warning for us:

> *And we desire that each one of you show the same*
> *diligence to the full assurance of hope until the end,*
> *that you do not become sluggish, but imitate those*
> *who through faith and patience inherit the promises.*
> *(Hebrews 6:11-12)*

We need to station ourselves in the work around us. Even when it seems that we are all alone, our hard working King will be right beside us. Paul learned this firsthand.

Colossians 1 is talking about Jesus Christ when Paul says:

> *Him we preach, warning every man and teaching*
> *every man in all wisdom, that we may present every*
> *man perfect in Christ Jesus. To this end I also labor,*
> *striving according to His working which works in*
> *me mightily. (Colossians 1:28-29)*

The word for 'striving' is 'agonizomai' It is where we get the English word 'agony'. Paul says, "*According to His working.*" According to who's working? The King's!! "*Which works in me mightily.*" I can labor and agonize according to what Christ is doing inside of me.

A disciple must work hard or he is not truly reflecting his King. He must be willing to say, "I will eat when I eat, I will sleep when I sleep." Or, as an old saint used to say when people would tell him to, "Take care of yourself" he'd reply, "God will do that, I'll take care of the King's business instead." (see Matthew 6:33)

How does the kingdom expand? Hard work.

Sometimes our hands feel like they are "cleaved to the sword". Sometimes we feel like we are the only one fighting and everyone else has left us. Shammah could have said, "Where is everyone?" Instead, he just stationed himself and worked hard and God elevated him to a mighty man.

When you are tired, keep on fighting! When you are alone, keep on fighting! When you have no weapons, keep on fighting! The Lord will have a great victory, and the increase of His kingdom shall have no end. AMEN!!!

i.   *What type of men were attracted to King David and why?*

ii. *David's mighty men knew that their bravery reflected on their king. How does your courage reflect on your King?*

iii. *What type of men did Christ reach out to?*

iv. *What is meant by fighting with your left and right arm spiritually?*

v.   *Compare how the kingdom of David expanded to how the kingdom of Christ grows?*

vi. *How much pain do you endure while the Lord fights the battle?*

vii. *What agony has entered your heart that God wants you to battle over?*

viii. *Surrender your agony to Christ and allow Him to battle through you. Realize your agony is part of walking with Christ because you are sharing His heart for the world as He walks with you.*

ix. *Memorize 1 Corinthians 9:24-25*

138

READY TO LOSE LIFE

A disciple must be unencumbered by the fear of death and this chapter is going to consider our readiness to lose our life for Christ. My friend, M. Paulose lives in Southern India. He has survived dozens of attempts to kill him and his family, everything from strangulation to skinning him alive. They have beaten his wife Sarajom. They have beaten his children. He has watched as his children nearly starved from lack of food when he was preaching the Gospel in difficult areas. His friends have been martyred. Yet, through all of this, the Lord has done a great work by this man's hand. Thousands of missionaries have been raised up and trained through M. Paulose and he has become like a general leading an army of native missionaries.

Why do I tell you this? Because this book is based upon tattered notes that the Lord had given him through the years. This man lives the life of a disciple more than anyone I have ever met in my travels, and everything we are about to learn, he has lived.

Inasmuch then as the children have partaken of flesh and blood, He Himself likewise shared in the same, that through death He might destroy him who had the power of death, that is, the devil, and release those who through fear of death were all their lifetime subject to bondage. (Hebrews 2:14-15)

We have already spoken about a disciple's willingness to suffer and 'take up the cross', but suffering is only temporary while dying is a bit more permanent. So if you will, it is a step beyond suffering.

Then He said to them all, "If anyone desires to come after Me, let him deny himself, and take up his cross daily, and follow Me. For whoever desires to save his life will lose it, but whoever loses his life for My sake will save it. For what profit is it to a man if he gains the whole world, and is himself destroyed or lost? (Luke 9:23-25)

In this Scripture, Jesus has given us three essential steps to becoming His disciple. Each of these has now received it's own chapter in this book. 'Deny Yourself', 'Take up the Cross', and now 'Ready to Lose Life' Are you ready?

He who finds his life will lose it, and he who loses his life for My sake will find it. (Matthew 10:39)

In the book of Matthew, Jesus begins to describe what He knows lies ahead of Him at Jerusalem.

From that time Jesus began to show to His disciples that He must go to Jerusalem, and suffer many things from the elders and chief priests and scribes, and be killed, and be raised the third day. (Matthew 16:21)

Peter, however, refuses to listen to such things.

Then Peter took Him aside and began to rebuke Him, saying, "Far be it from You, Lord; this shall not happen to You! (Matthew 16:22)

How does Jesus respond to Peter's plea to save His life?

But He turned and said to Peter, "Get behind Me, Satan! You are an offense to Me, for you are not mindful of the things of God, but the things of men." Then Jesus said to His disciples, "If anyone desires to come after Me, let him deny himself, and take up his cross, and follow Me. For whoever desires to save his life will lose it, but whoever loses his life for My sake will find it. For what profit is it to a man if he gains the whole world, and loses his own soul? Or what will a man give in exchange for his soul? For the Son of Man will come in the glory of His Father with His angels, and then He will reward each according to his works. (Matthew 16:23-27)

Here was perhaps Jesus' closest friend. Only Peter and a few others were allowed into the very heart of Jesus' private life. This was not an easy thing for Jesus to speak to Peter, but it was too important! Jesus reacted as strong as any friend could react when He spoke these words to Peter. Why? Jesus must suffer and die. It was God's will for the salvation of many, but Peter was thinking not like a disciple, but like a worldly man. Not only does Jesus say He has to die, but He goes on to say that all who follow Him have to be ready to die as well.

This particular quote by Jesus is found in Matthew, Mark and Luke. John, who wrote his Gospel last, also recorded these same words, but in a different context. In the book of John, it was after Jesus had gone into Jerusalem and had driven out the money changers. The crowd was very excited to see Jesus. And then a few gentiles show up.

> *Now there were certain Greeks among those who came up to worship at the feast. Then they came to Philip, who was from Bethsaida of Galilee, and asked him, saying, "Sir, we wish to see Jesus."* *(John 12:20)*

When Jesus is informed about these Greeks, He looks up and says:

> *"The hour has come that the Son of Man should be glorified. Most assuredly, I say to you, unless a grain of wheat falls into the ground and dies, it remains alone; but if it dies, it produces much grain."* *(John 12:23-24)*

Why did He say that right then? I believe I have an answer. The disciples had only been allowed to share the Gospel with the Jews up until that point. But the good news was going to come to all nations following Jesus' death and resurrection, for Paul writes: *for the Jew first and also for the Greek.* (Romans 1:16) So, Jesus tells them the great harvest (which includes the non-Jews) won't occur until after His death. He wasn't saying, "Get the Greeks away from Me." But rather, "I want the Greeks to be with me but it is going to cost Me My life."

> *He who loves his life will lose it, and he who hates his life in this world will keep it for eternal life. If anyone serves Me, let him follow Me. And where I am, there My servant will be also. If anyone serves Me, him My Father will honor. (John 12:25-26)*

Paul, who came later, summarizes this idea when he wrote,

> *"To live is Christ, to die is gain." (Philippians 1:21)*

If you are an American believer, then you are in a very unusual portion of the church. Throughout the history of Christianity, the Lord's people have been killed. In fact, they are being killed right now. Recently, Patras Masih was gunned down by three of his Muslim friends for not becoming a Muslim in a village of Pakistan. Swapan Mondol, an evangelist, was martyred in Bangladesh. Amina Muse was killed in Somalia for her Christian faith. Ri Hyon Ok was publicly executed in North Korea for distributing Bibles. The disciples of Jesus understand what it means to count their lives as nothing for Christ and His Gospel.

When Jesus' disciples departed to evangelize, they were not only prepared to preach, but they were ready to die for the Gospel. They purposed to tell others about the Gospel of Jesus, even though they had the ability to kill them. They were ready to lose their life for the Lord. In India, when I turned and walked toward a man who had a knife and wanted to end my life, I was simply acting like a disciple.

Let me share another personal story. There was a man who rode with the Hell's Angels motorcycle gang and was a methamphetamine cook for the West coast of the United States. This man had shot at one of my friends and had sliced another friend's stomach open with a knife, nearly killing him. One day the Lord told me to speak with him, so I went up into the woods to his little shack. At the end of his driveway was a large orange hazard cone. The gravel road behind it wandered up out of sight and into the woods. This man and I had never met. There I sat at the end of his driveway looking at this barrier and praying. It took everything I had to get out of my car, walk over and move the barrier so that I could proceed by myself up into the woods. As I slowly traveled up the road I passed Voodoo masks and headless dolls strewn everywhere. I had prepared to lose my life that day.

There have really only been two times in my life where I have faced such a dilemma. Both times I found myself praying for my wife and my children rather than myself. "God, if you are going to take my life today, please bring my wife a good husband for my children. Help her to make the right decisions." Both times that is exactly where my heart turned: to my family, rather than my life.

Will you choose to approach that drug dealer's house? Will you choose to put yourself in a situation that is foolish or dangerous, simply for the sake of the Gospel? Paul did it all the time. Jesus did it all the time.

I just want to look at a few verses, which give us examples of men and women who lived like this.

> *And David said with longing, "Oh, that someone would give me a drink of water from the well of Bethlehem, which is by the gate!" So the three broke through the camp of the Philistines, drew water from the well of Bethlehem that was by the gate, and took it and brought it to David. Nevertheless David would not drink it, but poured it out to the LORD. And he said, "Far be it from me, O my God, that I should do this! Shall I drink the blood of these men who have put their lives in jeopardy? For at the risk of their lives they brought it." Therefore he would not drink it. (1 Chronicles 11:17-19)*

This group of devoted followers of King David risked their very lives for a simple drink of water for their king. There have been many who have died on noble principles, perhaps trying to save a dog from getting hit by a car, or pulling photographs from a burning house. People who have purposely set aside the fear of death for some perishable things. But some reasons to risk your life seem greater than others. I once heard a World War II story about a man whose buddy was wounded and as they were removing him from the battlefield they had to strap him on the outside of the tank. Since there was absolutely no way to protect his friend, the unwounded man crawled out and laid upon his buddy. He took some of the bullets to preserve his friend's life. He had purposed to lose his life for his friend.

If the people of this world are willing to die for temporary things, how much more should the followers of the eternal God be willing to die when they know they have eternal life? Jesus said, "If you die, you will produce much fruit." (John 12:24) The moment I purpose that preserving my life is less important to me than reaching others with salvation is the beginning of great fruit and freedom. And if it means that I die, well, at least others might be saved.

You know, there are some things in the Old Testament that make you say, "Whoa"! One of them is in 1 Samuel 14, where Saul has just been anointed king of Israel. He gathers his mighty army of three thousand men together. He splits them up and two thousand go with him, while one thousand are assigned to his son, Jonathan. The Philistines gather their army of thirty thousand six hundred together and come against his little Hebrew army. How many swords were there in the hands of the Saul's army?

> *Now there was no blacksmith to be found throughout all the land of Israel, for the Philistines said, "Lest the Hebrews make swords or spears." But all the Israelites would go down to the Philistines to sharpen each man's plowshare, his mattock, his ax, and his sickle; and the charge for a sharpening was a pim for the plowshares, the mattocks, the forks, and the axes, and to set the points of the goads. So it came about, on the day of battle, that there was neither sword nor spear found in the hand of any of the people who were with Saul and Jonathan. But they were found with Saul and Jonathan his son. (1 Samuel 13:19-22)*

Two swords, two spears. Now, we read in 1 Samuel 13, that when the people saw the Philistines coming they crawled into the rocks and bushes and up the mountains. Wouldn't you hide if you were in a battle and didn't even have a sword? Don't forget there are also ten times as many people in the enemy's army and they are all fully armed. So, Jonathan gets up one day... (I love this story.)

> *Then Jonathan said to the young man who bore his armor, "Come, let us go over to the garrison of these uncircumcised; it may be that the LORD will work for us. For nothing restrains the LORD from saving by many or by few. (1 Samuel 14:6)*

Did he know if he was going to live? The word 'may be' means he didn't even know if he would live. 'Maybe' God will do something. "There are two of us: that should be enough against thirty thousand six hundred if the Lord is in it!" "Don't forget, I do have one of the swords!" Jonathan proclaims.

> *So his armor bearer said to him, "Do all that is in your heart. Go then; here I am with you, according to your heart." Then Jonathan said, "Very well,*

let us cross over to these men, and we will show ourselves to them. If they say thus to us, 'Wait until we come to you,' then we will stand still in our place and not go up to them. "But if they say thus, 'Come up to us,' then we will go up. For the LORD has delivered them into our hand, and this will be a sign to us." (1 Samuel 14:7-10)

Did God tell Jonathan to do this? He is risking a lot based on an assumption. So, what happens? They show themselves to the Philistines and the Philistines say, "Hey, the Hebrews are coming." I love what it says:

And the Philistines said, "Look, the Hebrews are coming out of the holes where they have hidden. Then the men of the garrison called to Jonathan and his armorbearer, and said, "Come up to us, and we will show you something." Jonathan said to his armorbearer, "Come up after me, for the LORD has delivered them into the hand of Israel." And Jonathan climbed up on his hands and knees with his armorbearer after him; and they fell before Jonathan. And as he came after him, his armorbearer killed them. (1 Samuel 14:11-13)

Jonathan and this armor bearer have placed their lives in immense risk. Do you remember the rest of the story? A great shaking and trembling in the Philistine camp occurs and Saul wonders what is happening. "It's your boy and he is chasing the entire Philistine army, thirty thousand six hundred men!" Was that a mighty deed? Was he ready to lose his life for the kingdom? It wasn't until this boy chose to die that great things happened.

How about the amazing story of Queen Esther? Mordecai the Jew has just informed his niece Esther that an evil man named Haman, has taken the king's seal and sent a decree to kill all the Jews in the land. Mordecai declares, "Esther, you are the queen. You must speak to the king about this wicked plan."

She responds:

All the king's servants and the people of the king's provinces know that any man or woman who goes into the inner court to the king, who has not been

*called, he has but one law: put all to death, except
the one to whom the king holds out the golden
scepter, that he may live. Yet I myself have not
been called to go in to the king these thirty days.
(Esther 4:11)*

Her uncle Mordecai replies:

*Do not think in your heart that you will escape in
the king's palace any more than all the other Jews.
For if you remain completely silent at this time,
relief and deliverance will arise for the Jews from
another place, but you and your father's house will
perish. Yet who knows whether you have come to the
kingdom for such a time as this? (Esther 4:13-14)*

Is Esther ready and willing to die for the deliverance of her
people?

*Go, gather all the Jews who are present in Shushan,
and fast for me; neither eat nor drink for three days,
night or day. My maids and I will fast likewise. And
so I will go to the king, which is against the law;
and if I perish, I perish! (Esther 4:16)*

If I perish, I perish! That is the call of a disciple. It is not
about my life. It is about what God wants. Paul and Barnabas
are described by the Jerusalem church in the following letter:

*It seemed good to us, being assembled with one
accord, to send chosen men to you with our
beloved Barnabas and Paul, men who have risked
their lives for the Name of our Lord Jesus Christ.
(Acts 15:25-26)*

When a person has risked his or her life for the Gospel, we
listen in awe. Yet, God has called every disciple to be ready to
risk his or her life. How quickly the kingdom of the Lord would
expand if every disciple risked his or her life for the sake of the
Name of Jesus Christ.

Paul commends one disciple named Epaphroditus:

*Receive him therefore in the Lord with all gladness,
and hold such men in esteem;*

Why?

Because for the work of Christ he came close to death, not regarding his life. (Philippians 2:30)

Just so you know: those who are believers and not disciples, they don't encourage this way of thinking. Oh, I've had many a Christian tell me, "Don't travel to those places: you might die." "Who will take care of your family?" "It is reckless and foolish to put yourself at risk." Well, what did Esther say? "If I perish, I perish!"

Jesus' disciple Thomas is often chided by believers, because he didn't believe Jesus had raised from the dead until he touched the wounds on his Lord's body. But there is another side to Thomas. In John chapter 11 Lazarus dies, but Jesus says He is going to be with Lazarus. Now we all know that Jesus is going to raise Lazarus from the dead, but His disciples didn't know it.

Then Jesus said to them plainly, "Lazarus is dead. And I am glad for your sakes that I was not there, that you may believe. Nevertheless let us go to him. (John 11:14-15)

So we have a little miscommunication between Jesus and the disciples. They were thinking Jesus was headed off to die. Look at what Thomas says:

Then Thomas, who is called the Twin, said to his fellow disciples, "Let us also go, that we may die with Him." (John 11:16)

Thomas understood that to follow Christ meant we must be ready to lose our life. Don't get me wrong: I don't think Thomas jumped up and down with joy as he spoke these words, but he did purpose this in his heart. As disciples, we also need to set our hearts so that we are able to say, "If I perish, I perish for Christ!"

Now there was Peter who was constantly saying, "I'm ready to die for you Jesus." And although Peter didn't yet understand the importance of prayer and the willingness to follow God's plans rather than man's, we must not overlook that he was fully ready to lose his life for the Lord. It was Peter who drew the sword to protect Jesus and took on a whole garrison of soldiers alone. Of course we know that Jesus commanded him to put his sword away, but in John 13:37 Peter openly states his readiness to lay down his life for the Lord.

> *Peter said to Him, "Lord, why can I not follow You now? I will lay down my life for Your sake."*
> *(John 13:37)*

Two other disciples, James and John also acknowledge this same thing when they came to Jesus and asked:

> *Grant us that we may sit, one on Your right hand and the other on Your left, in Your glory.*
> *(Mark 10:37)*

Jesus responds:

> *You do not know what you ask. Are you able to drink the cup that I drink, and be baptized with the baptism that I am baptized with? (Mark 10:38)*

They understood that this meant suffering and death. Were they ready to lose their lives?

> *They said to Him, "We are able." So Jesus said to them, "You will indeed drink the cup that I drink, and with the baptism I am baptized with you will be baptized; but to sit on My right hand and on My left is not Mine to give, but it is for those for whom it is prepared." (Mark 10:39-40)*

James became the first Apostle martyred. John survived until all the other Apostles had been martyred and Rome even tried to boil him to death in oil. However, history says that John died as an old man. God spared him, but was he ready to lose his life. Outside of John, were there any other Apostles not martyred for Jesus? History tells us that every single one of them was killed for their faith. They were all ready to lose their lives.

How about Stephen? Was Stephen ready to die for the Lord? Stephen was the first martyr in the book of Acts. He was stoned to death by the Jews while he prayed, *"Lord, do not charge them with this sin."* Jesus had said that if a grain of wheat falls into the ground it will produce much grain. Did Stephen's death bear fruit? First, the persecution that arose following his murder scattered the followers of Christ so that the Gospel spread to the known world. Second, I believe that this scene was the beginning of the conversion of Saul who later became Paul. Saul was sitting there watching Stephen's angelic face while he was looking up into heaven and crying out, "I see Jesus!"

Generally, if you are standing before a mad and violent crowd you try and speak calmly. When you are before a court that is ready to kill you, it is best not to call them 'vipers'. Read what Stephen said to this hostile crowd.

> *You stiffnecked and uncircumcised in heart and ears! You always resist the Holy Spirit; as your fathers did, so do you. Which of the prophets did your fathers not persecute? And they killed those who foretold the coming of the Just One, of whom you now have become the betrayers and murderers, who have received the law by the direction of angels and have not kept it. (Acts 7:51-53)*

He was preaching the very sermon that would kill him! He was ready to lose his life for his King!

Saul had taken part in killing Stephen and yet he was called to be an Apostle by the Lord. When Ananias was told to lay hands on him, listen to what God told him:

> *But the Lord said to him, "Go, for he is a chosen vessel of Mine to bear My name before Gentiles, kings, and the children of Israel. For I will show him how many things he must suffer for My name's sake." (Acts 9:15-16)*

From the very first day of Paul's discipleship training he was being taught about suffering.

In Acts chapter 20, Paul is on his way back to Jerusalem and at every stop the prophets are saying, "If you continue to Jerusalem you will be imprisoned and beaten." How does Paul respond?

> *And see, now I go bound in the spirit to Jerusalem, not knowing the things that will happen to me there, except that the Holy Spirit testifies in every city, saying that chains and tribulations await me. But none of these things move me; nor do I count my life dear to myself, so that I may finish my race with joy, and the ministry which I received from the*

Lord Jesus, to testify to the Gospel of the grace of God. (Acts 20:22-24)

Paul was a true disciple of the Lord Jesus and was ready and willing to lose his life for the Gospel. It didn't end there. In chapter 21, even more people plead with him and this time with tears; "Don't go! Don't go!"

Then Paul answered, "What do you mean by weeping and breaking my heart? For I am ready not only to be bound, but also to die at Jerusalem for the Name of the Lord Jesus." (Acts 21:13)

How hard would that choice be? His dearest friends are weeping and pleading. I personally know that it is extremely hard to leave my wife and children when I travel overseas. There is always a mourning when I get on the plane. I wonder if I will ever see my family again. Even if I don't die, perhaps one of my children will be harmed while I am away. I will be gone during their greatest need! And then I get on the plane. *"For I am ready not only to be bound, but also to die at Jerusalem for the Name of the Lord Jesus."* Stop crying, please! My heart is set. I am ready to lose my life: I'm headed for Jerusalem.

Romans 8:35 is so often memorized:

Who shall separate us from the love of Christ? Shall tribulation, or distress, or persecution, or famine, or nakedness, or peril, or sword? (Romans 8:35)

This verse has comforted many over the centuries. The Lord's love will never leave us, regardless of the situations we find ourselves in. But most people just 'pluck' this verse out of the middle of the chapter and rarely quote the very next verse:

As it is written: "For Your sake we are killed all day long; We are accounted as sheep for the slaughter." (Romans 8:36)

I never really understood this verse in Romans 8 until I stood next to real disciples in India. One time I was teaching a man Inductive Bible Study, and I was so excited to be helping him grow in his ministry. I was however, completely unaware that on the way to the seminar he was beaten severely and his wife was killed. Then there was the other man whom I asked why he wore no shoes. He responded, "I'm going to the Hindus. And devout Hindus don't wear shoes." One dear brother, Alexander, was repeatedly beaten at the bus stop when returning from evangelism. His persecutors would meet him and beat him wherever he would travel. So, pastor Moses Paulose bought him a bicycle. The next thing we heard was that he had been chased down by a 3-wheel auto rickshaw and beaten on his way to a village. So pastor Paulose bought him a motorcycle so he could get away. I don't know what's next: perhaps a racecar. But at least for now he can drive fast enough to get away from his persecutors.

Another brother is blind. Brother Isaac is blind because they have beaten his head so many times while he was sharing the Gospel. Now, being blind, someone has to lead him to the village center, where he sings and preaches. At one village a group of men said, "Hey, we'd like to hear more about this Jesus in our village. Could you come to our village?" So they took him into the middle of a thorn patch and tied him to a fire ant hill. (I was bitten by a fire ant once and it is very painful.) They tied him to this hill, where he sat for an hour being eaten alive by fire ants before God intervened miraculously. The Lord literally spoke to him, untied his ropes and led him home by the Spirit. So, guess what he did? He went back out and preached, ant bites and all! If I perish, I perish!

> *So, affectionately longing for you, we were well pleased to impart to you not only the Gospel of God, but also our own lives, because you had become dear to us. (1 Thessalonians 2:8)*

The whole book of 1 Thessalonians is about enduring trials while keeping our eye focused on the prize. Paul uses himself as an example in the verse above. "We gave you our lives, now you give your life. Come follow us."

> *Then Jesus said to His disciples, "If anyone desires to come after Me, let him deny himself, and take up his cross, and follow Me. For whoever desires to save his life will lose it, but whoever loses his life for My sake will find it. (Matthew 16:24)*

Follow me all the way...

*For to me, to live is Christ, and to die is gain.
(Philippians 1:21)*

Paul looked past his death every day. In 1 Corinthians 15:31
He says, *"I die daily"* Literally, "How anything affects me physically doesn't matter. I am going to heaven."

Dear reader, in Revelation, during the Great and Terrible
Tribulation, it says they overcame Satan by three things. Do you
remember what they were?

*And they overcame him by the blood of the Lamb
and by the word of their testimony, and they did
not love their lives to the death. (Revelation 12:11)*

Let me close with one last story: Robert Thomas was one of
the first protestant missionaries to Korea. This people group was
known as fierce warriors and had already killed others who had
tried to bring the Gospel into their land. However, Robert felt
that it was his duty. Many friends tried to discourage him from
going because the danger was "too great", but he chose to travel
to Korea in spite of this. In 1866 as he was traveling upriver, his
ship became grounded and was soon attacked by Korean warriors who lit it on fire. As the boat burned Robert threw Bibles
to his attackers. He was subsequently captured and executed, but
before his death he was able to give a Bible to the leader. This
man was unable to read, so he eventually lined the inside of his
house with the paper in the Bible. And, as God would have it,
word eventually spread that this man had the holy words of God
on the walls of his house and so Koreans began traveling great
distances to read these words. At the time of Robert Thomas'
death, the London Missionary Society felt that his mission had
been a complete and tragic failure. But today, Korean Christians
greatly honor this man's martyrdom because they can trace the
spread of the Gospel in their country back to the Bibles which
he threw from the deck of his burning ship and specifically, to
the Bible that he gave to his executioner.

Let God wash you in His Word and probe your heart. Am
I ready to lose my life? May your response be: "If I perish, I
perish!"

"He who finds his life will lose it, and he who loses his life for My sake will find it." (Matthew 10:39)

CHAPTER ELEVEN REVIEW

i.   Why must a disciple be unencumbered with the fear of death?

ii.   How does fear of death encumber you?

iii. What is the source of fear of death according to Hebrews 2:14-15?

iv.   How does God want you to respond to fearful circumstances?

v.   What does God offer in exchange for dying for His sake?

vi.   How does the death of a believer produce much fruit?

vii. Think through each of the stories about biblical saints who were willing to die for the Lord. What does each of their examples teach you?

viii. What circumstances bring fear into your life and need to be surrendered to the Lord so you can walk by faith?

ix.   Was Robert Thomas successful or not in his mission to Korea?

x.   Memorize Philippians 1:21

FORSAKING ALL

> *Now great multitudes went with Him. And He*
> *turned and said to them, "If anyone comes to Me*
> *and does not hate his father and mother, wife and*
> *children, brothers and sisters, yes, and his own life*
> *also, he cannot be My disciple. (Luke 14:25-26)*

*Y*ou couldn't pick a worse message to proclaim to those following you! "You have to hate your mom, your dad, your wife, your kids and yourself." What is He saying? Isn't this the same Lord who commands us to love our mother and father? Honor them - and good things will happen to us. Isn't that what the Bible promises?

> *"Honor your father and mother," which is the*
> *first commandment with promise: that it may be*
> *well with you and you may live long on the earth.*
> *(Ephesians 6:2-3)*

This is the same God! So, Jesus cannot be saying that He wants us to treat our families poorly. Instead He is saying we must have one Master, one Lord and one perfect love. Everything else must be 'forsaken.'

> *For which of you intending to build a tower, does*
> *not sit down first and count the cost, whether he*
> *has enough to finish it lest, after he has laid the*
> *foundation, and is not able to finish, all who see*
> *it begin to mock him, saying, 'This man began to*
> *build and was not able to finish.' Or what king,*
> *going to make war against another king, does not sit*
> *down first and consider whether he is able with ten*
> *thousand to meet him who comes against him with*
> *twenty thousand? Or, while the other is still a great*
> *way off he sends a delegation and asks conditions*
> *of peace. So likewise, whoever of you does not*
> *forsake all that he has cannot be My disciple.*
> *(Luke 14:28-33)*

The word 'forsake' literally means we are to say goodbye

and send it away. This Greek word is often translated in the following ways:

> *And when He had sent them away, He departed to the mountain to pray. (Mark 6:46)*

Or

> *"Lord, I will follow You, but let me first go and bid them farewell who are at my house." (Luke 9:61)*

'Sent' and 'Bid them farewell' come from the same Greek word. I experienced this part of discipleship when I came to a place in my life where the Lord was calling me to become a full time pastor. Yet my father considered me a fool and persecuted me. I have a friend even now who is going through this same struggle. His father is quoting Scriptures to him about how he needs to honor father and mother and care for them. But, God has been calling him to be a missionary, just as surely as God was calling me to become a pastor. I had to say in my own heart, just as he will eventually have to say, "Dad, I have forsaken my relationship with you and replaced it with God." If a disciple cannot do this, then they are like the man who half built a tower. He didn't finish what he had started to do.

In Mark 10:17-28, there is a story about a rich young ruler. The rich young ruler came running to Jesus. He wanted to follow Him, but had three difficulties to overcome. He was Rich, Young, and a Ruler. Wealth does make it difficult to follow God. (Matthew 19:23) Being young sometimes makes it difficult to follow God as well, because youth consider themselves invincible. And, to be a ruler at such a young age makes it extremely difficult to follow God because he would have to be very humble. So, this young man had a few struggles to overcome. Each of these spiritual struggles would actually be considered a 'success' by the unsaved world, but a barrier to discipleship in this instance. Which one do you think will keep him from following Christ?

> *Good Teacher, what shall I do that I may inherit eternal life? So Jesus said to him, "Why do you call Me good? No one is good but One, that is, God. You know the commandments: 'Do not commit adultery,' 'Do not murder,' 'Do not steal,' 'Do*

not bear false witness,' 'Do not defraud,' 'Honor your father and your mother.' And he answered and said to Him, "Teacher, all these things I have kept from my youth." Then Jesus, looking at him, loved him and said to him, "One thing you lack:" (Mark 10:17-21a)

This must have excited the young man. "One thing. That's it? One thing? Excellent! What is it, good Teacher?" Sometimes it becomes hard to tell the truth, but Jesus always did. In love.

"Go your way, sell whatever you have" (Mark 10:21b)

I looked that word up; it means sell 'what is in your hands', everything and anything you possess. Sell it all!

"and give to the poor, and you will have treasure in heaven; and come, take up the cross, and follow Me." (Mark 10:21c)

He wanted to follow God with his whole heart... well nearly his whole heart. He was willing to forsake most things: he just couldn't forsake all things. There were a few things in his life to which he was still attached.

It's not wrong to be rich. But it is wrong to not forsake your riches. It's not wrong to have a family, but it's wrong not to forsake your family. If something ties you down and keeps you from following Jesus, then you haven't forsaken it. You must "send away" your attachment to it and its control over you, or it will keep you from finishing what you start.

But he was sad at this word, and went away sorrowful, for he had great possessions. Then Jesus looked around and said to His disciples, "How hard it is for those who have riches to enter the kingdom of God!" (Mark 10:22-23)

Now that is a sad story!

It is easier for a camel to go through the eye of a needle than for a rich man to enter the kingdom of God. And they were greatly astonished, saying among themselves, "Who then can be saved?" But Jesus looked at them and said, "With men it

is impossible, but not with God; for with God all
things are possible." Then Peter began to say to
Him, "See, we have left all and followed You."
(Mark 10:25-28)

A disciple must 'forsake all' that keeps him from following the Lord. Peter tells him, "We have left all to follow You." Could he really say that? Let's see…

So it was, as the multitude pressed about Him to
hear the word of God, that He stood by the Lake
of Gennesaret, and saw two boats standing by the
lake; but the fishermen had gone from them and
were washing their nets. Then He got into one of the
boats, which was Simon's, and asked him to put out
a little from the land. And He sat down and taught
the multitudes from the boat. (Luke 5:1-3)

So, the Lord gets into Peter's boat and pulls away from the land slightly, so that He can preach to the crowd. Peter is sitting there with the best seat in the house listening to the Master. I imagine Peter is rejoicing greatly to be sitting at the feet of such a great Teacher.

When He had stopped speaking, He said to Simon,
"Launch out into the deep and let down your nets
for a catch." But Simon answered and said to
Him, "Master, we have toiled all night and caught
nothing; nevertheless at Your word I will let down
the net." (Luke 5:4-5)

There are two emerging problems with Jesus' fishing plan and Peter knows it. Jesus was a carpenter and not a fisherman, so Peter could overlook the fact that Jesus didn't know that people don't fish on the Sea of Galilee during the daytime. Even now, Galilean fishermen pull out in the evening and put lights on buoys to draw the fish in. The temperature of the lake forces fish to stay deep during the day and away from the surface except during the cool of the evening. The second problem with Jesus' command is that they didn't have very deep nets, because all of the nets must be pulled in by hand. Now, knowing all these facts, how many fish are hanging out in eight to ten-foot deep water in the middle of a deep pool during the heat of the day? Not many! So, from a fishing perspective, Jesus has just made a terrible error. Peter could have said, "Hey man, I fish; you preach." He did give a gentle resistance, but he didn't refuse to obey.

> *And when they had done this, they caught a great number of fish, and their net was breaking. (Luke 5:6)*

So I picture this in my mind: Peter lets down his net, and as he does, all the fish in the Sea of Galilee swim towards him. Soon the weight of the fish causes the net to begin breaking, and the boat tips sideways. He's excited and overwhelmed! He hadn't caught a single fish all night and now, in sixty seconds, he has caught them all!

> *So, they signaled to their partners in the other boat (James and John) to come and help them. And they came and filled both the boats, so that they began to sink. (Luke 5:7)*

It takes quite a bit of fish to sink a boat! Even if it is a small rowboat! I've never even heard of such a thing. The boats were so overfilled with fish that the fishermen would've been standing upon the piles while still trying to pull in more. Pretty soon the boats are just above the water line and they are slowly moving their way back to shore.

If you are a fisherman, how do you feel right now? You feel blessed! You have seen more fish today than you will see in an entire year. You are thinking that it is good to follow this Jesus! Then look what happens next:

> *When Simon Peter saw it, he fell down at Jesus' knees, saying, "Depart from me, for I am a sinful man, O Lord!" (Luke 5:8)*

He was completely overwhelmed with awe that at Jesus' word they had caught all these fish.

> *For he and all who were with him were astonished at the catch of fish which they had taken;* (I love that! What an understatement! Astonished. Yeah, the boats are sinking!) *and so also were James and John, the sons of Zebedee, who were partners with*

> *Simon. And Jesus said to Simon, "Do not be afraid.*
> *From now on you will catch men." So when they*
> *had brought their boats to land, they forsook all*
> *and followed Him. (Luke 5:9-11)*

So, when Peter tells Jesus, *"We have left all"*, in his mind, he was thinking about two boats so full of fish that they could barely make it to shore. When they landed and Jesus said, "Now leave it and follow Me." They left it all. They forsook the wealth, the occupation; the literal translation of the Greek is that they left 'every single one'. They forsook every one of those fish in the boat. They didn't stuff a few of them in their pockets before following. Could Peter say, "We left it all"? Oh, yeah. The fact is, every disciple will have to make a choice like this in their life. Some won't leave the fish at all. Some will leave most of them, only putting a couple in their pocket. But disciples (according to Jesus) will forsake it all. Peter simply accepted that someone else would eat those fish and their attraction no longer held power over him.

Now Judas is a good example of someone who chose not to become a disciple...

> *For Jesus knew from the beginning who they were*
> *who did not believe, and who would betray Him.*
> *(John 6:64b)*

Judas refused to forsake all. Wealth and greed still had power over him.

> *[H]e was a thief, and had the money box; and he*
> *used to take what was put in it. (John 12:6b)*

Even though the Lord personally called him and trained him, he was never able to finish, just like the parable in Luke 14: 28-30.

> *Then one of the twelve, called Judas Iscariot, went to*
> *the chief priests and said, "What are you willing to*
> *give me if I deliver Him to you?" And they counted*
> *out to him thirty pieces of silver. (Matthew 26:14-15)*

> *Then Judas, His betrayer, seeing that He had been*
> *condemned, was remorseful and brought back the*
> *thirty pieces of silver to the chief priests and elders,*
> *saying, "I have sinned by betraying innocent blood."*

And they said, "What is that to us? You see to it!"
Then he threw down the pieces of silver in the
temple and departed, and went and hanged himself.
(Matthew 27:3-5)

He didn't forsake all and therefore never finished. Peter forsook all and even though he had to overcome his own personal struggles; Peter finished well.

Dear reader, forsake and trust the Lord. In Luke chapter 18, immediately after Peter says, "We forsook all and followed you." Jesus responds:

Then Peter said, "See, we have left all and followed
You." So He said to them, "Assuredly, I say to
you, there is no one who has left house or parents
or brothers or wife or children, for the sake of the
kingdom of God, who shall not receive many times
more in this present time; and in the age to come
eternal life." (Luke 18:28-30)

When we forsake all, we will never regret it. I traded my career and prestige for the salvation of my entire biological family as well as gaining hundreds and thousands of brothers and sisters throughout the world. When I travel to a foreign land, my brothers and sisters in the Lord feed me, they offer me the best rooms to sleep in, they encourage me; they are my family! That is what Jesus meant. We receive a hundred fold *in this present time and, in the age to come, eternal life.* If you are held back by nothing, the Lord will give you everything. We can either have the Lord and His will or we can have the fish.

Let me close with a story: John Leonard Dober and David Nitschman are names you probably don't recognize. John was a simple potter and David a carpenter. Ordinary occupations. Extraordinary men. They left their jobs and families in 1732 to become the first Moravian missionaries.

These two men actually sold themselves into slavery in order to reach a group of slaves on an island in the West Indies. Their life's purpose was to follow Jesus, who had given His life for them and for all the world.

As their ship unfurled its sail and began pulling away from the dock, separating these two young men from the weeping families who would never see them again, they leaned over the rail and shouted across the water, "May the Lamb that was slain receive the reward of His suffering!" This heartfelt statement became the cry that sparked one of the greatest missionary movements of modern time, known as the Moravian Revival. I personally have been so touched by their willingness to give everything up to reach an island of slaves who would otherwise never hear the Gospel, that I have painted in 8-inch letters their statement on the wall of the dining room in my house. "May the Lord receive the reward of His suffering..." This is my daily reminder to forsake all and follow Christ.

CHAPTER TWELVE REVIEW

i. *In your own words re-write Luke 14:33 and then spend some time asking God to speak to you about this issue.*

ii. *What does 'forsake' mean?*

iii. *What is the difference between forsaking 'most' and forsaking 'all'? Which have you done?*

iv. *What has been the hardest thing to forsake as you have followed Christ?*

v. *How do you forsake your family and friends and yet still love them as the Scripture commands?*

vi. *What are the rewards promised by the Lord to those who forsake all?*

vii. *Memorize Luke 14:33*

he next characteristic of a disciple is discipline. Let's read what Paul wrote:

All things are lawful for me, but all things are not helpful. All things are lawful for me, but I will not be brought under the power of any. (1 Corinthians 6:12)

There is a great deal of freedom in the lifestyle of a Christian, but the moment my lifestyle controls my life, it is out of line.

Foods for the stomach and the stomach for foods, but God will destroy both it and them. Now the body is not for sexual immorality but for the Lord, and the Lord for the body. And God both raised up the Lord and will also raise us up by His power. (1 Corinthians 6:13-14)

In other words, earthly things are temporary. Good meals and a good nights' sleep all eventually fade away. Food is for the stomach and the stomach is for food, but both of them will pass away. As a disciple, the key to remaining disciplined is to recognize where I'm investing my life. It's as if I told you that you can put money into a certain account and receive thirty percent interest, but only for two and a half days, and then your whole investment disappears. Or you can put money into a long-term account and receive one hundred percent interest, but you are unable to withdraw it for a hundred years... Those are the two options we have as we live out our lives. Paul says, "I will not be put under the power of anything besides the Lord," so that leaves us two options, or two masters as Jesus referred to it.

No one can serve two masters; for either he will hate the one and love the other, or else he will be loyal to the one and despise the other. You cannot serve God and mammon. (Matthew 6:24)

Are you going to be ruled by the things of this world or will you be ruled by Him? If you are ruled by the things of this world, your investment is only temporary.

Let's look at some examples. What were the two desires mentioned by Paul in 1 Corinthians 6? Food and sexual immorality. Let's look at Esau and food.

Esau and Food

Now Jacob cooked a stew; and Esau came in from the field, and he was weary. (Genesis 25:29)

Esau was an undisciplined man who lived for the moment. All of his decisions were based upon how he felt right then. What is my stomach telling me? How do I feel? How should I react? I want it right now! He would have owned a microwave, because he wanted it instantly!

And Esau said to Jacob, "Please feed me with that same red stew, for I am weary." Therefore his name was called Edom (which means red) But Jacob said, "Sell me your birthright as of this day." (Genesis 25:30-31)

Which is a better investment? Feed the short-term hunger, or keep the long-term birthright? But Esau had no discipline in his life. It's like asking which is more valuable breathing or wearing shoes? They are incomparable.

And Esau said, "Look, I am about to die; so what is this birthright to me?" (Genesis 25:32)

Do you know how often we over exaggerate our temporary desires? In the United States, we often use the phrase, "Oh, I'm starving to death." Have you ever said that? "I'm starving to death!" If you are, then you must be the fattest starvation case I have ever seen! That was Esau. The stew and the birthright couldn't even be compared to each other, but his lack of discipline left him vulnerable.

Then Jacob said, "Swear to me as of this day." So he swore to him, and sold his birthright to Jacob. And Jacob gave Esau bread and stew of lentils; then he ate and drank, arose, and went his way. Thus Esau despised his birthright. (Genesis 25:33-34)

His hunger passed when his physical need was met, but it was too late, for he had despised his birthright. It was simply a lack of discipline that caused him to focus on short-term hunger rather than long-term birthrights.

Hebrews says something very interesting about Esau and what he did. Each of us has the ability to compromise. We struggle with discipline because we all have short-term desires that we want to fulfill! Sure, it feels good when we fulfill those desires, but only for a little while. Hebrews calls it the passing pleasures of sin (Hebrews 11:25). How many 'day-afters' has a Christian suffered due to a lack of discipline? How many times do they look back on yesterday and realize that they shouldn't have done what they did, having lived just for the moment? People who are dieting often give in to sudden hunger. Then they usually eat food of low nutritional value and high sugar content. The next morning they think, "Ahhh, I broke my diet! I really didn't need that cookie. I would have survived through the night." But they give in to the short-term and forsake the long-term. That is how it works spiritually. We can be like the boy who was asked, "Would you like a dime today or a dollar tomorrow?" And he answers, "Give me the dime."

> *Lest there be any fornicator or profane person like Esau, who for one morsel of food sold his birthright. (Hebrews 12:16)*

He sold his birthright for one meal. Not one hundred meals. Not all the meals he would eat until he grew old, but one thirty-minute meal.

> *For you know that afterward, when he wanted to inherit the blessing, he was rejected, for he found no place for repentance, though he sought it diligently with tears. (Hebrews 12:17)*

The moment passed and he regretted it, because he hadn't remained disciplined. Let's look at the second desire Paul mentioned.

Amnon and Sexual Immorality

King David had many wives and children. One of his sons, Amnon fell in love with a beautiful half sister named Tamar.

*After this Absalom the son of David had a lovely
sister, whose name was Tamar; and Amnon the son
of David loved her. (2 Samuel 13:1)*

Was this temporary? Do people 'fall in love' and find out
later it was lust? Amnon thinks, "I can't live without her!" How
many a young person has said those words? "Oh, my life will
end if I don't marry this person!" I tell them, "If your life will
end if you don't marry this person, then you have some real
emotional issues!"

*Amnon was so distressed over his sister Tamar that
he became sick; (2 Samuel 13:2a)*

Amnon is unable to eat or sleep because he can't have his
sister. She is so good looking! That's all it was: a temporary lustful passion in his heart

*for she was a virgin. And it was improper for Amnon
to do anything to her. But Amnon had a friend whose
name was Jonadab the son of Shimeah, David's
brother. Now Jonadab was a very crafty man. (2
Samuel 13:2b-3)*

A true friend would say to Amnon, "Get over it! There
are hundreds of beautiful women. Stay disciplined and don't be
driven by your passions!"

*And he said to him, "Why are you, the king's son,
becoming thinner day after day? Will you not tell
me?" Amnon said to him, "I love Tamar, my brother
Absalom's sister." So Jonadab said to him, "Lie
down on your bed and pretend to be ill. And when
your father comes to see you, say to him, 'Please
let my sister Tamar come and give me food, and
prepare the food in my sight, that I may see it and
eat it from her hand.'" (2 Samuel 13:4-5)*

I am not going to go through the entire story because it is
inappropriate, but he tricks her and rapes her. He was completely
controlled by his temporary lust. Could he have avoided this?
Yes. Were his feelings permanent? No!

However, he would not heed her voice; and being stronger than she, he forced her and lay with her. Then Amnon hated her exceedingly, so that the hatred with which he hated her was greater than the love with which he had loved her. (2 Samuel 13:14-15)

How quickly did his 'love' fade? Just like Esau, he has now traded the blessing of being the prince of Israel, for a single lustful moment. Instead of remaining disciplined, his passions ruled his life.

What was the result? In 2 Samuel 13:23-29, Tamar's full brother, Absalom murders Amnon two years later for this act. Do you think this passionate 'love' was worth it? Was it worth dying at the age of twenty simply because of lust? The fruit of living without discipline is always destruction. Amnon didn't invest in the future, Esau didn't invest in the future, and they both suffered destruction.

No temptation has overtaken you except such as is common to man. (1 Corinthians 10:13)

What does 1 Corinthians 10:13 tell us? Temptations are not unusual to the Christian. Stay disciplined.

Do you not know that those who run in a race all run, but one receives the prize? Run in such a way that you may obtain it. And everyone who competes for the prize is temperate (That means self-disciplined.) in all things. Now they do it to obtain a perishable crown, but we for an imperishable crown. (1 Corinthians 9:24-25)

If we are disciplined, we gain a crown that will never pass away. We enter into heaven with unseen treasures that have been rewarded for our discipline. The word 'competes' is 'agonizomai'. In English it sounds like 'agony'. If you compete for the Olympics or, in this case, the Isthmian Grecian games, you starve yourself. You run until exhaustion. You do pushups until your joints feel like they'll burst. You work, work, work, setting aside every relationship you have; all the fun, all the excitement. You do nothing but focus on the prize. You are disciplined! And the prize for winning the race, in Paul's day, was a leafy stick formed into a crown. Paul uses this to show how disciplined an athlete can be for a dead plant. How much more we who will receive an eternal crown!

Paul says,

> *Therefore I run thus: not with uncertainty.*
> *Thus I fight: not as one who beats the air. But I*
> *discipline my body and bring it into subjection...*
> *(1 Corinthians 9:26-27b)*

Which means his body's desires often differed from his heart's. So will yours. Your body will say, "Let's enjoy ourselves today and not worry about tomorrow." But Paul says, remain disciplined...

> *...lest, when I have preached to others, I myself*
> *should become disqualified. (1 Corinthians 9:27)*

In Matthew chapter 4:1-4 Satan attacks Jesus with a temptation similar to that of Esau's - Hunger. "You're going to starve Jesus!" But, Jesus knew He wasn't going to die in the desert, but upon the cross. Still Satan tempts Him to live for the moment, "Just give up your Father's plans. Forget the long term Jesus; think about the 'right now'. You're really hungry aren't you?"

> *Then Jesus was led up by the Spirit into the*
> *wilderness to be tempted by the devil. And when He*
> *had fasted forty days and forty nights, afterward He*
> *was hungry. (Matthew 4:1-2)*

Now, it is a biological fact that after you fast for a certain period of time your body will lose the desire for food. But after you've lost your hunger; when it does finally come back, you are near to death. Jesus had fasted for forty days and was now hungry. This means that He was near death. Satan says, "Eat a little bit. You're hungry. Just eat a little bit right now." This is the same temptation that came to Esau.

> *"If You are the Son of God, command that these*
> *stones become bread." But He answered and said,*
> *"It is written, 'Man shall not live by bread alone,*
> *but by every word that proceeds from the mouth of*
> *God.'" (Matthew 4:3-4)*

In other words, Jesus refused to live for the moment, but chose to live for God.

CHAPTER THIRTEEN REVIEW

i. *There are two masters: which one rules your life the most?*

ii. *How is becoming disciplined investing in the future?*

iii. *1 John 2:16 lists three temptations which all mankind struggles with. What are they? Which one challenges your discipline the most?*

iv. *What does the Lord promise in 1 Corinthians 9 to those who remain disciplined? (There is a hint found in Revelation 4:10)*

v. *What should Esau and Amnon have done when they were overwhelmed by physical temptation?*

vi. *Pick a temptation that overwhelms you and devise a plan of escape for the next time it happens.*

vii. *Memorize 1 Corinthians 6:12*

O/V hat does the word wisdom mean? It is the application of knowledge for practical use. Have you ever met someone who knows a great deal of information, yet is incapable of doing anything? They might be able to tell you how to do something, but if you ask them to do it, they themselves are unable. They aren't able to apply what they know. My wife calls that 'Book Smart'. When you look up the word 'wise', you find that it means 'useful, well thought out, practical intelligence'. It is the difference between being able to describe a hammer, and use one. That is wisdom.

Jesus said to His disciples:

"Behold, I send you out as sheep in the midst of wolves. Therefore be wise as serpents and harmless as doves. (Matthew 10:16)

Be wise! You don't often see serpents in the middle of an open area, do you? They hang out and watch things. They sneak up on you. Be wise. Think it out. He doesn't say be evil, but harmless, like a dove. In other words, don't be a serpent; just be wise as a serpent. There is a great deal of persecution in India, but Pastor Paulose has more than once reminded me that some missionaries are beaten for Jesus while others are beaten for foolishness. Know the difference. Disciples are called to be wise.

"Who then is that faithful and wise steward, whom his master will make ruler over his household, to give them their portion of food in due season? Blessed is that servant whom his master will find so doing when he comes. Truly, I say to you that he will make him ruler over all that he has." (Luke 12:42-43)

He says those servants who make good use of today will be given greater authority tomorrow. These are the people who think things through practically and have a plan, rather than saying, "I have faith! I have faith!" Wisdom and practical planning makes a ministry more effective and less burdensome.

If the ax is dull, and one does not sharpen the edge,

then he must use more strength; But wisdom brings success. (Ecclesiastes 10:10)

You can get along without wisdom, but there is a price. Have you ever done something foolish and paid a price? "Oh, I should get down off this ladder, it's kind of dangerous. Oh, I'll just try to reach a little further..." and you hear a little voice inside saying, "Foolish!" and then you fall. When serving the Lord, sometimes we do foolish things, but God has called us to wisdom.

If the ax is dull and one does not sharpen the edge, then he must use more strength; If we don't use wisdom then we replace it with effort. If we would stop and sharpen the axe it would cut a great deal more! Wisdom brings success. Doing ministry hastily and without wisdom is like swinging that dull axe. You will eventually break the wood, but there is a better way.

So teach us to number our days, that we may gain a heart of wisdom. (Psalms 90:12)

What does that mean? We will make better decisions in life if we realize life is almost over. If you only have a little bit of time to invest, don't dilly-dally! Be wise. The wisest man on earth invests for the day after his death.

He also said to His disciples:

There was a certain rich man who had a steward, and an accusation was brought to him that this man was wasting his goods. So he called him and said to him, "What is this I hear about you? Give an account of your stewardship, for you can no longer be steward." Then the steward said within himself, "What shall I do? For my master is taking the stewardship away from me. I cannot dig; I am ashamed to beg. I have resolved what to do, that when I am put out of the stewardship, they may receive me into their houses." So he called every one of his master's debtors to him, and said to the first, "How much do you owe my master?" And he said, "A hundred measures of oil." So he said to him, "Take your bill, and sit down quickly and write fifty." Then he said to another, "And how much do you owe?" So he said, "A hundred measures of wheat." And he said to him, "Take your bill, and write eighty." So the master commended the unjust steward because he had dealt shrewdly. For the sons of this world are more shrewd in their generation than the sons of light. "And I say to you, make friends for yourselves by unrighteous mammon, that when you fail, they may receive you into an everlasting home." (Luke 16:1-9)

This shrewd (yet evil) servant was wise enough to plan beyond his employment. He knew that he was about to be fired and so planned out a way to help him after his termination. Jesus tells us to invest into eternity, so that when *we fail*, it will be waiting for us. Your life is a little blip on a screen, compared to eternity. If you had a scale from zero to one billion years (which is not very long from God's viewpoint) how big would your life be on that scale? So, what should we do in those few seconds we are alive? Fruit flies have one of the shortest life spans of any insect. Do you know what they do with their lives? They multiply! Stick a rotten banana on the table and, where there are two fruit flies today, there will be two hundred in two days. What does that tell you? The sooner we become wise about the length of our lives the quicker we multiply.

Getting back to wisdom: how do I get it?

The fear of the LORD is the beginning of wisdom. (Psalms 111:10)

If you meet someone reverent, you will have met someone wise. Someone who has a fear of God and knows that they are going to give account for their lives will be wise. They will not make rash decisions.

When pride comes, then comes shame; but with the humble is wisdom. (Proverbs 11:2)

You get wisdom by being humble. You want to be wise? Don't always talk. When was the last time you learned something from yourself? Never. When you are talking, you are not learning.

By pride comes nothing but strife, but with the well-advised is wisdom. (Proverbs 13:10)

You become wise by listening to counselors. You want to be wise? Ask godly people before you make a decision. "Should I marry this person?" Don't make the decision on your own. Ask the people around you who know the person. Ask them what they think. Find out! Do they say, "No, don't marry that person." Or, "Yeah, that's a good idea." We don't have to make all our decisions based upon what others think, but we are wise if we ask them.

> *Do not speak in the hearing of a fool, for he will despise the wisdom of your words. (Proverbs 23:9)*

So, *not* listening to counselors makes us a fool then. Are you independent? Are you the one who knows everything? Or do you ask people?

Finally, the one my children love the most,

> *The rod and rebuke give wisdom, but a child left to himself brings shame to his mother. (Proverbs 29:15)*

Wisdom comes from the rod of discipline! My children have learned that it is a bad thing to touch a fire because every time they get close to touching it, I apply the rod of discipline. And, when they get older they thank me for spanking them because they don't have scars on their hands! They were protected by discipline. Spank your children and you will make them wise. Don't spank your children and you will make them fools and shameful. There are a lot of fools running around out there! A disciple shouldn't be one.

A great illustration of wisdom comes from a Pakistani friend name Mujahid El Masih, a former Muslim who now follows Jesus. The Holy Spirit's wisdom literally saved his life. One day he was in a village giving out the gospel of John. As he was moving through the dusty streets of the village an angry mob arrived from the local mosque. They were yelling violent threats, some had clubs in their hand and Mujahid knew they were ready to kill him. The leader demanded to know why Mujahid was poisoning the people with these Christian materials. He screamed that these are corrupt books full of lies. Mujahid knew that if he answered foolishly it would likely cost him his life. Mujahid prayed a quick prayer for wisdom and then asked, "Have you read this book?"

The man admitted that he had not read it. "How you can judge a book that you have not read?" The leader then told Mujahid that he would read the book but that Mujahid must immediately stop giving it away and leave. This bit of wisdom brought peace to an explosive situation and saved Mujuhid's life. The disciples of Jesus need to exercise wisdom.

CHAPTER FOURTEEN REVIEW

i. *What is wisdom and how do you get it?*

ii. *What does God think wisdom is?*

iii. *What is the difference between wisdom and knowledge?*

iv. *How does the fear of God bring wisdom?*

v. *Why did the master commend the sinful steward in Luke 16:1-9?*

vi. *Memorize Matthew 10:16*

A HEART FOR RECONCILIATION

*T*he heart of a disciple is the heart of reconciliation. The opposite of this is a heart of division. Within every person there is a temptation to create division.

Blessed are the peacemakers, for they shall be called sons of God. (Matthew 5:9)

Now all things are of God, who has reconciled us to Himself through Jesus Christ, and has given us the ministry of reconciliation. (2 Corinthians 5:18)

The word for 'peace' that Jesus used means 'to cause joining' or 'to mend together'. Let me give you an example: If you break a bone then you must put the two pieces together so that they can mend. This often takes effort and time, both with bones and brethren. Jesus says when you do this you are blessed.

For first of all, when you come together as a church, I hear that there are divisions among you, and in part I believe it. For there must also be factions among you, that those who are approved may be recognized among you. (1 Corinthians 11:18-19)

God asks the peacemaker to mend the broken parts of His body, the church. He has given us the ministry of reconciliation. Reconciliation centers around two types of 'mending' or peacemaking: peace with men and peace with God.

First, we declare peace with God through the death and resurrection of Jesus Christ and because of that people can be 'mended' to Him.

That they all may be one, as You, Father, are in Me, and I in You; that they also may be one in Us, that the world may believe that You sent Me. (John 17:21)

Our ministry of reconciliation brings people to a loving God who desires a relationship with us. Adam broke that relationship, and Jesus 'mended' it.

But there is also a 'mending' of men. As a disciple we have been given the ministry of removing divisions between people.

Our ministry is to stand in between people and love them together. This may mean (as we will see) that we rebuke them so
that they can come together in truth.

How important are peacemakers?

> *Therefore if you bring your gift to the altar, and there*
> *remember that your brother has something against*
> *you, leave your gift there before the altar, and go*
> *your way. First be reconciled to your brother, and*
> *then come and offer your gift. (Matthew 5:23-24)*

Jesus says first be reconciled to your brother and then offer
the gift. If you have an issue between you and your brother, deal
with the issue first. We all understand that we must first remove
our clothes and then bathe rather than bathing and then removing our garments. No man is foolish enough to do the latter, but
many a Christian is doing just this when they bring their gift
to the Lord and have not been reconciled to their brother. The
sacrificial gifts of a New Testament Christian aren't goats and
gold, but praise and prayer (Hebrews 13:15-16). Therefore, if
you have division with your brother and are spending your time
praising and praying, God does not want your gift. Jesus commands that you set down your gift, take care of this issue and
then come back to worship and praise. Jesus tells us:

> *...the hour is coming, and now is, when the true*
> *worshipers will worship the Father in spirit and*
> *truth; for the Father is seeking such to worship Him.*
> *God is Spirit, and those who worship Him must*
> *worship in spirit and truth. (John 4:23a)*

The Father is looking for those who worship in spirit and
in truth, not in lies. When we pray, "I come before you Father,
please convict me of my sin." And He responds, "Deal with the
issue between you and your brother." Don't expect more, because
He won't receive your gift until you have addressed what He has
told you. John says, in his letter:

> *If someone says, "I love God," and hates his brother,*
> *he is a liar; for he who does not love his brother*
> *whom he has seen, how can he love God whom he*
> *has not seen? (1 John 4:20)*

It is a serious thing not to be reconciled with others. But how do you reconcile? Can you reconcile every problem and situation? No. You can only reconcile the part that you have control over. For example, if I sin against my brother and repent but he responds, "I will never forgive you." Can I do anything about that? No. I have peace with God, but my brother refuses to have peace with me.

We are told in Romans chapter 12 that we are to be reconciled to the degree that we are responsible.

Repay no one evil for evil. Have regard for good things in the sight of all men. If it is possible, as much as depends on you, live peaceably with all men. (Romans 12:17-18)

That means we have to be able to say, "I made every effort, God. Every effort to be at peace with this person but they have refused it." As much as depends on you, live peaceably with all men. God holds us accountable for what He knows we are capable of.

In Romans, Paul goes on to tell us

...don't argue over doubtful things. (Romans 14:1)

This word literally means 'arguable' things. You *do* have control over 'arguable things'. Don't argue about what day of the week to worship or what food to eat. These things are 'arguable' according to Romans 14. Head coverings. Baptism methods. Don't argue about these.

Therefore let us pursue the things which make for peace and the things by which one may edify another. (Romans 14:19)

We as disciples of Jesus may still have our issues. But we should build each other up rather than tear each other down. However, Luke chapter 17 instructs us that this does not mean that we are to let sin go unexposed when it is keeping us from being reconciled. If I can't be reconciled to my brother because he is in sin, then I haven't done all that depends on me. If he is a brother, I have an obligation and a command by God to rebuke him. And until I rebuke him, I cannot say that I have done all

I can.

> *Take heed to yourselves. If your brother sins against*
> *you, rebuke him; and if he repents, forgive him.*
> *(Luke 17:3)*

What does rebuke mean? Go to him and say, "This is sin."
But do it in love. If you ignore his sin, then don't expect the Lord
to accept your gift. We are commanded to rebuke him. Not as
judge and ruler, but as an ambassador of Jesus Christ. Correct
it and forgive him. That fast. Just exactly like Nathan, who con-
fronted King David in his sin. David responded, "I have sinned
against the LORD." So Nathan tells him, "The LORD also has
put away your sin; you shall not die." God's grace is just that fast.

Matthew chapter 18 tells us the proper steps to take when
trying to reconcile a sinning brother. These are the Biblical steps
of rebuke.

Step #1 *Privately Rebuke Them*

> *Moreover if your brother sins against you, go and*
> *tell him his fault between you and him alone.*
> *(Matthew 18:15)*

Don't make it public. Do not bring other people into this
division. Go speak to that person quietly and alone. The purpose
is not to humiliate them, but to draw them closer to God. Go
alone!

Step #2 *Bring Witnesses*

> *If he hears you, you have gained your brother. But*
> *if he will not hear, (If he is unrepentant) take with*
> *you one or two more, that by the mouth of two*
> *or three witnesses every word may be established.*
> *(Matthew 18:16)*

Quietly take one or two people who are respected by your
brother and confront him again. Seek someone who is respected
by that person so that they will be more apt to listen. The whole
goal is to win them to Christ, not to beat them in a fight. This
sometimes takes thought. Remember, mending takes time and

effort. Which witnesses would they respect? Also, remember that these witnesses may end up rebuking you. They are to establish the truth and there is a possibility that you don't have the truth. At the end, *you* may be the one repenting. So, take someone who walks closely with the Lord.

Step #3 *Confront Publicly*

And if he refuses to hear them, tell it to the church. (Matthew 18:17)

Now it becomes public. For the most part, this last verse means that you and the witnesses give a report to the church of what is occurring so that it can be dealt with openly. Sin is very dangerous within a church. Many can be hurt when even one brother or sister is allowed to continue in sin, especially if in leadership. When the Corinthians didn't rebuke a sinning brother, Paul said,

> *"Your glorying is not good. Do you not know that a little leaven leavens the whole lump?" (1 Corinthians 5:6)*

Step #4 *Separate From Them*

But if he refuses even to hear the church, let him be to you like a heathen and a tax collector. Assuredly, I say to you, whatever you bind on earth will be bound in heaven, and whatever you loose on earth will be loosed in heaven. Again I say to you that if two of you agree on earth concerning anything that they ask, it will be done for them by My Father in heaven. For where two or three are gathered together in My name, I am there in the midst of them. (Matthew 18:17-20)

In other words, Jesus casts His vote when we are rebuking someone. We are now to treat them like a tax collector. Paul tells us what this last action looks like.

But now I have written to you not to keep company

with anyone named a brother, who is sexually immoral, or covetous, or an idolater, or a reviler, or a drunkard, or an extortioner--not even to eat with such a person. For what have I to do with judging those also who are outside? Do you not judge those who are inside? But those who are outside God judges. Therefore "put away from yourselves the evil person." (1 Corinthians 5:11-13)

Now I urge you, brethren, note those who cause divisions and offenses, contrary to the doctrine which you learned, and avoid them. (Romans 16:17)

But we command you, brethren, in the name of our Lord Jesus Christ, that you withdraw from every brother who walks disorderly and not according to the tradition which he received from us. (2 Thessalonians 3:6)

And if anyone does not obey our word in this epistle, note that person and do not keep company with him, that he may be ashamed. (2 Thessalonians 3:14)

It doesn't say you are to hate the person, but that the church needs to 'uncover' him.

In the name of our Lord Jesus Christ, when you are gathered together, along with my spirit, with the power of our Lord Jesus Christ, deliver such a one to Satan for the destruction of the flesh, that his spirit may be saved in the day of the Lord Jesus. (1 Corinthians 5:4-5)

Take away the covering. Don't minister to them and don't let them believe that they are right with God. They have no reconciliation with God or men when they reject the Lord's commands. Let them have an earthly taste of the separation that has occurred in heaven.

When do we know that they are repentant? Is it when they are sorry?

Now I rejoice, not that you were made sorry, but that your sorrow led to repentance. For you were made sorry in a godly manner, that you might suffer

loss from us in nothing. For godly sorrow produces
repentance leading to salvation, not to be regretted;
but the sorrow of the world produces death. For
observe this very thing, that you sorrowed in a godly
manner: What diligence it produced in you, what
clearing of yourselves, what indignation, what fear,
what vehement desire, what zeal, what vindication!
In all things you proved yourselves to be clear in this
matter. (2 Corinthians 7:9-11)

Sorrow does not necessarily equal repentance but it MAY lead to it. There are two types of sorrow mentioned. *Godly Sorrow* that leads to repentance and reconciliation and *Worldly Sorrow*, which brings regret, depression and death. Many a person has been depressed and sorrowful for the consequences of their actions. Prisons are full of these individuals. But sorrow does not necessarily mean that they are repentant. Godly sorrow, as described above, brings about a passionate, almost desperate desire to get things cleared up and to be restored to God and His church.

However, no matter what the sin is, when a person is truly repentant, the Lord emphasizes how important it is that we quickly and genuinely restore them:

Then Peter came to Him and said, "Lord, how often
shall my brother sin against me, and I forgive him?
Up to seven times?" Jesus said to him, "I do not say
to you, up to seven times, but up to seventy times
seven. (Matthew 18:21-22)

Now that doesn't mean four hundred and ninety, but means every single time they repent forgive them.

Here is the spiritual reason why this must be so:

Therefore the kingdom of heaven is like a certain
king who wanted to settle accounts with his servants.
And when he had begun to settle accounts, one
was brought to him who owed him ten thousand
talents. But as he was not able to pay, his master
commanded that he be sold, with his wife and
children and all that he had, and that payment be
made. The servant therefore fell down before him,

saying, "Master, have patience with me, and I will pay you all." Then the master of that servant was moved with compassion, released him, and forgave him the debt. But that servant went out and found one of his fellow servants who owed him a hundred denarii; and he laid hands on him and took him by the throat, saying, "Pay me what you owe!" So his fellow servant fell down at his feet and begged him, saying, "Have patience with me, and I will pay you all." And he would not, but went and threw him into prison till he should pay the debt. So when his fellow servants saw what had been done, they were very grieved, and came and told their master all that had been done. Then his master, after he had called him, said to him, "You wicked servant! I forgave you all that debt because you begged me. Should you not also have had compassion on your fellow servant, just as I had pity on you?" And his master was angry, and delivered him to the torturers until he should pay all that was due to him. (Matthew 18:23-34)

Here is Peter's question again: "Lord, how often shall my brother sin against me and I forgive him?" Jesus' answer is:

So My heavenly Father also will do to you if each of you, from his heart, does not forgive his brother his trespasses. (Matthew 18:35)

If Peter chooses not to forgive a brother, God's forgiveness for Peter will end. That's what is at stake if we harbor unforgiveness in our heart when they ask us to forgive. Do you see why Jesus told us at the beginning of the chapter that this was more important than the gift we might bring to Him? Your salvation is at risk. No one will enter heaven without forgiveness and you can't receive forgiveness if you refuse to give it.

But if you do not forgive men their trespasses, neither will your Father forgive your trespasses. (Matthew 6:15)

It is best to walk in forgiveness towards others, because if we decide to take the place of judge, then we will be judged in the same way we judge others.

For with what judgment you judge, you will be judged; and with the measure you use, it will be measured back to you. (Matthew 7:2)

Just as Jesus described in Matthew 18 the steps for confronting a sinning brother; Paul describes in 2 Corinthians 2, the steps for restoring a brother who has sinned against you. In this chapter, there seems to be a brother who was separated from the church because of an unrepentant sin, but has now asked for forgiveness. Paul notes that he has truly repented and needs to be restored to the church. Here are the steps of restoration that Paul lays out.

Step #1 *Forgive Willfully*

This punishment which was inflicted by the majority is sufficient for such a man, so that, on the contrary, you ought rather to forgive. (2 Corinthians 2:6-7a)

Forgiveness is not an emotion of happiness or joy, but a willful choice not to hold the sin against them any longer. Jesus did not feel happy when they were killing Him on the cross, but was still willing to say, *"Father, forgive them, for they do not know what they do."* Forgiveness means that you choose not to speak about their sin to them, to yourself or to others. It has been forgiven.

Step #2 *Comfort Personally*

And comfort him, lest perhaps such a one be swallowed up with too much sorrow. (2 Corinthians 2:7b)

The word 'comfort' means to "call near and encourage." It implies a willingness to spend time with them. It is the picture of someone putting their arm around another and walking with them for a while.

Step #3 *Reaffirm Publicly*

Therefore I urge you to reaffirm your love to him.
(2 Corinthians 2:8)

This word in Greek means 'to ratify or publicly endorse.' The intent is that you have not only spoken forgiveness to them and have interacted with them, but are willing to publicly endorse them. This means that you give them your stamp of approval before others by showing that there is nothing between you and them.

So, how about your own heart? Do you have reconciliation that needs to happen? Is there somebody in sin that you need to lovingly rebuke? Is there someone who has sinned against you that you need to restore? Can you see that unforgiveness threatens salvation? As a word of warning, I have witnessed unforgiveness slowly kill a pastor's wife. She has led hundreds of children to the Lord and at this point in her life, I don't know if she will be in heaven because she has so much unforgiveness and bitterness. The potential for this kind of bitterness is there for all believers.

Therefore let him who thinks he stands take heed lest he fall. No temptation has overtaken you except such as is common to man. (1 Corinthians 10:12-13a)

We must have the heart of reconciliation to be a disciple of Jesus Christ.

CHAPTER FIFTEEN REVIEW

i.   *What does the word 'reconcile' mean in your own words?*

ii. *What are we supposed to do 'first' before we bring our gifts to God ?*

iii. *What are the four steps of reconciliation of Mathew 18?*

iv. *What is the difference between Godly sorrow and worldly sorrow?*

v.   *How often do you restore a repentant believer?*

vi. *What are the three steps of restoration?*

vii. *Memorize Matthew 5:23-24*

Blessed are the pure in heart, for they shall see God.
(Matthew 5:8)

*P*urity is about righteousness and holiness. According to Ezekiel 42:14, the priests were given two garments to wear. One that the Lord had prepared for them, and they were to wear before Him in the Temple, and one that they were to wear among the people. We too have two sets of garments:

The righteousness of Christ, which allows us to be in His Presence:

For He made Him who knew no sin to be sin for us,
that we might become the righteousness of God in
Him. (2 Corinthians 5:21)

And the righteous actions that can be seen by others:

Let us be glad and rejoice and give Him glory, for
the marriage of the Lamb has come, and His wife
has made herself ready." And to her it was granted
to be arrayed in fine linen, clean and bright, for
the fine linen is the righteous acts of the saints.
(Revelation 19:7-8)

We must be very careful not to confuse purity and righteousness with salvation because of good works. The Scriptures clearly say no one is righteous enough to be saved by their good works but all are saved by grace:

For by grace you have been saved through faith, and
that not of yourselves; it is the gift of God, not of
works, lest anyone should boast. (Ephesians 2:8-9)

But the Scriptures also say we are to make every effort to be free from sin!

What then? Shall we sin because we are not under
law but under grace? Certainly not! (Romans 6:15)

"Cheap grace" is a phrase that some use. Cheap grace is

when a believer doesn't worry about his/her lifestyle. That's not
following Christ. A disciple will be pure in heart!

Romans 6:19 is very powerful:

For just as (In the exact same way) *you presented
your members as slaves of uncleanness, and of
lawlessness leading to more lawlessness, so now
present your members as slaves of righteousness for
holiness. (Romans 6:19)*

What does that mean personally? Think about your life
before Christ. Did you stay up late doing what you wanted?
Do you stay up late doing what's godly? What surrounded your
life? Was it an addiction? If you were passionate about sin, how
passionate are you about righteousness? The word, 'just as'
means 'to the exact same degree.' To the exact same degree that
you presented your lives as sinful vessels, now present them *in
that degree* as righteous vessels. If you are a follower of Christ,
in Romans it says to present your body as a slave for righteousness. I know people who watch sports and store up in their mind
every score, and statistic - worthless nothing! When that person
becomes a Christian, they should begin memorizing Scripture
with that same passion.

Purity brings peace, because I am not hiding sin in my life.
In the Scriptures, impurity is like a dirty dish. If I wash a dish
lightly, and leave a little egg stuck to it, then the next time I eat,
I will carefully avoid that plate because it is defiled. Some people
live their lives before God in a similar way.

*But in a great house there are not only vessels of gold
and silver, but also of wood and clay, some for honor
and some for dishonor. Therefore if anyone cleanses
himself from the latter, he will be a vessel for honor,
sanctified and useful for the Master, prepared for
every good work. (2 Timothy 2:20-21)*

Some refuse to 'cleanse' their life, while others scrub it with
passion. Which way do you live as a Christian? Do you say, "It's
nothing." and put the dirty vessel back on the shelf? Or, do you
say, "I'm going to try and keep myself unspotted from the world!"

Pure religion and undefiled before God and the

*Father is this, To visit the fatherless and widows in
their affliction, and to keep himself unspotted from
the world. (James 1:27)*

God calls us to righteousness the same way Satan called us
to sin...wholeheartedly.

*For when you were slaves of sin, you were free in
regard to righteousness. (Romans 6:20)*

Satan didn't say, "Leave your sin behind and do something
good." He said, "Don't worry about righteousness, live your
whole life for sin." Christ now says, "You have a new Master;
live your whole life for righteousness."

*But now having been set free from sin, and having
become slaves of God, you have your fruit to
holiness, and the end, everlasting life. (Romans 6:22)*

In 1 Timothy Paul tells Timothy that he is to be an example
for others to follow:

*Let no one despise your youth, but be an example to
the believers in word, in conduct, in love, in spirit,
in faith, in purity. (1 Timothy 4:12)*

In purity Timothy! Don't choose anything that is even ques-
tionable to those watching you.

*Abstain from every form of evil.
(1 Thessalonians 5:22)*

Purity doesn't save me: I'm saved by grace. But now I am
fully living for Christ. Do you see the difference? If you don't
have a clear conscience when death comes, then fear creeps in.
You begin to second-guess. "Maybe I didn't get it right. How
could I have continued in my secret sin if I was truly born again?
How could I have done that?" Sin places doubt in my heart.
Don't allow that doubt to be there. Be pure!

What are some practical ways to live a pure life? In 1 Corinthians 15:33 it says,

*Do not be deceived: "Evil company corrupts good
habits." (1 Corinthians 15:33)*

The word for corrupt is 'rot'. If you choose to stand in the path of sinners (Psalm 1:1), you will sin. You won't necessarily want to sin, but it will happen. One day you will be weak in your faith and the evil company will corrupt your life. If you place a single rotting vegetable in a bag of vegetables, the mold spreads and the other vegetables begin to rot. Have you heard that old proverb? "One bad apple will spoil the whole bunch." Try it for yourself. Stick a ripe banana on top of some green bananas and watch them rot. That's what the Scripture is talking about. We are told to be separate from evil company and remain holy.

Do not be unequally yoked together with unbelievers. For what fellowship has righteousness with lawlessness? And what communion has light with darkness? And what accord has Christ with Belial? Or what part has a believer with an unbeliever? And what agreement has the temple of God with idols? For you are the temple of the living God. As God has said: "I will dwell in them and walk among them. I will be their God, And they shall be My people." Therefore "Come out from among them and be separate, says the Lord. Do not touch what is unclean, and I will receive you. I will be a Father to you, and you shall be My sons and daughters, Says the LORD Almighty." (2 Corinthians 6:14-18)

It is okay to share the Gospel with those in sin and to spend time with them (Jesus did), but we must remain separate from their sins. They may judge and condemn us, but we need to respond in truth.

Another path of purity is to stay focused on eternal things.

But the day of the Lord will come as a thief in the night, in which the heavens will pass away with a great noise, and the elements will melt with fervent heat; both the earth and the works that are in it will be burned up. Therefore, since all these things will be dissolved, what manner of persons ought you to be in holy conduct and godliness... (2 Peter 3:10-11)

Knowing the end helps us to live in purity.

Therefore, beloved, looking forward to these things, be diligent to be found by Him in peace, without spot and blameless. (2 Peter 3:14)

If I'm expecting Jesus' return today, I will live differently than if I think He's coming back in a year. Awaiting His return motivates me to holiness.

To remain pure, we must also stay in God's Word. Psalm 119 asks:

> *How can a young man cleanse his way? By taking heed according to Your word. With my whole heart I have sought You; Oh, let me not wander from Your commandments! Your word I have hidden in my heart, That I might not sin against You! (Psalm 119:9-11)*

One way to live a pure life is to put the Word of God in your heart. How do you do that? Memorize it, meditate on it, and practice it. Don't just read it! Ask God to help you apply it to your life. Be active in your faith 'to the same degree' you were active in your sin.

Jesus said:

> *If you abide in My word, you are My disciples indeed. And you shall know the truth, and the truth shall make you free." (John 8:31-32)*

That's how my life in Christ began and that's how I will continue to be free from sin. Ephesians says we are Christ's bride and that even now He washes us with water which is the Word of God.

> *Husbands, love your wives, just as Christ also loved the church and gave Himself for her, that He might sanctify and cleanse her with the washing of water by the word, that He might present her to Himself a glorious church, not having spot or wrinkle or any such thing, but that she should be holy and without blemish. (Ephesians 5:25-27)*

Jesus gave us a living example of this washing. Do you remember John 13?

> *Jesus, knowing that the Father had given all things into His hands, and that He had come from God and was going to God, rose from supper and laid aside His garments, took a towel and girded Himself.*

After that, He poured water into a basin and began to wash the disciples' feet, and to wipe them with the towel with which He was girded. Then He came to Simon Peter. And Peter said to Him, "Lord, are You washing my feet?" (John 13:3-6)

Jesus had chosen the role of the lowest slave in the household and began washing men's feet. Peter was ashamed to have Him do this. But listen to what Jesus says:

Jesus answered and said to him, "What I am doing you do not understand now, but you will know after this." Peter said to Him, "You shall never wash my feet!" Jesus answered him, "If I do not wash you, you have no part with Me." Simon Peter said to Him, "Lord, not my feet only, but also my hands and my head!" Jesus said to him, "He who is bathed needs only to wash his feet, but is completely clean; and you are clean... (John 13:7-10a)

You are already clean because of the word which I have spoken to you. (John 15:3)

He was showing them a spiritual lesson. Peter said, "If not being washed will keep me from heaven then wash my whole body." Jesus tells him, "Those who have bathed need only wash their feet and they will be clean. I only need to wash your feet, Peter, because you're already clean." Spiritually Peter was clean before the Father, but his feet were still dirty. We can be saved and bound for heaven, yet we still need to be regularly cleansed.

When a Christian begins to harden their heart and say, "No, I'm not repenting of this particular sin, I'm keeping it", they are doing exactly what Peter did when he said, "I will follow you Jesus, but don't wash my feet. Leave my dirty feet out of our relationship." Even today Jesus responds, "Let Me wash!" Purity means you let Jesus wash you.

On a daily basis I get spiritually dirty feet. I am angry with my kids or I mistreat my loving wife. I have bad thoughts or begin to harbor bitterness against someone. Throughout the day these things build on us, like filth on our feet. So what do I do? I let Jesus wash my feet with His Word. Jesus even now kneels beside you with His waist girded, asking, "May I?" Picture this in your mind the next time you repent. No, you're not getting saved again. But Jesus is washing you pure like Ephesians 5 says:

> *Christ also loved the church and gave Himself for her, that He might sanctify and cleanse her with the washing of water by the word, that He might present her to Himself a glorious church, not having spot or wrinkle or any such thing, but that she should be holy and without blemish. (Ephesians 5:25b-27)*

What an awesome picture! Dear reader, the choice is now ours...

> *And he said to me, "Do not seal the words of the prophecy of this book, for the time is at hand. "He who is unjust, let him be unjust still; he who is filthy, let him be filthy still; he who is righteous, let him be righteous still; he who is holy, let him be holy still." "And behold, I am coming quickly, and My reward is with Me, to give to every one according to his work. (Revelation 22:10-12)*

I end this chapter with one dramatic story of a couple who remained pure in their walk with Christ through great difficulties. Methu and Adel are Christians from Indonesia. Their village was attacked by Islamic fundamentalists in January 2000. In one night their home was burned to the ground. Their youngest son was killed. Methu's parents and mother-in-law were also killed. Adel was captured while fleeing and the fundamentalists forced her to marry a Muslim man. She soon bore this man a son. But for two years Methu never gave up hope of reuniting with his wife. He kept remembering the words he had said on his wedding day. "Do you, Methu, take Adel in joy and in sorrow?" Only death could separate him from his love and faithfulness to Adel. He would remain pure. After relentless searching he finally located Adel. She also had kept a secret hope that she might one day escape and reunite with her husband. She had been forced to convert as a Muslim but always held onto her faith in Jesus in her heart. In a very courageous act, Methu was able to rescue his wife along with her child. He then adopted this son and loves him as his own. He had devoted himself to one wife before God and remained pure even though the situation seemed hopeless. Remarriage was not an option for him. Since this time the two of them have forgiven those who violated their lives and today Methu is a pastor and continues to advance the gospel in Indonesia as a beautiful example of purity, faith and obedience.

CHAPTER SIXTEEN REVIEW

i. Describe the difference between being righteous for the Lord and being righteous for salvation.

ii. List 5 ways that God has called you to live in purity.

iii. Based upon Ephesians 5:25-27 and Revelation 21:1-2, why do you think the Lord desires purity?

iv. What is the garment of righteousness God gives us to wear?

v. How does sin place doubt in our heart?

vi. How does purity place peace in our heart?

vii. Why does God command us to be pure?

viii. Are you as passionate about purity or holiness as you were about sin?

ix. Memorize Romans 6:19

....

*T*he next characteristic of a disciple is faithfulness. What does 'faithful' mean? To be counted faithful literally means to be 'trustable'.

God is ultimately our standard for faithfulness.

> *Now may the God of peace Himself sanctify you completely; and may your whole spirit, soul, and body be preserved blameless at the coming of our Lord Jesus Christ. He who calls you is faithful, who also will do it. (1 Thessalonians 5:23-24)*

We have faith in God because He is trustworthy and does what He says. We don't have faith in God because we decided it was a neat idea. I trust a person because they are trustworthy. I trust God because He is faithful.

> *He who is faithful in what is least is faithful also in much; and he who is unjust in what is least is unjust also in much. (Luke 16:10)*

This particular Scripture is referring to money. The Lord considers money and worldly possessions as some of the least important things we will ever have. If we are faithful in our finances, then God will give us more important things. But first we have to prove our faithfulness in the little things.

Look at what it says in 2 Timothy about preaching the Gospel.

> *You therefore, my son, be strong in the grace that is in Christ Jesus. And the things that you have heard from me among many witnesses, commit these to faithful men who will be able to teach others also. (2 Timothy 2:2)*

Commit these teachings to men who are trustworthy. Don't just pick someone from the crowd and say, "I'd like to make you a teacher." Remember: God rewards those who are faithful in the little things with these greater things. It is those who are willing to do the small tasks that are entrusted with the great responsibilities.

My friend Pastor Paulose has a saying about missionaries, "They will be given no motorcycles unless they have been faithful with bicycles."

Even the very families of church leaders must be faithful.

Likewise their wives must be reverent, not slanderers, temperate, faithful in all things. (1 Timothy 3:11)

If a man is blameless, the husband of one wife, having faithful children not accused of dissipation or insubordination. (Titus 1:6)

Paul commands Timothy and Titus to find these faithful men and teach them. In other words, find disciples not believers.

Now when He was in Jerusalem at the Passover, during the feast, many believed (literally: trusted) in His name when they saw the signs which He did. But Jesus did not commit (literally: trust) Himself to them, because He knew all men, and had no need that anyone should testify of man, for He knew what was in man. (John 2:23-25)

This Scripture used the same word twice, 'pisteuo'. It means 'to have faith in or trust something'. The people had faith and trusted in Jesus, but He did not trust them, because He knew what was in their hearts. They were believers, not faithful disciples. We know that eventually Jesus did entrust Himself to His disciples.

When Jesus came into the region of Caesarea Philippi, He asked His disciples, saying, "Who do men say that I, the Son of Man, am?" So they said, "Some say John the Baptist, some Elijah, and others Jeremiah or one of the prophets." He said to them, "But who do you say that I am?" Simon Peter answered and said, "You are the Christ, the Son of the living God." Jesus answered and said to him, "Blessed are you, Simon Bar-Jonah, for flesh and blood has not revealed this to you, but My Father who is in heaven. "And I also say to you that you are Peter, and on this rock I will build My church, and the gates of Hades shall not prevail against it. And I will give you the keys of the kingdom of heaven, and whatever you bind on earth will be

*bound in heaven, and whatever you loose on earth
will be loosed in heaven." Then He commanded His
disciples that they should tell no one that He was
Jesus the Christ. (Matthew 16:13-20)*

How did these men become trustworthy? By being faithful.

*These twelve Jesus sent out and commanded them,
saying: "Do not go into the way of the Gentiles,
and do not enter a city of the Samaritans. But go
rather to the lost sheep of the house of Israel. And
as you go, preach, saying, 'The kingdom of heaven
is at hand.' Heal the sick, cleanse the lepers, raise
the dead, cast out demons. Freely you have received,
freely give. Provide neither gold nor silver nor copper
in your money belts, nor bag for your journey, nor
two tunics, nor sandals, nor staffs; for a worker is
worthy of his food. (Matthew 10:5-10)*

Here was a faithfulness test. Will they put a little money
in their pocket before they go? Will they charge a small fee for
healing people? It was a test of their faithfulness.

*When it was evening, His disciples came to Him,
saying, "This is a deserted place, and the hour
is already late. Send the multitudes away, that
they may go into the villages and buy themselves
food." But Jesus said to them, "They do not need
to go away. You give them something to eat."
(Matthew 14:15-16)*

Another test. Were they faithful to give up their food, or did
they go eat it in a corner?

*And they said to Him, "We have here only five loaves
and two fish." He said, "Bring them here to Me."
Then He commanded the multitudes to sit down
on the grass. And He took the five loaves and the
two fish, and looking up to heaven, He blessed and
broke and gave the loaves to the disciples; and the
disciples gave to the multitudes. So they all ate and
were filled, and they took up twelve baskets full of
the fragments that remained. (Matthew 14:17-20)*

Since they were faithful in the little things, they offered up

their small lunch and so Jesus entrusted them with greater things.
You can look at the time that Jesus spends with His disciples
and see how often He gave them tasks to test their faithfulness.
Some tasks were great, like stepping out of a boat onto water
(Matthew 14:29) while others were small like casting a hook
into the sea (Matthew 17:27).

God uses tests to strengthen our faith and faithfulness. God
tested Abraham's faith with Isaac, right? But, that wasn't the first
test of faith Abraham experienced. God tested his faithfulness
by delaying Sarah from having even a single child for years. God
tested Abraham's faithfulness through the famine that caused him
to flee to Egypt. God tested his faithfulness by calling him out
of his hometown and to leave his family. God built Abraham's
faith one test at a time.

We want spiritual power and maturity to happen right now!
But God says, "Be faithful in what is little." There is always
more for those who are faithful. Always. He who is faithful in
little will be faithful in much. If I give my child ten cents and tell
him to save it yet he buys bubble gum, what will happen when
he asks for more?

*Therefore if you have not been faithful in the
unrighteous mammon, (Or literally, the money of
this world) who will commit to your trust the true
riches? "And if you have not been faithful in what
is another man's, who will give you what is your
own? (Luke 16:11-12)*

Do you see that? According to Jesus, our money doesn't
belong to us. If we die, it becomes someone else's. You don't take
it with you. You are simply borrowing another man's things. If
you can't be faithful in that, how are you going to be faithful in
what belongs to you?

Jesus said,

*For everyone to whom much is given, from him
much will be required; and to whom much has
been committed, of him they will ask the more.
(Luke 12:48)*

To be a servant of the Lord is to be entrusted with responsibility.

> *Let a man so consider us, as servants of Christ and stewards of the mysteries of God. Moreover it is required in stewards that one be found faithful. (1 Corinthians 4:1-2)*

Moses

> *Hear now My words: If there is a prophet among you, I, the LORD, make Myself known to him in a vision; I speak to him in a dream. Not so with My servant Moses; He is faithful in all My house. I speak with him face to face, even plainly, and not in dark sayings; (Numbers 12:6-8)*

Hebrews says Moses was faithful when he realized that he was a Jew and chose not to live with the Egyptians. Instead, he chose to suffer with those who were God's people, rather than enjoy the fleeting pleasures of sin.

> *By faith Moses, when he became of age, refused to be called the son of Pharaoh's daughter, choosing rather to suffer affliction with the people of God than to enjoy the passing pleasures of sin. (Hebrews 11:24-25)*

Moses was faithful in his actions. What was the reward God gave him for being faithful?

Moses was given an encounter with God unsurpassed by any human on the face of the earth. God came down in a fire and Moses lived in that fire for forty days and forty nights speaking face to face with God. It says in Hebrews that he received the Ten Commandments from the very hand of God through angels. God wrote it, gave it to the angels, and they gave it to Moses. The priests had to put blood on the altar and on the tabernacle to pay for their sins before they were even allowed into the Presence of the Lord. But any time the cloud of glory fell on the tabernacle, Moses walked right into the very Presence of God because he was counted faithful.

> *So the people stood afar off, but Moses drew near the thick darkness where God was. (Exodus 20:21)*

So it was, whenever Moses went out to the tabernacle, that all the people rose, and each man stood at his tent door and watched Moses until he had gone into the tabernacle. And it came to pass, when Moses entered the tabernacle, that the pillar of cloud descended and stood at the door of the tabernacle, and the LORD talked with Moses. All the people saw the pillar of cloud standing at the tabernacle door, and all the people rose and worshiped, each man in his tent door. So the LORD spoke to Moses face to face, as a man speaks to his friend. (Exodus 33:8-11)

God rewarded his faithfulness.

[Moses] esteem[ed] the reproach of Christ greater riches than the treasures in Egypt; for he looked to the reward. (Hebrews 11:26)

David

In 1 Samuel the priest of the Tabernacle spoke to King Saul about David in such a way:

"who among all your servants is as faithful as David..." (1 Samuel 22:14)

Up until that very day, David had been known for his faithfulness. This began early in David's life:

And Samuel said to Jesse, "Are all the young men here?" Then he said, "There remains yet the youngest (David), and there he is, keeping the sheep." (1 Samuel 16:11)

The whole family had gathered to meet the prophet, but David was being faithful to tend the sheep. A little thing. As a shepherd, David was often tested in faithfulness.

But David said to Saul, "Your servant used to keep his father's sheep, and when a lion or a bear came and took a lamb out of the flock, I went out after it and struck it, and delivered the lamb from its mouth; and when it arose against me, I caught it by its beard, and struck and killed it. (1 Samuel 17:34-35)

Did God reward David's faithfulness in the little things? Read the next verse.

Your servant has killed both lion and bear; and this uncircumcised Philistine will be like one of them, seeing he has defied the armies of the living God." Moreover David said, "The LORD, who delivered me from the paw of the lion and from the paw of the bear, He will deliver me from the hand of this Philistine." And Saul said to David, "Go, and the LORD be with you!" (1 Samuel 17:36-37)

So it was, when the Philistine arose and came and drew near to meet David, that David hastened and ran toward the army to meet the Philistine. Then David put his hand in his bag and took out a stone; and he slung it and struck the Philistine in his forehead, so that the stone sank into his forehead, and he fell on his face to the earth. So David prevailed over the Philistine with a sling and a stone, and struck the Philistine and killed him. But there was no sword in the hand of David. Therefore David ran and stood over the Philistine, took his sword and drew it out of its sheath and killed him, and cut off his head with it. And when the Philistines saw that their champion was dead, they fled. (1 Samuel 17:48-51)

What if David hadn't been faithful with sheep?

Hananiah

I bet you don't even know who this man is. But the Lord God does and has recorded his name down as "faithful". In Nehemiah chapter 7, Nehemiah has completed his journey to Jerusalem to rebuild the walls. Now as he prepares for his return to Persia he selects one individual to govern over God's people.

Then it was, when the wall was built and I had hung the doors, when the gatekeepers, the singers, and the Levites had been appointed, that I gave the charge of Jerusalem to my brother Hanani, and Hananiah the leader of the citadel, for he was a faithful man and feared God more than many. (Nehemiah 7:1-2)

He was a faithful man, so the Lord gave him responsibility over much. Does that sound like a parable?

> *'Well done, good and faithful servant; you have been faithful over a few things, I will make you ruler over many things. Enter into the joy of your lord.'*
> *(Matthew 25:23)*

Daniel

> *So the governors and satraps sought to find some charge against Daniel concerning the kingdom; but they could find no charge or fault, because he was faithful; nor was there any error or fault found in him. (Daniel 6:4)*

Daniel was faithful. When the commander over the eunuchs told him to eat and drink the food from the king's table, he realized that the meal had been sacrificed to false gods, so his response was one of faithfulness. He asked for vegetables and relied upon the Lord to keep him healthy. Now, not eating meat and bread is a pretty small test of faith compared to being thrown into a fire or a lion's den but first we must be faithful in the little things. So God gave him and his friends health as well as recognition from the king. Every mighty man or woman of God has proven themselves faithful in the little things. As we read the stories, we tend to remember the amazing acts of faith and forget all of the others. Daniel was faithful in bread and water and became prime minister of two world kingdoms. Simply by faithfulness.

Timothy

> *For this reason I have sent Timothy to you, who is my beloved and faithful son in the Lord, who will remind you of my ways in Christ, as I teach everywhere in every church. (1 Corinthians 4:17)*

Timothy's reward for faithfulness was authority. It seems from the book of Acts that Paul led Timothy to the Lord and the next time he came through Timothy's hometown, he took him into his charge and let him travel alongside him. Timothy was still young when he was given a leadership role in Ephesus. Paul tells him not to let anyone "despise your youth". Don't you think there were some older disciples whom Paul could have sent to Corinth? Why did he choose a boy? Because he was faithful. It isn't about age. It isn't about how long you have been a Christian. It is whether or not you have been faithful. If you want more from God, then be faithful in what you have.

Look at what it says in the Psalms.

My eyes shall be on the faithful of the land, that they may dwell with me. (Psalm 101:6)

God is actively looking across the land for faithful men and women. I believe he is looking to give them more.

Jesus is of course our perfect example.

Therefore, holy brethren, partakers of the heavenly calling, consider the Apostle and High Priest of our confession, Christ Jesus, who was faithful to Him who appointed Him, as Moses also was faithful in all His house. For this One has been counted worthy of more glory than Moses, inasmuch as He who built the house has more honor than the house. (Hebrews 3:1-3)

Jesus Christ's faithfulness gave him more glory than Moses.

So, what does faithfulness look like practically? First, it does not draw back from difficulty.

Now the just shall live by faith; But if anyone draws back, My soul has no pleasure in him." But we are not of those who draw back to perdition, but of those who believe to the saving of the soul. (Hebrews 10:38-39)

Based on this Scripture, faithfulness is not turning back. Do you remember the man in Luke 9:61-62 who said, "Master, Master, I'm coming, I'm coming. But, let me get things settled with my family"?

And another also said, "Lord, I will follow You, but let me first go and bid them farewell who are at my house." But Jesus said to him, "No one, having put his hand to the plow, and looking back, is fit for the kingdom of God." (Luke 9:61-62)

Jesus said that anyone who puts his hand to the plow and turns back is not faithful. Faithfulness is knowing that there may be other things that you could be doing and yet not turning back from serving the Lord. As Paul said,

I press toward the goal for the prize of the upward call of God in Christ Jesus. (Philippians 3:14)

Secondly, faithfulness focuses on little things!

He who is faithful in what is least is faithful also in much; and he who is unjust in what is least is unjust also in much. (Luke 16:10)

An example of this comes from one of my favorite Scriptures. Let me set the scene for you. Zerubbabel is supposed to rebuild the Temple, which has been destroyed, but there is a problem. When Nebuchadnezzar took Jerusalem, he utterly destroyed the Temple and razed it with fire. At this point it is nothing but a large pile of rubble. So, here's Zerubbabel, looking at this mountain of rocks where the Temple used to be and wondering, "How are we ever going to accomplish this?" Now with this in mind, read what the Lord says:

The hands of Zerubbabel Have laid the foundation of this temple; His hands shall also finish it. Then you will know that the LORD of hosts has sent Me to you. For who has despised the day of small things? For these seven rejoice to see the plumb line in the hand of Zerubbabel. They are the eyes of the LORD, which scan to and fro throughout the whole earth. (Zechariah 4:9-10)

God says, "Zerubbabel, it may be a mound right now, but I see it completed. The Temple will be built. Don't despise the day of *small things*." What was the small thing Zerubbabel was being asked to do? He was being asked to pick up rocks and haul them down a hill. Here is the mighty man of God, the leader of the free Israelites, pushing a cart full of rocks.

The Lord says to Zerubbabel, be faithful in the little things and I will give you strength to complete the Temple.

So, we see that faithfulness does not turn back when things are hard and faithfulness focuses on the little things. But it also keeps secrets.

> *A talebearer reveals secrets, but he who is of a faithful spirit conceals a matter. (Proverbs 11:13)*

How can you tell if someone is faithful? Can they keep a secret? If they can't, then they aren't faithful. That's a simple test.

Faithfulness doesn't lie...

> *A faithful witness does not lie, but a false witness will utter lies. (Proverbs 14:5)*

Faithfulness serves others...

> *Like the cold of snow in time of harvest is a faithful messenger to those who send him, for he refreshes the soul of his masters. (Proverbs 25:13)*

Have you ever been in scorching heat and wished for a cool breeze? That is what a faithful messenger is like. A cool breeze. A faithful person is helpful and brings refreshment with them. If a person refuses to serve others they are not faithful.

Let me end with a story. Richard Wurmbrand is a great hero of the faith, as attested by the large scar on his neck and the seventeen major scars on his body. Of his fourteen years spent in a Romanian prison for preaching the gospel, three were in solitary confinement thirty feet below ground. During his solitary confinement he had no book, no pen, no paper and no visitors. So, every day he would start with the Lord's Prayer. Then he would begin praying for believers around the world. Next he would prepare a sermon. With no paper he would simply memorize his sermon and then preach to the walls, remembering that Scripture declares that angels desire to observe the preaching of the Word of God. (1 Peter 1:12) During that season he memorized 350 sermons. Many of them have been published today and have touched the lives of millions. Alone for years, he remained faithful, preaching to the smallest congregation in the world (none) and God has entrusted him with so much more.

CHAPTER SEVENTEEN REVIEW

i.   *Why didn't Jesus trust those who believed in him in John 2:23-25?*

ii.   *How do we become faithful?*

iii.   *Name one additional character from the Scriptures who was faithful and tell why.*

iv.   *In what things are you most faithful to the Lord? What things are you least faithful?*

v.   *Pick one thing that you are least faithful in and purpose to be faithful to God in that one thing for an entire week. Watch the blessings that come.*

vi.   *Memorize Luke 16:10*

*T*his is probably the most crucial of all the topics we will cover. The Scriptures say that a disciple is not above his master, nor is a student above his teacher. But that it is enough for a disciple to be like his master, or student like his teacher. Our Master and Teacher is Jesus the Christ, the Son of God, the Holy One of Israel, the Name above every name that will ever be named in heaven or on earth: our God - and no other. And our Lord Jesus Christ devoted himself to prayer.

In Luke we find Jesus being baptized:

> **When all the people were baptized, it came to pass that Jesus also was baptized; and while He prayed, the heaven was opened. And the Holy Spirit descended in bodily form like a dove upon Him, and a voice came from heaven which said, "You are My beloved Son; in You I am well pleased." (Luke 3:21)**

During His baptism, Our Lord prays and the Holy Spirit falls upon Him. The heavens open up. The dove descends. The voice of God speaks, "The One praying is my beloved Son."

In Mark chapter 1 we saw how hard working our Master is. Jesus gets up early, goes to the synagogue, casts out demons, goes home, heals Peter's mother-in-law, and then when dusk comes, the whole town comes to Him and He stays awake through the night to heal them all. Then, the very next verse says:

> **Now in the morning, having risen a long while before daylight, He went out and departed to a solitary place; and there He prayed. (Mark 1:35)**

Being utterly exhausted, He arose and prayed.

In Matthew 14: do you remember the story? There was no food for them, so Jesus multiplied the loaves for the people. John the Baptist has just been martyred, the disciples have just returned, exhausted from their first missionary trip: there was no time to eat, and the crowd wouldn't leave them alone. It had been a very long day. Finally Jesus sends His disciples away and climbs up a mountain that night to pray.

Immediately Jesus made His disciples get into the boat and go before Him to the other side, while He sent the multitudes away. And when He had sent the multitudes away, He went up on the mountain by Himself to pray. Now when evening came, He was alone there. (Matthew 14:22-23)

In Luke He climbs another mountain with Peter, John and James for a time of prayer.

Now it came to pass, about eight days after these sayings, that He took Peter, John, and James and went up on the mountain to pray. As He prayed, the appearance of His face was altered, and His robe became white and glistening. (Luke 9:28)

There was no Holy Spirit dove this time, but while He is praying He is transformed before their eyes. Not while He's teaching or preaching; but praying. The glory of God doesn't come upon Him as before, but comes from within Him. Matthew says, *"His face shone like the sun, and His clothes became as white as the light." (Matthew 17:2)* While He's praying!

In John chapter 17, Jesus is on the way to Gethsemane. This is after He has broken the bread and drank the wine, after He has told them what is about to happen according to John 17. He then prays out loud the whole way to Gethsemane. And can anyone tell me why He is going to Gethsemane? TO PRAY! He is praying on His way to pray. How important must prayer be?

If that's not enough, early the next morning as they nail Him to the cross, according to Luke, He prays while hanging from that very cross!

Then Jesus said, "Father, forgive them, for they do not know what they do." (Luke 23:34)

As a disciple, our hope is to become like our Master.

A disciple is not above his teacher, but everyone who is perfectly trained will be like his teacher. (Luke 6:40)

Jesus was never too busy to pray! No matter how hard the times were, He believed that prayer was as important as food and sleep. It may be hard to find time to pray, but Jesus found it. Even when He was bleeding to death on the cross!

How essential is prayer? Yet, how hard is it for a disciple to live a life of prayer?

How many chapters are there in the book of Acts? Twenty-eight. In fourteen out of twenty-eight chapters, guess what we see the disciples and the Apostles doing? Fourteen out of twenty-eight chapters, *half the biblical history of the church,* we find the disciples praying. But so few believers gather at the prayer meetings today. I tell you; it was the heartbeat of the early disciples. It was, in fact, so important that we find the Apostles refusing to start a widow's ministry because they had to pray.

> *Therefore, brethren, seek out from among you seven men of good reputation, full of the Holy Spirit and wisdom, whom we may appoint over this business; but we will give ourselves continually to prayer and to the ministry of the word. (Acts 6:3-4)*

The Apostles must stay devoted to two things. The first one is prayer. The second is the ministry of the Word.

The church should be praying. The leaders should be praying. The disciples should be praying. Our Master knew that He couldn't complete the tasks set before Him without the Father, and if the Lord had to pray, how much more do we?

Let's look in Matthew at His prayer in Gethsemane.

> *Then Jesus came with them to a place called Gethsemane, and said to the disciples, "Sit here while I go and pray over there." And He took with Him Peter and the two sons of Zebedee, and He began to be sorrowful and deeply distressed. Then He said to them, "My soul is exceedingly sorrowful, even to death. Stay here and watch with Me."(Matthew 26:36-38)*

Now this is really important. If you have your Bible out and are willing, circle the word 'watch'. We are going to talk about that word in detail. It means 'to be awake or alert'. "Stay here and watch with Me."

> *He went a little farther and fell on His face, and prayed, saying, "O My Father, if it is possible, let this cup pass from Me; nevertheless, not as*

*I will, but as You will." Then He came to the
disciples and found them asleep, and said to Peter,
"What? Could you not watch with Me one hour?"
(Matthew 26:39-40)*

Sleeping. This is the second word we need to look at because
it is the exact opposite of watching. Now very carefully read the
next verse.

*Watch and pray, lest you enter into temptation.
The spirit indeed is willing, but the flesh is weak.
(Matthew 26:41)*

It literally reads, in the Greek, stay awake so that you do
not enter into temptation. He just gave a spiritual truth. Prayer
is the single greatest tool for keeping a disciple from falling into
temptation. What do I mean? How many people do you know
who have a devoted prayer life and whose lives are falling apart
spiritually? I don't know a single one. How many people do you
know who go to Bible study regularly and their lives are spiritually falling apart? I know hundreds! How many do you know
who go to church regularly and yet their lives are spiritually
falling apart? Hundreds! I don't know a single person actually
devoted to prayer whose life is spiritually falling apart. Do you
see that? Do you grasp that?

He said:

*"Watch and pray, lest you enter into temptation.
The spirit indeed is willing, but the flesh is weak."
(Matthew 26:41)*

The spirit of a believer is indeed willing to avoid sin, but
our flesh is too weak without prayer.

The Lord God Himself openly pleads with us to pray.

In Mark chapter 13 Jesus says, *"The end of the world will
come but I am also coming. And when I come back it will be in
the troublesome times."* He gives us some warnings about what
the end will be like.

*For many will come in My name, saying, 'I am
He,' and will deceive many. But when you hear of
wars and rumors of wars, do not be troubled; for*

such things must happen, but the end is not yet. (Mark 13:6-7)

But when they arrest you and deliver you up, do not worry beforehand, or premeditate what you will speak. But whatever is given you in that hour, speak that; for it is not you who speak, but the Holy Spirit. Now brother will betray brother to death, and a father his child; and children will rise up against parents and cause them to be put to death. And you will be hated by all for My name's sake. But he who endures to the end shall be saved. (Mark 13:11-13)

Most believers are keeping an eye out for the false Christs. They are watching the increasing wars and famines, they are preparing for persecution, and yet they don't read the rest of what Jesus said...

But of that day and hour no one knows, not even the angels in heaven, nor the Son, but only the Father. Take heed, watch and pray; for you do not know when the time is. (Mark 13:32-33)

After telling us not to worry about the troublesome times ahead, He then warns us, not about the wars, the persecutions, the famines or the false Christs, but about a lack of watching and praying.

Those are the exact words spoken to the Apostles at Gethsemane during the darkest time in history (Luke 22:53). However, the Apostles didn't heed the warning and fell asleep. What was the result? Was Peter prepared for his trial? The one who had boldly proclaimed that he was willing to be thrown into prison or face crucifixion for Jesus is also the only one mentioned as denying Jesus that night! Jesus knew that Peter wasn't prepared for his trial, and He warned him about his need for prayer.

Watch and pray, lest you enter into temptation. (Matthew 26:41a)

Like Peter, we may feel prepared for the troublesome times ahead. We may have the plans all laid, but that didn't work for Peter and Jesus warns us that it won't work for us.

*The spirit indeed is willing, but the flesh is weak.
(Matthew 26:41b)*

To make His point even stronger, Jesus tells a parable in Mark.

It is like a man going to a far country, who left his house and gave authority to his servants, and to each his work, and commanded the doorkeeper to watch. Watch therefore, for you do not know when the master of the house is coming--in the evening, at midnight, at the crowing of the rooster, or in the morning-- lest, coming suddenly, he find you sleeping. (Mark 13:34-36)

That does not mean I cannot physically sleep at night. It does not mean that my wife and I have to take turns staying awake through the night so that we don't miss Jesus' return. He is referring to a spiritual sleep, a weakness towards temptation and deception. Don't fall asleep spiritually! "Lest coming suddenly Jesus finds you sleeping." And just in case we think this is not a command for all disciples in all generations:

*And what I say to you, I say to all: Watch!
(Mark 13:37)*

The Apostle Paul understood this.

And do this, knowing the time, that now it is high time to awake out of sleep; for now our salvation is nearer than when we first believed. The night is far spent, the day is at hand. Therefore let us cast off the works of darkness, and let us put on the armor of light. Let us walk properly, as in the day, not in revelry and drunkenness, not in lewdness and lust, not in strife and envy. But put on the Lord Jesus Christ, and make no provision for the flesh, to fulfill its lusts. (Romans 13:11-14)

Again, spiritual strength comes from prayer. When you are awake spiritually, you will make no provision for the flesh. It is once again the same words spoken to Peter, "*The spirit is willing, but the flesh is weak.*" If you don't pray you will fall. You can attend every church service. You can memorize the entire Bible. But without prayer you will fall.

Romans 13:11 says stay awake and pray. 1 Corinthians 16:13 says: *Watch, stand fast in the faith, be brave, be strong.* He links 'staying awake' with standing fast in the faith.

Many memorize Ephesians 6. The belt of truth. The breastplate of righteousness. The helmet of salvation. The sword of the spirit. The shield of faith. But Paul goes on and we stop memorizing!

> *praying always with all prayer and supplication in the Spirit, being watchful to this end with all perseverance and supplication for all the saints (Ephesians 6:18)*

A disciple must persevere in prayer.

> *Continue earnestly in prayer, being vigilant in it with thanksgiving; (Colossians 4:2)*

> *But the end of all things is at hand; therefore be serious and watchful in your prayers. (1 Peter 4:7)*

> *Therefore let us not sleep, as others do, but let us watch and be sober...pray without ceasing (1 Thessalonians 5:6, 17)*

In Revelation chapter 3 Jesus talks to the church of Sardis.

> *I know your works, that you have a name that you are alive, but you are dead. (Revelation 3:1)*

They looked alive, but they were spiritually dead. What did they need?

> *Be watchful, and strengthen the things which remain, that are ready to die. (Revelation 3:2)*

Watchfulness! They hadn't been praying and weren't awake.

> *Therefore if you will not watch, I will come upon you as a thief, and you will not know what hour I will come upon you. (Revelation 3:3b)*

Then after Revelation chapter 3 we have thirteen chapters without a red letter in it. Not a single word from the Lord Jesus in all of those pages. We are supplied with vivid details about what is happening in heaven and on earth during the Great Tribulation period. We learn about the terrible rule of the antichrist and the great sorrow of those dwelling on earth. People are dying left and right. The earth is burning up: plagues, locusts, and all kinds of horrors. If you are a believer at this time, you would think that there would be no possible way that you wouldn't be prepared for the Son of God's return. But, in the middle of this unprecedented time of sorrow and 13 chapters of silence, Jesus makes a single statement!

Behold, I am coming as a thief. Blessed is he who watches, and keeps his garments, lest he walk naked and they see his shame. (Revelation 16:15)

Blessed is he who is praying and awake! Watching! Six specific times Jesus COMMANDS His disciples:

Watch therefore, for you do not know what hour your Lord is coming. (Matthew 24:42)

Watch therefore, for you know neither the day nor the hour in which the Son of Man is coming. (Matthew 25:13)

Watch and pray, lest you enter into temptation. The spirit indeed is willing, but the flesh is weak." (Matthew 26:41)

Take heed, watch and pray; for you do not know when the time is. (Mark 13:33)

And if he should come in the second watch, or come in the third watch, and find them so, blessed are those servants. But know this, that if the master of the house had known what hour the thief would come, he would have watched and not allowed his house to be broken into. Therefore you also be ready, for the Son of Man is coming at an hour you do not expect. (Luke 12:38-40)

Watch therefore, and pray always that you may be counted worthy to escape all these things that will come to pass, and to stand before the Son of Man." (Luke 21:36)

Every single one of these commands meant do not spiritually sleep, but pray. Disciples must pray! The church that doesn't pray doesn't survive. Not a single revival in recorded history occurred without a revival of prayer first! They even call it 'The Great Awakening' in America. Awakening from what? From spiritual sleep! Oh, how my heart yearns and God's heart yearns for us to pray! Then we will be prepared for the things that are coming. We will be able to love our neighbor, carry our cross and endure to the end.

Let's look at Luke chapter 18, a parable about praying. It is a story about a judge who didn't fear God, or regard men. But there was a persistent widow in that city who pestered him until this evil judge gave her justice.

Then He spoke a parable to them, that men always ought to pray and not lose heart, saying: "There was in a certain city a judge who did not fear God nor regard man. saying: "There was in a certain city a judge who did not fear God nor regard man. Now there was a widow in that city; and she came to him, saying, 'Get justice for me from my adversary.' And he would not for a while; but afterward he said within himself, 'Though I do not fear God nor regard man, yet because this widow troubles me I will avenge her, lest by her continual coming she weary me.' Then the Lord said, "Hear what the unjust judge said. And shall God not avenge His own elect who cry out day and night to Him, though He bears long with them? I tell you that He will avenge them speedily. (Luke 18:1-8a)

What was the purpose of the parable? *"That men always ought to pray and not lose heart."* He is instructing us to continually come before our Father. But, how many of us will? Jesus summarizes the result of prayerlessness at the end of His parable...

Nevertheless, when the Son of Man comes, will He really find faith on the earth? (Luke 18:8b)

In other words, our faith isn't going to make it unless we continue praying. Did you know that it is a great falling away of the church that allows the rise of the antichrist?

> *Now, brethren, concerning the coming of our Lord*
> *Jesus Christ and our gathering together to Him, we*
> *ask you, not to be soon shaken in mind or troubled,*
> *either by spirit or by word or by letter, as if from*
> *us, as though the day of Christ had come. Let no*
> *one deceive you by any means; for that Day will*
> *not come unless the falling away comes first, and*
> *the man of sin is revealed, the son of perdition...*
> *(2 Thessalonians 2:1-3)*

Don't worry about the antichrist sneaking up on you: that's not our danger. The greatest danger for the church is falling asleep through prayerlessness and becoming apostate.

Welcome to America! According to a recent survey only around 3% of the entire United States actually has a Biblical worldview. 26% of born again Christians believe all religions are essentially the same. 50% believe we are saved by works. 35% don't even believe in the resurrection of Jesus. According to Romans 10:9, that means these people are not saved. What would Paul call that? A great falling away!

Prayerlessness is killing the American church. We are now in the 'Great Falling Asleep', rather than the 'Great Awakening'. We *"have a name that [we] are alive, but [we] are dead."*

Just look at Samson in Judges chapter 16. He is the strongest man on the face of the earth. He picks up a donkey jaw and whips an army. When he wants to go home he takes the gate out of the wall and packs it with him. Nothing can defeat Samson, *except sleep*. In Judges chapter 16 he meets a woman named Delilah. And she puts him to sleep. Just like the world puts us to sleep.

> *So Delilah said to Samson, "Please tell me where*
> *your great strength lies, and with what you may be*
> *bound to afflict you." (Judges 16:6)*

You know the story: first seven bowstrings are put on him while he sleeps, but he overcomes these, then new ropes are put upon him while he sleeps, but he is still stronger than these; and then a loom:

> *But he awoke from his sleep, and pulled out the*
> *batten and the web from the loom. (Judges 16:14)*

Finally, Samson grew tired of Delilah's persistence and told her the source of his strength was in his hair, which dedicated him to the Lord. Now Delilah could never have overcome such a mighty man, just as Satan could never overcome the kingdom of God (Matthew 16:18). So what do Delilah and Satan do?

> *Then she lulled him to sleep on her knees, and called for a man and had him shave off the seven locks of his head. Then she began to torment him, and his strength left him. (Judges 16:19)*

Samson is asleep in the arms of the adversary! He thinks the gates of his enemies cannot prevail against him.

> *So he awoke from his sleep, and said, "I will go out as before, at other times, and shake myself free!" But he did not know that the LORD had departed from him. (Judges 16:20)*

Dear reader, a note has just been received from the Lord in heaven, which reads:

> *Take heed, watch and pray: for you do not know when the time is.*
> *(Mark 13:33)*

CHAPTER EIGHTEEN REVIEW

i. *What does Jesus mean when He commands us to 'watch'?*

ii. *What does prayer have to do with temptation?*

iii. *How important was prayer to Jesus? How important is it to you?*

iv. *How much time of your day is actually spent in prayer?*

v. *What steps are you going to take in order that you don't fall asleep spiritually?*

vi. *Memorize Mark 13:33*

ATTITUDES OF THE HEART

Not a Hypocrite

> *Therefore, laying aside all malice, all deceit, hypocrisy, envy, and all evil speaking, as newborn babes, desire the pure milk of the word, that you may grow thereby, if indeed you have tasted that the Lord is gracious. (1 Peter 2:1-3)*

Hypocrisy. What does it mean?

*I*t means to say one thing and do another. To be untrue or have double standards. It literally means to put on a mask. The word, 'hupokrites', is the Greek word for actor. In Greek dramas, one person might play two, three, or maybe four different characters. So, they would put on a mask for each character. Their attitude changed with the donning of a new mask. Hypocrisy.

Now Jesus was pretty clear about hypocrisy. Look at Matthew 23:15-33. He calls the Scribes and the Pharisees hypocrites. Face changers. Let's look at what Jesus considers hypocrisy.

> *Woe to you, scribes and Pharisees, hypocrites! For you travel land and sea to win one proselyte, and when he is won, you make him twice as much a son of hell as yourselves. (Matthew 23:15)*

Jesus states that one characteristic of hypocrisy is to want people to be like you rather than the Lord. These are those who work hard for themselves not God. "Come to my group. Don't be like those people. We are better than they." That's hypocrisy.

> *Woe to you, scribes and Pharisees, hypocrites! For you pay tithe of mint and anise and cummin, and have neglected the weightier matters of the law: justice and mercy and faith. These you ought to have done, without leaving the others undone. (Matthew 23:23)*

Another characteristic of hypocrisy is to be extremely strict about religious rules while acting completely contrary to the character of God.

> *And though I bestow all my goods to feed the poor,*
> *and though I give my body to be burned, but have*
> *not love, it profits me nothing. (1 Corinthians 13:3)*

It isn't wrong to tithe small herbs to the Lord, but it is wrong to focus on them and forget justice, mercy and faith. Jesus referred to this as *"strain[ing] out a gnat and swallow[ing] a camel!"* Neither animal was proper to eat, but we shouldn't focus so hard on the little one that we end up eating the big one. Keeping religious rules can sometimes eclipse the true character of God.

Hypocrites are unconcerned about what's really going on inside their hearts, but are interested in how their lives are viewed by others. If other people respect them, it is of little concern how their lives are viewed by God. "As long as I look good on the outside and no one knows my secret life, I'm okay." That is the essence of hypocrisy. Outward appearance rather than inward truth. My goal is to impress others with the fact that I have memorized Scripture, or with my ability to speak eloquently. As long as men are impressed, I'm satisfied. That's hypocrisy.

> *Woe to you, scribes and Pharisees, hypocrites! For*
> *you cleanse the outside of the cup and dish, but*
> *inside they are full of extortion and self-indulgence.*
> *Blind Pharisee, first cleanse the inside of the cup*
> *and dish, that the outside of them may be clean*
> *also. Woe to you, scribes and Pharisees, hypocrites!*
> *For you are like whitewashed tombs which indeed*
> *appear beautiful outwardly, but inside are full of*
> *dead men's bones and all uncleanness. Even so*
> *you also outwardly appear righteous to men, but*
> *inside you are full of hypocrisy and lawlessness.*
> *(Matthew 23:25-28)*

> *Take heed that you do not do your charitable deeds*
> *before men, to be seen by them. Otherwise you have*
> *no reward from your Father in heaven. Therefore,*
> *when you do a charitable deed, do not sound a*
> *trumpet before you as the hypocrites do in the*
> *synagogues and in the streets, that they may have*
> *glory from men. Assuredly, I say to you, they have*
> *their reward. (Matthew 6:1-2)*

If I am actually a hypocrite, then when I do a good deed, I'm compelled to tell you about it. I make it look like I am sharing, but if other people don't know what I have done, then I am unsatisfied.

We each have a desire to maintain a good reputation or appearance. We all crave someone to say, "Hey, what are you doing is wonderful." But we must be careful that praise from men doesn't become the reason we serve the Lord.

> *And when you pray, you shall not be like the hypocrites. For they love to pray standing in the synagogues and on the corners of the streets, that they may be seen by men. Assuredly, I say to you, they have their reward. (Matthew 6:5)*

What was the purpose of their praying?

> *Moreover, when you fast do not be like the hypocrites, with a sad countenance. For they disfigure their faces that they may appear to men to be fasting. Assuredly, I say to you, they have their reward. But you, when you fast, anoint your head and wash your face, "so that you do not appear to men to be fasting, but to your Father who is in the secret place; and your Father who sees in secret will reward you openly. (Matthew 6:16-18)*

The remedy to not fasting hypocritically is to avoid letting others know that you're fasting at all. Trying to hide your fasting can sometimes become ridiculous. It's okay to say, "I'm fasting." It's not okay to say, "Boy, I'm sure hungry. I have been fasting and I'm so hungry. I'd like to have your food...." That's hypocrisy.

What is the remedy for not praying in a hypocritical way? Avoid letting anyone know you're praying.

> *But you, when you pray, go into your room, and when you have shut your door, pray to your Father who is in the secret place; and your Father who sees in secret will reward you openly. (Matthew 6:6)*

Instead of being the one who has to pray the loudest and longest, just pray to God and don't pay attention to those listening. Again, don't make 'hiding your prayer' a rigid rule either, but if you find that you are praying the longest, the loudest, and the last, you are probably the hypocrite.

How do I give generously without becoming a hypocrite?

> *But when you do a charitable deed, do not let your left hand know what your right hand is doing, "that your charitable deed may be in secret; and your Father who sees in secret will Himself reward you openly. (Matthew 6:3-4)*

Avoid letting anyone know what you are doing. Once more, don't make this a legalistic rule that causes you to keep secrets from your wife or husband. Just don't give so that you receive applause. Because when we give for the purpose of applause, Jesus said, "That's all we get!" Oh, how people have ripped themselves off by giving a generous gift and then telling everyone what they have done. They get nothing in heaven. They have just traded all of that money for a pat on the back. The gift has been erased from God's ledger.

> *But the wisdom that is from above is first pure, then peaceable, gentle, willing to yield, full of mercy and good fruits, without partiality and without hypocrisy. (James 3:17)*

God is not a hypocrite. And those who are full of God's wisdom will not be hypocrites. If they are, it's not from God. A disciple must be more concerned about what God sees than what man sees. Remember when Samuel was selecting the next king of Israel and David's strong good looking brother Eliab walked into the room? God knew his heart.

> *So it was, when they came, that he looked at Eliab and said, "Surely the LORD'S anointed is before Him." But the LORD said to Samuel, "Do not look at his appearance or at the height of his stature, because I have refused him. For the LORD does not see as man sees; for man looks at the outward appearance, but the LORD looks at the heart." (1 Samuel 16:6-7)*

God sees a person's heart, not his actions. A brother could give a generous gift and I could give the same gift, but based upon our hearts, he might receive eternal reward, while I receive

nothing. God weighs the hearts, not the actions. Hearts don't lie!
Paul says,

> *But with me it is a very small thing that I should*
> *be judged by you or by a human court. In fact, I do*
> *not even judge myself. For I know nothing against*
> *myself, yet I am not justified by this; but He who*
> *judges me is the Lord. (1 Corinthians 4:3-4)*

In other words, my opinion about myself doesn't even matter. God's opinion is the only one that counts. Paul says, "I can judge and you can judge, but God knows!"

2 Timothy 2:15 says, *"Be diligent to present yourself approved to God"*, not approved of men! Ultimately, I hope that others like me and look to me as someone they can respect. But I don't care if they don't. Because I'm alive for Christ.

Let's look at some Biblical examples of hypocrisy. First, the early church!

Ananias and Sapphira

> *Now the multitude of those who believed were of*
> *one heart and one soul; neither did anyone say*
> *that any of the things he possessed was his own,*
> *but they had all things in common. And with great*
> *power the apostles gave witness to the resurrection*
> *of the Lord Jesus. And great grace was upon them*
> *all. (Acts 4:32-33)*

This is a great work of God, where an entire group of people is living selflessly.

> *Nor was there anyone among them who lacked;*
> *for all who were possessors of lands or houses sold*
> *them, and brought the proceeds of the things that*
> *were sold, and laid them at the apostles' feet; and*
> *they distributed to each as anyone had need. And*
> *Joses, who was also named Barnabas by the apostles*
> *(which is translated Son of Encouragement), a Levite*
> *of the country of Cyprus, having land, sold it, and*
> *brought the money and laid it at the apostles' feet.*
> *(Acts 4:34-37)*

This guy was so generous that they changed his name and called him a Son of Encouragement! Now what happens is, in the back of this congregation a couple named Ananias and Sapphira are thinking, "Wow! Look at the recognition this guy received. The Apostles themselves changed his name. That's awesome. Hey, Sapphira, we have some property. Why don't we sell our property just like they did and then we'll give the money to the church. Then maybe they'll change our names too! We'll be somebody just like Barnabas!" Did they desire to be approved by men or God? They were worrying about what the Apostles and the church thought.

So they went and sold their property. Only when they sold it they hadn't realized how much money they were going to receive. Then they said, "Well, let's just give part of it to the church and say that's how much it sold for."

> *But a certain man named Ananias, with Sapphira his wife, sold a possession. And he kept back part of the proceeds, his wife also being aware of it, and brought a certain part and laid it at the apostles' feet. But Peter said, "Ananias, why has Satan filled your heart to lie to the Holy Spirit and keep back part of the price of the land for yourself? "While it remained, was it not your own? And after it was sold, was it not in your own control? Why have you conceived this thing in your heart? You have not lied to men but to God." (Acts 5:1-4)*

How does God respond to their hypocrisy?

> *Then Ananias, hearing these words, fell down and breathed his last. So great fear came upon all those who heard these things. And the young men arose and wrapped him up, carried him out, and buried him. (Acts 5:5-6)*

Now that's a church service! Anyone else want to lie?

> *Now it was about three hours later when his wife came in, not knowing what had happened. And Peter answered her, "Tell me whether you sold the land for so much?" She said, "Yes, for so much." Then Peter said to her, "How is it that you have agreed together to test the Spirit of the Lord? Look,*

*the feet of those who have buried your husband
are at the door, and they will carry you out." Then
immediately she fell down at his feet and breathed
her last. And the young men came in and found
her dead, and carrying her out, buried her by her
husband. (Acts 5:7-10)*

How would you like to be the young men? "Oh, Peter's
preaching? I'm not going to church today! We had to bury two
people last time."

Think about what this reveals. They were going to lay down
their possessions at the feet of the Apostles, but due to their hypocrisy, they laid down their lives. Did they receive fame? Yep,
the Lord recorded them in His Holy Bible as two of the first
hypocrites in the church!

Achan

In Joshua Chapter 7, the Lord commanded them to conquer
Jericho. Everything within those walls was to be dedicated to
Him. They were to take nothing for themselves. No Gold. No
animals. Nothing.

*But the children of Israel committed a trespass
regarding the accursed things, for Achan the son of
Carmi, the son of Zabdi, the son of Zerah, of the
tribe of Judah, took of the accursed things; so the
anger of the LORD burned against the children of
Israel. Now Joshua sent men from Jericho to Ai,
which is beside Beth Aven, on the east side of Bethel,
and spoke to them, saying, "Go up and spy out the
country." So the men went up and spied out Ai.
(Joshua 7:1-2)*

Jericho was a big city and Ai was a little village.

*And they returned to Joshua and said to him, "Do
not let all the people go up, but let about two or
three thousand men go up and attack Ai. Do not
weary all the people there, for the people of Ai are
few." So about three thousand men went up there
from the people, but they fled before the men of Ai.
(Joshua 7:3)*

Their hidden sin had removed the blessing of God. They destroy Jericho with the shout of their voices and now they are being chased away from a village by women and dogs.

What happened? Hypocrisy! Achan had put on a good face before everyone in the camp, but his heart was far from God.

So Joshua complains before God:

> *O Lord, what shall I say when Israel turns its back before its enemies? (Joshua 7:8)*

And the Lord replies, "There is no power because there is sin in the camp."

> *Israel has sinned, and they have also transgressed My covenant which I commanded them. For they have even taken some of the accursed things, and have both stolen and deceived; and they have also put it among their own stuff. (Joshua 7:11)*

From Joshua's eyes, everything looked fine in the camp, but God could see beyond the acting, into the very heart of Achan and his family.

> *So Joshua rose early in the morning and brought Israel by their tribes, and the tribe of Judah was taken. He brought the clan of Judah, and he took the family of the Zarhites; and he brought the family of the Zarhites man by man, and Zabdi was taken. Then he brought his household man by man, and Achan the son of Carmi, the son of Zabdi, the son of Zerah, of the tribe of Judah, was taken. (Joshua 7:16-18)*

I wonder how many of these men were nervous while the lot was being thrown. He rolled again and again until he was down to one family. Can you imagine what Achan is thinking? Achan is probably hypocritically praying that the lot won't fall upon him. But God knows the heart.

> *Now Joshua said to Achan, "My son, I beg you, give glory to the LORD God of Israel, and make confession to Him, and tell me now what you have done; do not hide it from me." (Joshua 7:19)*

"Achan, you have been a hypocrite until now. You have hidden sin from all of us, confess the truth!" The Bible commands us to confess our sins to one another, because it exposes our heart and humbles us. Hypocrites don't like being humbled; it's bad for the reputation.

> *And Achan answered Joshua and said, "Indeed I have sinned against the LORD God of Israel, and this is what I have done: "When I saw among the spoils a beautiful Babylonian garment, two hundred shekels of silver, and a wedge of gold weighing fifty shekels, I coveted them and took them. And there they are, hidden in the earth in the midst of my tent, with the silver under it." So Joshua sent messengers, and they ran to the tent; and there it was, hidden in his tent, with the silver under it. (Joshua 7:18-22)*

That's hypocrisy. The tent looked fine, he looked fine, but there was hidden sin. You can read the rest of the story yourself. God doesn't like hypocrisy. His lie was counted against the whole family, because they all knew that it was hidden under the tent. Similar to how Ananias' lie brought destruction to his wife.

> *He began to say to His disciples first of all, "Beware of the leaven of the Pharisees, which is hypocrisy. For there is nothing covered that will not be revealed, nor hidden that will not be known." (Luke 12:1-2)*

Controls the Tongue

This is very practical, for those of us who preach the Word.

> *If anyone among you thinks he is religious, and does not bridle his tongue but deceives his own heart, this one's religion is useless. (James 1:26)*

Now put that in your own words.

Given enough time your mouth will sin. Or as Solomon said, "*In the multitude of words sin is not lacking.*" (Proverbs 10:19) If you want to truly know somebody, listen to them carefully. Jesus says in Matthew that the great lie detector is the mouth.

> *Either make the tree good and its fruit good, or*

*else make the tree bad and its fruit bad; for a
tree is known by its fruit. Brood of vipers! How
can you, being evil, speak good things? For out
of the abundance of the heart the mouth speaks.
(Matthew 12:33-34)*

What comes out of our mouth is really from the depths of
our heart. When we are in a heated argument, we sometimes
blurt out what we didn't want anyone to know was in us.

*A good man out of the good treasure of his heart
brings forth good things, and an evil man out of
the evil treasure brings forth evil things. But I say
to you that for every idle word men may speak,
they will give account of it in the day of judgment.
(Matthew 12:35-36)*

That phrase means, 'every casual and relaxed word'. Think
about that! When we let our guard down and just say how we
feel, God listens and writes the words down.

*For by your words you will be justified, and by your
words you will be condemned. (Matthew 12:37)*

Repent quickly. If there is nastiness in your heart and your
mouth spills it out, what you need to do is confess it immediately
rather than cover it up, like Achan.

Addressing the mouth, James says:

*With it we bless our God and Father, and with it we
curse men, who have been made in the similitude of
God. Out of the same mouth proceed blessing and
cursing. My brethren, these things ought not to be
so. Does a spring send forth fresh water and bitter
from the same opening? (James 3:9-11)*

Who would want a well like that? Can you see the conversation around the well each morning? "What's the water like
today?" "I don't know. I'm afraid to try it! It was good yesterday;
it's probably terrible today." Can you imagine a spring like that?
You'd quickly abandon such a watering hole.

Can a fig tree, my brethren, bear olives, or a

grapevine bear figs? Thus no spring yields both salt water and fresh. (James 3:12)

And no mouth should bless God and curse men. A disciple must learn to control his/her tongue. How do I do it?

For He who would love life and see good days, Let him refrain his tongue from evil, And his lips from speaking deceit. Let him turn away from evil and do good; Let him seek peace and pursue it. (1 Peter 3:10-11)

What is the meaning of 'refrain'? It means to restrain or keep something from continuing. Police officers often have to restrain criminals. The word literally means, "pause". It means, in the middle of my speaking I purposely stop talking! Have you ever said something completely inappropriate, and for some reason you just keep on talking, hoping that you can cover up what you just spoke? We think that if we talk enough maybe somehow it will never have happened. We have a phrase in the U.S. about 'putting our foot in our mouth'. The godly way to respond to this type of situation is to 'pause' your talking and repent. Sinfulness inside of you has just been revealed to others. Use this as an opportunity to grow in the Lord by pausing your mouth...

Is Content

Likewise the soldiers asked him, saying, "And what shall we do?" So he said to them, "Do not intimidate anyone or accuse falsely, and be content with your wages." (Luke 3:14)

This is a quote from John the Baptist who is preparing the people for the Messiah. People are coming up to him and asking, "What must I do to be saved?" He responds, "Repent. Repent!" In Luke 3:14 he tells this certain group of soldiers to repent in a very specific way. "Be content!" The word means, 'be satisfied'. How many people do you know who are satisfied with their wages? I owned a business once and had somewhere around thirty employees. And I never once met a man who was satisfied with his wages. Even when we would receive a new contract and their wages would double, they were still unhappy. Mainly because contentment has nothing to do with circumstances, but is an attitude of the heart. Everyone has the ability to be discontent, because there is always more than they currently have.

Notice, John didn't even ask how much they were making. He didn't say, "Well, how much do you make? Oh, that's a fair wage for a soldier. Be happy with that." He simply said, "Whatever you're making, it's good enough." Contentment is an attitude of the heart.

Paul spends quite a few verses discipling Timothy about this characteristic.

Now godliness with contentment is great gain.
(1 Timothy 6:6)

This particular verse is, of course, in reference to money. Paul is telling him how to gain the most out of life. It's an attitude of the heart.

For we brought nothing into this world, and it
is certain we can carry nothing out. And having
food and clothing, with these we shall be content.
(1 Timothy 6:7-7)

Again, he says it a second time. But, this time he describes what is necessary for a disciple to be content. Not money. Not a house. Food and Clothing! Because, you know what? When I die nothing goes with me. It's the old joke. You've never seen a coffin with luggage compartments. I like what Solomon says about it:

When goods increase, they increase who eat them;
So what profit have the owners except to see them
with their eyes? (Ecclesiastes 5:11)

What's the use of earning more money, because everybody just shows up and eats it! Be content with what you have.

But those who desire to be rich fall into temptation
and a snare, and into many foolish and harmful
lusts which drown men in destruction and perdition.
(1 Timothy 6:9)

According to the Word of God, discontentment will cause us to fall into temptation, snares and foolish and harmful lusts that will eventually drown us in destruction. Whereas, if we have the heart attitude of contentment, we will have great gain.

> *For the love of money is a root of all kinds of evil,*
> *for which some have strayed from the faith in their*
> *greediness, and pierced themselves through with*
> *many sorrows. (1 Timothy 6:10)*

He tells Timothy to look around and see how many believers have fallen into this trap and have destroyed their lives. Do you realize that Jesus said there was a particular type of believer who would receive the Word and begin growing, but never produce fruit?

> *Now these are the ones sown among thorns; they are*
> *the ones who hear the word, and the cares of this*
> *world, the deceitfulness of riches, and the desires*
> *for other things entering in choke the word, and it*
> *becomes unfruitful. (Mark 4:18-19)*

This is a temptation to those who are paid for ministry. The love of money can lead us astray. You probably don't have to look very far to find an example of a brother or sister who has fallen into such a snare.

> *...for which some have strayed from the faith in*
> *their greediness, and pierced themselves through*
> *with many sorrows. (1 Timothy 6:10)*

It is the picture of a man taking a spear with the word 'GREED' engraved on it, and falling on its tip. They destroy themselves!

> *But you, O man of God, flee these things and pursue*
> *righteousness, godliness, faith, love, patience,*
> *gentleness. (1 Timothy 6:11)*

Flee discontentment.

> *Let your conduct be without covetousness; be*
> *content with such things as you have. For He*
> *Himself has said, "I will never leave you nor forsake*
> *you." (Hebrews 13:5)*

As a disciple, when I am tempted to become discontent with my position in life, I am called to remember that my position is

right beside the Lord! I can never lose that Treasure. And since
we always have the Best with us, we should always be content.

Paul wrote from a prison cell:

> *Not that I speak in regard to need, for I have learned
> in whatever state I am, to be content: I know how to
> be abased, and I know how to abound. Everywhere
> and in all things I have learned both to be full and
> to be hungry, both to abound and to suffer need.*
> *(Philippians 4:11-12)*

I have *learned*. That means it is something we as disciples
must learn. Paul didn't wake up one day and find that he was
content with the prison cell and the rats. He learned to rejoice
whether he had food, or health, or freedom. What was the key
to finding contentment according to the Hebrews passage above?
The Presence of the Lord! What is the key that Paul found to
learn contentment through his circumstances? The Presence of
the Lord!

> *I can do all things through Christ who strengthens
> me. (Philippians 4:13)*

That is the proper context for this often misquoted verse.
"I can suffer or be rich. I can starve or be full. None of it brings
discontentment, because Jesus is with me."

The final example for contentment is our Lord Himself. How
much did Jesus own? Or, how much did He earn? How many
camels could He call His own? How many goats? Carts? Robes?

When a man came to Him and said, "I will follow you
wherever you go, Master", He revealed His great wealth.

> *Foxes have holes and birds of the air have nests,
> but the Son of Man has nowhere to lay His head."*
> *(Luke 9:58)*

He wanted the man to realize that He wasn't offering luxury,
but His eternal love.

> *Who shall separate us from the love of Christ? Shall
> tribulation, or distress, or persecution, or famine,
> or nakedness, or peril, or sword?... Yet in all these
> things we are more than conquerors through Him
> who loved us. For I am persuaded that neither death*

nor life, nor angels nor principalities nor powers, nor things present nor things to come, nor height nor depth, nor any other created thing, shall be able to separate us from the love of God which is in Christ Jesus our Lord. (Romans 8:35, 37-39)

CHAPTER NINETEEN REVIEW

i. Describe how being an actor and being a hypocrite are similar.

ii. What is the most important thing to a hypocrite?

iii. What is the best indicator of a man's heart?

iv. When was the last time you were discontent? Why?

v. Which of these three characteristics do you struggle with the most? And what steps are you going to take to overcome that struggle?

vi. Memorize 1 Samuel 16:7b

Loves Christ's Appearing

 et's speak about the church's uniting with the Lord which is spoken about in 1 Thessalonians.

Then we who are alive and remain shall be caught up together with them in the clouds to meet the Lord in the air. And thus we shall always be with the Lord. (1 Thessalonians 4:17)

Many believe this event occurs prior to the Tribulation. Some believe it occurs three and one-half years into the Tribulation and others believe that it occurs immediately following the Tribulation. Which is it? Here is the final answer for all who would debate what is referred to as the rapture of the church: *We don't know*! Isn't that what Jesus said in Mark 13:33-37?

Therefore, we must be prepared today! That much is clear and inarguable. In fact, it removes all discussion about the timing, because it is of no concern to a disciple. Jesus said I am to expect His imminent return. It is not based upon world events. We are not looking for the Tribulation. We are not looking for the rebuilding of the Temple. We are not looking for the Sanhedrin to reconvene. We are not looking for the antichrist to be revealed. We are not looking for the ten horns of the Roman Empire to assemble. We are looking for Jesus.

We often become excited about the daily events that we see in the news. There are many prophecies being fulfilled in these last few years with Russia, Iran, Israel, and the world economy. We live in a good time for those who study prophecy. This should encourage us to be more ready for His appearing.

Then He spoke to them a parable: "Look at the fig tree, and all the trees. When they are already budding, you see and know for yourselves that summer is now near. So you also, when you see these things happening, know that the kingdom of God is near. Assuredly, I say to you, this generation will by no means pass away till all things take place. (Luke 21:29-32)

In Genesis 15:13, the Lord revealed to Abraham that his offspring would be in bondage for four hundred years. Yet, why would he tell this to Abraham when it was so far away? The Lord showed me that He spoke these words to Abraham in order that when Israel was eventually enslaved, they would know that the Lord was with them in it and that they should look for the coming redeemer. Their redeemer was Moses, but ours is the Lord Jesus. This is the very reason that Jesus revealed the troublesome times which lie ahead (Matthew 24 and 25): so that this generation might be looking for the Lord's return.

Now when these things begin to happen, look up and lift up your heads, because your redemption draws near. (Luke 21:28)

Just a side note, based upon current events, Jesus might return for you before you finish this chapter. Be ready!

Since we don't know the exact timing of His return, we are commanded to watch and pray! We covered this topic in detail in a previous chapter. And we do know that *our salvation is nearer than when we first believed* (Romans 13:11). We are one day closer than yesterday!

It is like a man going to a far country, who left his house and gave authority to his servants, and to each his work (Mark 13:34a)

God has also given us an authority and a task. If you don't think so, re-read Matthew 28:18-20

and commanded the doorkeeper to watch. Watch therefore, for you do not know when the master of the house is coming--in the evening, at midnight, at the crowing of the rooster, or in the morning— (Mark 13:34b-35)

Here's the warning: if we don't watch,

...lest, coming suddenly, he find you sleeping. And what I say to you, I say to all: Watch! (Mark 13:36-37)

Is Jesus' coming going to be slow? What does it say in Revelation?

He who testifies to these things says, "Surely I am coming quickly." Amen. Even so, come, Lord Jesus! (Revelation 22:20)

His return will be very sudden and based upon this Scripture, there will be some believers who are not watching and will not be prepared.

> *Finally, there is laid up for me the crown of righteousness, which the Lord, the righteous Judge, will give to me on that Day, and not to me only but also to all who have loved His appearing. (2 Timothy 4:8)*

Paul was waiting excitedly to meet the Lord. Are you? There is a unique crown for those who are in love with the day of His appearing. It is both a time of reward for those longingly watching and a time of judgment for those who are against Him.

> *And then the lawless one will be revealed,* (The antichrist) *whom the Lord will consume with the breath of His mouth and destroy with the brightness of His coming. (2 Thessalonians 2:8)*

So the Lord's appearing is a good day for a disciple and a bad day for the antichrist. Just like when a nuclear bomb is detonated and incinerates everything for miles, when the Lord returns, His glory will incinerate the antichrist. His appearing is wonderful and fearful.

Paul uses our Lord's appearing as a motivational tool to exhort his disciple Timothy.

> *I charge you therefore before God and the Lord Jesus Christ, who will judge the living and the dead at His appearing and His kingdom: (2 Timothy 4:1)*

> *Keep this commandment without spot, blameless until our Lord Jesus Christ's appearing, which He will manifest in His own time, He who is the blessed and only Potentate, the King of kings and Lord of lords, who alone has immortality, dwelling in unapproachable light, whom no man has seen or can see, to whom be honor and everlasting power. Amen. (1 Timothy 6:14-16).*

"Keep this commandment Timothy, because the Lord is coming and He is coming in power." The Lord's sudden appearing

should make us shudder at the thought of doing wrong things.
You don't want to be in the middle of a sin when He arrives! He
is coming in unapproachable consuming light. Great and terrible!

For the day of the LORD is great and very terrible (Joel 2:11)

A great day for us and a terrible day for the unsaved. For
His glory will come and with it comes His righteousness. For
us who are in Christ, we rejoice! But, for those who hate God,
and have rejected His Son, it's a terrible day. It's the great and
terrible day of the Lord.

Paul uses the same word of encouragement with his other
disciple, Titus.

> *For the grace of God that brings salvation has
> appeared to all men, teaching us that, denying
> ungodliness and worldly lusts, we should live
> soberly, righteously, and godly in the present
> age, looking for the blessed hope and glorious
> appearing of our great God and Savior Jesus Christ
> (Titus 2:11-13)*

That word 'looking' means '*to wait with confidence*'. It is
not the word you would use to describe looking out a car window, but rather looking at a ball that was being thrown towards
you. You know that it is on its way. Zacchaeus knew that Jesus
was on His way, so he climbed a tree to be in a better position
when He arrived (Luke 19). Paul says in the same way, get rid
of ungodliness and worldly lusts so that we might be in a better
position when He arrives. Wait confidently!

Paul had a great desire to be in the Presence of the Lord:

> *For to me, to live is Christ, and to die is gain. But
> if I live on in the flesh, this will mean fruit from my
> labor; yet what I shall choose I cannot tell. For I
> am hard pressed between the two, having a desire
> to depart and be with Christ, which is far better.
> (Philippians 1:21-23)*

Paul was so in love with Christ's appearing that he actually
longed for death. Not from despair, but from joy! He wasn't
discouraged when he wrote his final letter to Timothy. He was

rejoicing that he would soon see the Lord.

> *For I am already being poured out as a drink*
> *offering, and the time of my departure is at hand.*
> *(2 Timothy 4:6)*

We should have this same attitude! If there is truly a special crown awaiting all who love Christ's appearing, then we should never be found saying, "O Lord, don't come today." Now I understand those whose heart's desire is to see every person saved. My own heart longs for the same, but when the Lord comes, it will be the right time, for he knows the hearts of all men.

> *Shall not the Judge of all the earth do right?*
> *(Genesis 18:25)*

Love those around you. Pray for the lost and share the Gospel. Do something while you're still alive. But be sure to ask God to send His Son quickly.

Paul's head was continually in heaven rather than on earth.

> *For our citizenship is in heaven, from which we also*
> *eagerly wait for the Savior, the Lord Jesus Christ,*
> *(Philippians 3:20)*

From which we also *eagerly wait*...Can you think of a word picture for someone eagerly waiting? Perhaps a child unwrapping a gift, or a hungry man awaiting a meal. That's the disciple's attitude. Is Jesus coming today? Maybe today? Eagerly waiting for the Savior!

> *The Lord Jesus Christ, who will transform our lowly*
> *body that it may be conformed to His glorious body,*
> *according to the working by which He is able even to*
> *subdue all things to Himself. (Philippians 3:20-21)*

I'm ready to leave this lowly house and gain that glorious one that the Lord will bring with Him.

Paul had watched the lives of the Thessalonians become transformed by the Gospel.

> *For they themselves declare concerning us what*
> *manner of entry we had to you, and how you turned*
> *to God from idols to serve the living and true God,*

and to wait for His Son from heaven, whom He raised from the dead, even Jesus who delivers us from the wrath to come. (1 Thessalonians 1:9-10)

They had turned from idols to serve the living and true God: to serve God *and to wait for His Son from heaven*. What marked these believers? Service and expectation. The word used for 'wait' in this particular Scripture differs from the previous two and means to 'wait with endurance'.

We are told to 'wait confidently' in Titus, to 'wait eagerly' in Philippians and now we are told to *'wait with endurance'* in 1 Thessalonians. These are the characteristics of a disciple who is loving Christ's appearing, thinking, "Tonight, tonight, yes! Tonight!" I am hoping that when you hear the trumpet of the Lord sound, the very next sound you hear is me screaming "YAHOO!"

I've had people say to me, "I'm not ready for Jesus to come tonight." So, I reply, "You'd better start getting ready because He is coming quickly!" There's a song with the lyrics, "People get ready, Jesus is coming. Soon we'll be going home…"

Once saved, the Thessalonians started serving, but they always had one eye looking up. Kind of like the people who rebuilt the Jerusalem walls during the time of Nehemiah; with one hand they worked at construction, and with the other they were prepared to meet the enemy. (Nehemiah 4:17) Only we're the opposite. Like them, we have one hand reaching the lost but the other is in the air waiting to grab the hand that will soon appear. Amen!

And may the Lord make you increase and abound in love to one another and to all, just as we do to you, so that He may establish your hearts blameless in holiness before our God and Father at the coming of our Lord Jesus Christ with all His saints. (1 Thessalonians 3:13)

Paul wants the Thessalonians to keep growing so that when the Lord returns they will have nothing to be ashamed of.

For the Lord Himself will descend from heaven with a shout, with the voice of an archangel, and with the trumpet of God. And the dead in Christ will rise first. Then we who are alive and remain shall be caught up together with them in the clouds to meet the Lord in the air. And thus we shall always be with the Lord. Therefore comfort one another with these words. (1 Thessalonians 4:16-18)

Are you sad? Wait eagerly! (Philippians 3:20) Jesus is coming soon.

Are you discouraged? Wait confidently! (Titus 2:13) Jesus is coming soon.

Are you beat down? Wait with endurance! (1 Thessalonians 1:10)...

JESUS IS COMING SOON!

CHAPTER TWENTY REVIEW

i.   What was the Lord's first supernatural message to the church in Acts 1:10-11 and what was the last in Revelation 22:20?

ii. What are the three words that Scripture uses to describe waiting or looking for Jesus' return and how do they apply to you?

iii. Why does the Lord's soon coming bring so much comfort to the believer?

iv. Why is the day of the Lord referred to as great and terrible?

v.   Memorize Hebrews 9:28

his final chapter is the result of the Lord speaking to my heart. Jesus lovingly taught His disciples for years, taking great pain to instill in them the principles of the Kingdom of God and of His Father's will. But after all had been taught and the lessons were complete, He told them they should not continue without the Holy Spirit (Acts 1:4). While the commandments of the Lord have been clearly taught in this book, He has reminded me that *it is God who works in you both to will and to do for His good pleasure.* (Philippians 2:13). Until completing this last chapter, the Lord has continually said to me, "Do not leave them as orphans." (John 14:18) With this preface, I now present to you:

A Spirit Filled Life

In John 16:7, Jesus says this to His disciples on the way to Gethsemane:

> *Nevertheless I tell you the truth. It is to your advantage that I go away; for if I do not go away, the Helper will not come to you; but if I depart, I will send Him to you. (John 16:7)*

That was one of the most troublesome verses in my life for a very long time. How is it to my advantage that Jesus would go away? How did the disciples feel about this? Did they grasp it?

The word for "advantage" in Greek, is 'sumfero', a compound word which literally means, "to bear together" and make things easier. You have heard the phrase: "Many hands makes the load light"? That is the idea behind this word. When you have 'sumfero' it is better or easier to carry the load. Jesus is telling His disciples that His Father will send aid if He goes away. We won't be carrying out the remaining work alone: there will be a Helper.

Up until this final chapter, this book on discipleship has focused upon our spiritual life. God has been developing Christ-like characteristics within each one of us as His disciples. But in this chapter I want to focus on a different, and yet vitally important aspect of the Lord's work within each one of His disciples. Not the *spiritual life* of a disciple, but the *Spirit-filled life* of a disciple.

The Holy Spirit is mentioned greater than one hundred times in the New Testament.

He is the Author behind conviction that leads to salvation:

And when He has come, He will convict the world of sin, and of righteousness, and of judgment (John 16:8)

He is our protection from sin.

I say then: Walk in the Spirit, and you shall not fulfill the lust of the flesh. (Galatians 5:16)

He is even the power behind our resurrection.

But if the Spirit of Him who raised Jesus from the dead dwells in you, He who raised Christ from the dead will also give life to your mortal bodies through His Spirit who dwells in you. (Romans 8:11)

The things that we have talked about in discipleship; being faithful, not being a hypocrite, being a lover of God and of others, being diligent, being prayerful: these are all good works which we should desire to do. However, there is an even greater work, which we cannot do because it is the work of the Holy Spirit.

First, for simplicity, I wish to summarize the various ministries of the Holy Spirit into three Biblical categories represented by three "relationships" He has with us. These three categories are described by our Lord Jesus Himself in John 14:16-17 and Acts 1:8.

And I will pray to the Father, and He will give you another Helper, that He may abide with you forever-- the Spirit of truth, whom the world cannot receive, because it neither sees Him nor knows Him; but you know Him, for He dwells with you and will be in you. (John 14:16-17)

When Jesus made this statement he had not yet been crucified and resurrected. At that point, the Spirit of God had not been given. And yet, Jesus describes that the Holy Spirit of God was already *with* them. Then He tells them that in the future the Holy Spirit shall be *in* them. The Spirit had clearly been with them through His signs and wonders while they were preaching. Just by the very Name of Jesus, even if He wasn't present, the Spirit would deliver people from sickness and demons. But there was more coming. He would soon be *in* them and later He said...

> *[Y]ou shall receive power when the Holy Spirit has come upon you; (Acts 1:8)*

Three relationships the Holy Spirit would have with them. He was *with* them, will be *in* them and then shall be *upon* them. There is surely an important difference between these words. If I tell you that I have coffee *with* me, it brings to mind a certain picture. Now, if I say that I have coffee *in* me, it is a completely different picture. What about if I say that I have coffee *upon* me? These are three unique relationships. Let's look at them more closely.

THE HOLY SPIRIT'S MINISTRY TO THE WORLD

In John 14:17, the Greek word for "with" is 'para'. It means to be alongside. We are familiar with the word "parable". It means an earthly story placed alongside a spiritual truth so that it can be understood. When Jesus says, "I will give you a Helper" He uses a similar word, 'parakletos'which means someone who will come alongside and help. Before they were born again, Jesus told His disciples that the Spirit was already alongside them. This is the Holy Spirit's relationship to the entire world and has been true from the very first day of creation.

> *The earth was without form, and void; and darkness was on the face of the deep. And the Spirit of God was hovering over the face of the waters. (Genesis 1:2)*

Even though Adam sinned, God's Spirit did not leave His creation. Long after creation we find the Spirit of God striving with man prior to the flood (Genesis 6:3). John 16:8 tells us that the work of the Holy Spirit is to convict the lost world of sin and according to John 6:44, those who become convicted are then led to Jesus.

> *No one can come to Me unless the Father who sent*
> *Me draws him; and I will raise him up at the last*
> *day. (John 6:44)*

The Holy Spirit comes alongside every human that has ever been born and reveals God to them.

> *[W]hat may be known of God is manifest in them,*
> *for God has shown it to them. For since the creation*
> *of the world His invisible attributes are clearly seen,*
> *being understood by the things that are made, even*
> *His eternal power and Godhead, so that they are*
> *without excuse, because, although they knew God,*
> *they did not glorify Him as God, nor were thankful,*
> *but became futile in their thoughts, and their foolish*
> *hearts were darkened. Professing to be wise, they*
> *became fools...(Roman 1:19-22)*

The Holy Spirit has a relationship with this world. He is "clearly" revealing God to us, so that we have no excuse for being lost. Remember back to those times when He revealed God to you, prior to your salvation? If you are saved, then you have probably realized that the Holy Spirit was with you during the years of rebellion and sin. If you are not saved, then the Holy Spirit at this very moment is with you and revealing the truth of this to your heart as you read. As Paul said, *God will reveal even this to you.* (Philippians 3:15)

It is the Holy Spirit who convicts the world of their sins. Not the saints. Not the church. We might call it our conscience before we are saved, but God is with us. This is the Holy Spirit's primary ministry to the world and explains why Jesus reacted so strongly about blaspheming the Holy Spirit.

> *[H]e who blasphemes against the Holy Spirit*
> *never has forgiveness, but is subject to eternal*
> *condemnation. (Mark 3:29)*

In this situation, God had been revealing who Jesus was through His miracles and the Jews responded that this was not God's Spirit, but the power of Satan. This is when Jesus tells them that they should not speak against the Spirit or they will not be able to be saved. If you reject and blaspheme the Holy Spirit then there is no forgiveness, because it is the only ministry available to a lost and sinful world which leads them to salvation. Needless to say, I believe that if a person dies unsaved, that they must have blasphemed or rejected the ministry of the Holy Spirit in their life.

THE HOLY SPIRIT'S REGENERATION MINISTRY

In

In John 14:17, the Greek word for "in" is 'en'. It means "inside". On the night that Jesus spoke these words, it was still a future ministry to them because the Spirit would not dwell within man until after the resurrection of our blessed Lord.

> *He showed them His hands and His side. Then the disciples were glad when they saw the Lord. So Jesus said to them again, "Peace to you! As the Father has sent Me, I also send you." And when He had said this, He breathed on them, and said to them, "Receive the Holy Spirit. (John 20:20-22)*

The Lord's breath gave eternal life to His disciples just as God's breath had done for Adam.

> *And the LORD God formed man of the dust of the ground, and breathed into his nostrils the breath of life; and man became a living being. (Genesis 2:7)*

Jesus chose to breathe life into His disciples in the same way He had Adam.

> *For as the Father raises the dead and gives life to them, even so the Son gives life to whom He will. (John 5:21)*

The Greek word for spirit and breath are the same. And so Jesus breathes on them and says, *Receive the Holy Spirit*. When He blew on them and commanded this, I believe that they were born again by the Spirit.

> *That which is born of the flesh is flesh, and that which is born of the Spirit (or breath) is spirit. Do not marvel that I said to you, 'You must be born again.' The wind blows where it wishes, and you hear the sound of it, but cannot tell where it comes*

*from and where it goes. So is everyone who is born
of the Spirit. (John 3:6-8)*

There were no outward manifestations at this time, but I
believe that the Holy Spirit regenerated them and they entered
the kingdom of God. This is the Holy Spirit's regeneration ministry in us. This ministry doesn't lead us to salvation. It saves us!

*And if Christ is in you, the body is dead because of
sin, but the Spirit is life because of righteousness. But
if the Spirit of Him who raised Jesus from the dead
dwells in you, He who raised Christ from the dead
will also give life to your mortal bodies through His
Spirit who dwells in you. Therefore, brethren, we
are debtors--not to the flesh, to live according to the
flesh. For if you live according to the flesh you will
die; but if by the Spirit you put to death the deeds
of the body, you will live. For as many as are led
by the Spirit of God, these are sons of God. For you
did not receive the spirit of bondage again to fear,
but you received the Spirit of adoption by whom we
cry out, "Abba, Father." The Spirit Himself bears
witness with our spirit that we are children of God.
(Romans 8:10-16)*

*Now He who establishes us with you in Christ and
has anointed us is God, who also has sealed us
and given us the Spirit in our hearts as a guarantee
['arrabown']. (2 Corinthians 1:21-22)*

'Arrabown': is a Hebrew word that made it into the New
Testament and means 'down payment'.

Hallelujah!!! God has given the Holy Spirit inside of us,
not only to regenerate us, not only to bear witness that we are
saved, but He has become the guaranteed down payment of
our salvation! This is why Paul was so serious when he wrote 2
Corinthians 13:5:

*Examine yourselves as to whether you are in the
faith. Test yourselves. Do you not know yourselves,
that Jesus Christ is in you? --unless indeed you are
disqualified. (2 Corinthians 13:5)*

If we do not have the Holy Spirit within us, declaring that we are children of God, then we are not saved! No man can say you are saved. Only the Holy Spirit can testify that you are saved. I can tell you the way of salvation. I can tell you what salvation looks like and about God's promises. I can help you with fear in your life. But, I cannot confirm your salvation. Only the Holy Spirit can do this. Many people are relying on some evangelist who told them, "You are saved!" It is possible that they might get to heaven and find out that the evangelist was wrong! We must know within our hearts. The Holy Spirit must say to us, "You are saved", and then we are guaranteed. Jesus said,

Many will say to Me in that day, 'Lord, Lord'... And then I will declare to them, 'I never knew you'? (Matthew 7:22-23)

They thought they were saved, but they weren't. They had outward assurances that they were saved,

"have we not prophesied in Your name, cast out demons in Your name, and done many wonders in Your name?" (Matthew 7:22)

But they didn't have the inner guarantee. I ask you right now to please make sure that you have the Holy Spirit *in* you. He must dwell *in* you for you to be saved. Does Jesus Christ live in you? It's not about doing what is right or saying 'yes' to the correct questions. It's about whether or not the living God is *in* you. He should exist - In you! This is the mystery of regeneration.

[T]he mystery which has been hidden from ages and from generations, but now has been revealed to His saints. To them God willed to make known what are the riches of the glory of this mystery among the Gentiles:

Do you know what the mystery is?

which is Christ in you, the hope of glory. (Colossians 1:26-27)

Christ in you! That's the mystery that the Lord has made known to us. Christ is in us! If Christ is not in you, then you have no hope of glory. Not just God *with* us, but God *in* us.

The Holy Spirit's Empowering Ministry

Upon

The third ministry is "upon".

But you shall receive power when the Holy Spirit has come <u>upon</u> you (Acts 1:8)

Were the disciples saved prior to the day of Pentecost? Yes! This third ministry has nothing to do with conviction of sin or salvation, but is a completely different word. 'Epi'. Jesus tells us this ministry is one of power.

Before our Lord's revealing, there was a man named John the Baptist who stated:

I indeed baptized you with water, but He (Jesus) will baptize you with the Holy Spirit. (Mark 1:8)

This baptism John refers to is the same as the ministry Jesus is talking about in Acts 1:8 and is also referred to as being "filled with the Holy Spirit" in Acts 2:4. According to Acts 2:17, we are told by Peter that the ministry of being filled with or baptized by the Holy Spirit is available to anyone who comes to Christ.

And it shall come to pass in the last days, says God, That I will pour out of My Spirit <u>upon</u> all flesh; Your sons and your daughters shall prophesy, your young men shall see visions, your old men shall dream dreams. And on My menservants and on My maidservants I will pour out My Spirit in those days; And they shall prophesy. (Acts 2:17-18)

As a disciple of Jesus, how important is this ministry? Well, in Acts chapter 8, it says that when the Apostles who were at Jerusalem heard that Samaria had received the Word of God, they sent Peter and John to them. These were already followers of Christ; Philip had already baptized them in water and by all outward marks they were saved. But, they had not received something important. The baptism of the Holy Spirit. What is the first thing the Apostles did when they came to this group of new believers?

> *Now when the apostles who were at Jerusalem heard
> that Samaria had received the word of God, they
> sent Peter and John to them, when they had come
> down, prayed for them that they might receive the
> Holy Spirit. For as yet He had fallen upon none of
> them. They had only been baptized in the name of
> the Lord Jesus. Then they laid hands on them, and
> they received the Holy Spirit. (Acts 8:14-17)*

They prayed for them to receive the Holy Spirit. How important is this? There are entire denominations and groups who think that this is unimportant. Was it unimportant to the Apostles? Look at Acts chapter 19, when Paul is coming through Ephesus.

> *And it happened, while Apollos was at Corinth,
> that Paul, having passed through the upper regions,
> came to Ephesus. And finding some disciples he
> said to them, "Did you receive the Holy Spirit when
> you believed?" So they said to him, "We have not
> so much as heard whether there is a Holy Spirit."
> (Acts 19:1-2)*

Don't you find that an interesting question for Paul to ask? How important did he think the ministry of the Holy Spirit was?

> *And he said to them, "Into what then were you
> baptized?" So they said, "Into John's baptism." Then
> Paul said, "John indeed baptized with a baptism of
> repentance, saying to the people that they should
> believe on Him who would come after him, that is,
> on Christ Jesus." When they heard this, they were
> baptized in the name of the Lord Jesus. (Acts 19:3-5)*

Will everyone agree that they are now saved? Yes! But, Paul didn't stop there.

> *And when Paul had laid hands on them, the Holy
> Spirit came upon them, and they spoke with tongues
> and prophesied. Now the men were about twelve in
> all. (Acts 19:6-7)*

Why did he lay hands on them when they had already been baptized? He wanted the Holy Spirit to come upon them. They were saved, according to Romans 6, when they were baptized into Christ's death and resurrection; however, they needed the Holy Spirit upon them. It is a shame what churches have done with this doctrine. They have made the baptism of the Holy Spirit so cheap and ridiculous that people walk away from an essential ministry of God to His people. I'm telling you that if the Apostles heard you didn't have the Holy Spirit they would send someone right now to lay hands upon you. It was that important.

At one point it became the sole reason for Peter to water baptize a group of gentiles. Do you remember the story? In Acts 10 he went to Cornelius' house. God had just told him that believing gentiles were accepted by Him.

What God has cleansed you must not call common. (Acts 10:15)

So Peter enters a gentile's house. I'm not sure what kind of a struggle was going on in his heart, but I doubt he was ready for what happened. He obeyed God, even though it was against Jewish tradition (even telling them that he was breaking Jewish law [Acts 10:28]). Then Peter began preaching Jesus and...

While Peter was still speaking these words, the Holy Spirit fell upon all those who heard the word. And those of the circumcision who believed were astonished, as many as came with Peter, because the gift of the Holy Spirit had been poured out on the Gentiles also. For they heard them speak with tongues and magnify God. Then Peter answered, "Can anyone forbid water, that these should not be baptized who have received the Holy Spirit just as we have?" And he commanded them to be baptized in the Name of the Lord. (Acts 10:44-48)

When Peter returns to Jerusalem, trouble comes from the devout Jewish believers for breaking their laws. He answers:

And as I began to speak, the Holy Spirit fell upon them, as upon us at the beginning. Then I remembered the word of the Lord, how He said, 'John indeed baptized with water, but you shall be baptized with the Holy Spirit.' "If therefore God gave them the same gift as He gave us when we believed on the Lord Jesus Christ, who was I that I could withstand God?" When they heard these things they became silent; and they glorified God, saying, "Then God has also granted to the Gentiles repentance to life." (Acts 11:15-18)

What was his point of argument? The Holy Spirit was upon them. The gentiles had received this third ministry and so must already have the second ministry which is regeneration. Do we need to prophesy or speak in tongues before we are saved? No! God gave tongues to this group of Gentiles for a specific reason. He needed to reveal to Peter that He had already saved them. Peter might have said, "Become a Jew and then God will save you!" but they were already baptized by the Spirit and so it was unnecessary to become a Jew first. It's as if you are watching someone drive a car. You automatically know that they must have the keys because they are driving. That is why God showed them the Holy Spirit's baptism before they were water baptized. God was saying, "I have already given them salvation."

Being baptized with the Holy Spirit is so essential, that Christ Himself *commanded* them to *wait* until they received this ministry before proceeding. How many people is God saying that to today?

And being assembled together with them, He commanded them not to depart from Jerusalem, but to wait for the Promise of the Father, "which," He said, "you have heard from Me; (Acts 1:4)

It is essential for a disciple to be baptized in the Holy Spirit. This is why Peter and John went up to Samaria and why Paul asked the disciples whether they had received the Holy Spirit.

There are a couple things I want to note about this spiritual baptism. Just as is the case of water baptism, no one can spiritually baptize himself.

Then Jesus came from Galilee to John at the Jordan to be baptized by him. And John tried to prevent Him, saying, "I need to be baptized by You, and are You coming to me?" But Jesus answered and said to him, "Permit it to be so now, for thus it is fitting for us to fulfill all righteousness." Then he allowed Him. (Matthew 3:13-15)

When receiving water baptism, even Jesus Himself was baptized by another. This is the first thing we must note about *all* baptisms, We cannot "self-baptize". There are those who will try and teach us how to receive the baptism of the Holy Spirit, perhaps by talking rapidly or continuously repeating some action. Holy Spirit baptism often occurs by the laying on of hands of men (as seen in Acts chapter 8 and 19), but it is always based upon God Himself pouring the Spirit upon an individual. Cornelius was baptized in the Holy Spirit by God. The disciples, in Acts chapter 2, were praying as a group and were baptized in the Holy Spirit by God. It is clear that we cannot baptize ourselves in the Holy Spirit, however Jesus does encourage us to ask our Father to baptize us.

If you then, being evil, know how to give good gifts to your children, how much more will your heavenly Father give the Holy Spirit to those who ask Him! (Luke 11:13)

Now, sadly, there is controversy surrounding baptism of the Holy Spirit, because some teach that the only true mark of this baptism is to speak in tongues and they refuse to believe someone is baptized in the Holy Spirit unless they can speak a new language. The result of this doctrine has left people trying to baptize themselves in the Holy Spirit by making up words or talking quickly until they speak a non-understandable language. Is "tongues" speaking a foreign language as in Acts 2:6 and 8? Or, is it speaking an angelic language as in 1 Corinthians 13:1? Do we have to know? We should not enter into unfruitful arguments about gifts that God gives; just simply agree with Paul and wish that all spoke with tongues.

I wish you all spoke with tongues, but even more that you prophesied (1 Corinthians 14:5)

He couldn't have made this statement unless they didn't all speak with tongues could he? Conclusion? In the church of Corinth, not everyone spoke with tongues. So, first of all, let me tell you that we will not all speak in tongues or be prophets or do miracles.

Now you are the body of Christ, and members

individually. And God has appointed these in the church: first apostles, second prophets, third teachers, after that miracles, then gifts of healings, helps, administrations, varieties of tongues. Are all apostles? Are all prophets? Are all teachers? Are all workers of miracles? Do all have gifts of healings? Do all speak with tongues? Do all interpret? (1 Corinthians 12:27-30)

Some will speak in tongues and some won't, but all should be baptized in the Holy Spirit, because it is Jesus' empowering ministry to His disciples and is essential.

If it's true that speaking in tongues is not the identifying mark of the baptism of the Holy Spirit, what is? I studied the biblical account of what the Holy Spirit baptism looks like. I referenced every instance in the book of Acts where an individual was 'filled with the Holy Spirit' or 'full of the Holy Spirit' or 'baptized with the Holy Spirit'. There are seven occurrences in the book of Acts. Guess what I found? Twice, those being baptized began boldly praising God (Ac 2:4, 11 and 10:44, 46), four times they became courageously bold in their witness of Christ (Ac 4:8, 13, 4:31, 7:55 and 13:9) and once they boldly rejoiced in their persecution (Ac 13:52).

Do you see a theme? The baptism of the Holy Spirit we find in the book of Acts is associated with boldness. Boldness in praise, boldness in witnessing and boldness in suffering. Baptism of the Holy Spirit is not about miracles, signs and wonders. The Apostles had already done many of these prior to being baptized in the Holy Spirit. They had already raised the dead. They had already cast out demons. They had already healed the sick, cleansed the lepers, given sight to the blind.

Yes, sometimes people being baptized in the Holy Spirit spoke in tongues, but, when the tongues were translated by the listeners, what do we find them saying? According to the interpreters they were saying praises to God. In the book of Acts it says,

...we hear them speaking in our own tongues the wonderful works of God. (Acts 2:11)

That is the true Pentecost! It is not the speaking in tongues that is important, but an overflow of praise and worship from the heart.

Paul gives us a biblical definition of being filled with the Holy Spirit. Let's see how it contrasts to the one being taught by men today. Ephesians 5:15-20 gives us Paul's definition of what it is to be filled with the Holy Spirit.

> *See then that you walk circumspectly, not as fools but as wise, redeeming the time, because the days are evil. Therefore do not be unwise, but understand what the will of the Lord is. And do not be drunk with wine, in which is dissipation; but be filled with the Spirit, (Ephesians 5:15-18)*

The word for dissipation means "an empty rip-off". Nothing wholesome and nothing fulfilling. That's what drunkenness offers. We think wine brings relief: Paul is telling us that it is a rip-off and can never give real joy. Don't be drunk with wine, because that doesn't do any good! When we wake up, our troubles are still there. Instead, be filled with the Spirit.

It's important to make note that a couple of times drunkenness and being filled with the Holy Spirit is contrasted. This leaves us with the hint that there must be some similarity between being drunk and being filled with the Holy Spirit. First, Paul contrasts the two in this statement and secondly, whatever the disciples were doing on Pentecost must have had some resemblance to drunkenness because of the crowd's response.

> *Others mocking said, "They are full of new wine."* (Acts 2:13)

So what is the filling of the Spirit?

> *speaking to one another in psalms and hymns and spiritual songs, singing and making melody in your heart to the Lord, giving thanks always for all things to God the Father in the name of our Lord Jesus Christ, (Ephesians 5:19-20)*

According to this Scripture being filled with the Holy Spirit manifests an unrestrained joy that rivals the cheap substitute of alcohol. A biblical description of being filled with the Holy Spirit would be unrestrained worship and praise. That is exactly what happened at Pentecost (Acts 2), it is exactly what happened at Cornelius' house (Acts 10), it is exactly what happened to Stephen while he was being stoned (Acts 7), it is exactly what happened when the disciples were being persecuted in Antioch in Pisidia (Act 13:52).

When I say, "unrestrained" I must point out that unrestrained does not mean disorderly.

> *God is not the author of confusion but of peace, as in all the churches of the saints. (1 Corinthians 14:33)*

In other words, don't create chaos so that no one else can worship God but you. This is selfishness not godliness. It might be a filling of the Holy Spirit but God isn't selfish as are many modern day contrivances of being baptized in the Holy Spirit.

The next verse in Ephesians says that this baptism will overflow into submission not dominance.

> *submitting to one another in the fear of God. (Ephesians 5:21)*

Bold, powerful worship of God is the true biblical mark of baptism in the Holy Spirit. Unrestrained love for God. *That* is what happened to the miracle working Apostles. They were sitting in a room timid and afraid and the next moment they became bold and unrestrained in their worship of the Lord and Savior Jesus.

Outside of Jesus Himself, there is only one other example in the Gospels of an individual being filled with the Holy Spirit...a little boy named John the Baptist.

> *"For he will be great in the sight of the Lord, and shall drink neither wine nor strong drink. He will also be filled with the Holy Spirit, even from his mother's womb. (Luke 1:15)*

Was John unrestrained in his worship of God? *Even from his mother's womb?* It says that when Mary came in that the 1-pound pre-born baby John leapt for joy. He wasn't simply moving around stretching, making more room. *He leapt for joy!* And she knew it was Holy Spirit unrestrained joy that had made the baby move.

*For indeed, as soon as the voice of your greeting
sounded in my ears, the babe leaped in my womb
for joy. (Luke 1:44)*

There is one more clear evidence of being baptized with the
Holy Spirit. Fearless bold witnessing. We clearly see in the Spirit
filled disciples of Acts an unrestrained boldness in proclaiming
the Word of God. Do we see that in John the Baptist?

He called the Jews a brood of vipers! He told them they had
better produce fruit or God was going to chop them down and
they were going to hell! That sounds bold! He told King Herod
that his marriage was an abomination to God. Herod's queen
finally shut his mouth by removing his head. Was John filled
with the Holy Spirit from the womb? Did he exhibit Holy Spirit
boldness? Yes! But, was his Holy Spirit baptism accompanied
by signs and wonders? How many miracles did he do? None!
How many times did he speak in tongues? None! So, what does
baptism of the Holy Spirit really bring? It is the Holy Spirit's
ministry to empower God's people to be bold and unrestrained
in their praise and worship and in their witnessing to the lost.

Here are some other examples:

*Then Peter, filled with the Holy Spirit, said to them,
"Rulers of the people and elders of Israel: Now
when they saw the boldness of Peter and John, and
perceived that they were uneducated and untrained
men, they marveled. And they realized that they had
been with Jesus. (Acts 4:8, 13)*

What was the baptism of the Holy Spirit in that instance?
Bold witnessing. He just stood up and spoke the truth to those
who would probably kill him! Then, after receiving chastisement
from the leaders, they returned home to the other disciples and...

*And when they had prayed, the place where they
were assembled together was shaken; and they were
all filled with the Holy Spirit, and they spoke the
word of God with boldness. (Acts 4:31)*

The biblical mark that identifies if someone is a spirit filled
believer is unrestrained and joyful boldness in worship and unrestrained courageous boldness in witnessing.

Look at Paul. As he was trying to witness to the proconsul, this wicked sorcerer kept interfering.

> *Then Saul, who also is called Paul, filled with the Holy Spirit, looked intently at him (Acts 13:9)*

Look out! Paul is being filled with the Holy Spirit...

> *and said, "O full of all deceit and all fraud, you son of the devil, you enemy of all righteousness, will you not cease perverting the straight ways of the Lord? "And now, indeed, the hand of the Lord is upon you, and you shall be blind, not seeing the sun for a time." And immediately a dark mist fell on him, and he went around seeking someone to lead him by the hand. (Acts 13:10-11)*

Can you imagine? What incredible boldness! He didn't go around and do this to every evil person he met. He was filled with the Holy Spirit and had enough. How can I be a witness to someone if I'm timid? Jesus knew that the Apostles couldn't serve Him without the Holy Spirit's empowering. He knew that they would soon be standing up in the Temple and preaching against the rulers of the Jews without Him. He knew that they would be stoned to death and some would be cut in half. He knew they needed to be baptized with the Holy Spirit.

Yes, you can be saved without the baptism of the Holy Spirit, but you cannot walk in the power God has given you without it. Do you know that the life of every great preacher I am aware of, from the extremely conservative to the extremely Pentecostal, from staunch Calvinists to Armenianists all point to a moment in their lives when they received the baptism of the Holy Spirit for their ministry? Jesus told the disciples that they must wait until they had received this power before continuing.

Peter thought it was essential, John thought it was essential, Paul thought it was essential, but most importantly, Jesus told us that it is essential.

> *Do not quench the Spirit. (1 Thessalonians 5:19)*

i.   What are the three relationships that the Holy Spirit has with an individual? List them and then describe the purpose of them.

ii. Have you ever asked the Lord to give you His Holy Spirit? Ask Him!

iii. Review the seven occurrences of Holy Spirit baptism in the book of Acts and write down the details for yourself. What do you find is the common theme?

iv. Have you ever considered John the Baptist as a spirit filled believer? Do you think he would be accepted in any of the modern Holy Spirit movements? Why or why not?

v.   If the Holy Spirit has used this book to draw you closer to Christ and to becoming a disciple rather than just a believer, then please take the time to give it to someone else, so that they too might be blessed by it. Thank you, and may God in heaven bless His beloved church. Amen!